THE TROUBLE
WITH KINGS

SUPPLEMENTS

TO

VETUS TESTAMENTUM

EDITED BY
THE BOARD OF THE QUARTERLY

J.A. EMERTON – W.L. HOLLADAY – A. van der KOOIJ
A. LEMAIRE – R.E. MURPHY – B. OTZEN – R. SMEND
J.A. SOGGIN – M. WEINFELD

VOLUME XLII

THE TROUBLE WITH KINGS

THE COMPOSITION OF THE BOOK OF KINGS IN THE DEUTERONOMISTIC HISTORY

BY

STEVEN L. McKENZIE

E.J. BRILL

LEIDEN · NEW YORK · KØBENHAVN · KÖLN

1991

The paper in this book meets the guidelines for permanence and durability of the Committee on Production Guidelines for Book Longevity of the Council on Library Resources.

BS
1335.2
. M355
1991

Library of Congress Cataloging-in-Publication Data

McKenzie, Steven L., 1953-
    The trouble with Kings: the composition of the book of Kings in the Deuteronomistic history / by Steven L. McKenzie.
        p.   cm.—(Supplements to Vetus testamentum, ISSN 0083-5889; v. 42)
    Includes bibliographical references and indexes.
    ISBN 90-04-09402-4 (alk. paper)
    1. Bible. O.T. Kings—Criticism, Redaction. 2. Bible. O.T. Kings—Sources. 3. D document (Biblical criticism) I. Title. II. Series.
BS1335.2.M355   1991
222'.5066—dc20
                                  91-10144
                                  CIP

ISSN   0083-5889
ISBN   90 04 09402 4

© *Copyright 1991 by E. J. Brill, Leiden, The Netherlands*

All rights reserved. No part of this book may be reproduced or translated in any form, by print, photoprint, microfilm, microfiche or any other means without written permission from the publisher

Authorization to photocopy items for internal or personal use is granted by E. J. Brill provided that the appropriate fees are paid directly to Copyright Clearance Center, 27 Congress Street, SALEM MA 01970, USA. Fees are subject to change.

PRINTED IN THE NETHERLANDS

I dedicate this book to my parents,

Wilfred and Germaine McKenzie.

CONTENTS

FOREWORD

My interest in the composition of the Deuteronomistic History and the focus of that issue in the book of Kings began, as is frequently the case for such interests, with a doctoral dissertation. The topic of my 1983 Harvard dissertation, "The Chronicler's Use of the Deuteronomistic History" was an ideal one for a nascent biblical scholar because it introduced me to two large and very important bodies of literature besides touching on a wide variety of related areas. I shall always be indebted to Professor Frank Moore Cross for his direction on the initial writing of that dissertation and on its 1985 publication in the Harvard Semitic Monographs. If the present volume demurs from his views on some key texts it is with the utmost esteem for him and his work which has only increased since I left his direct tutelage.

Like many dissertations my 1985 monograph was too much an "in house" product. Ironically, it ushered me into the fellowship of two of the most productive and congenial groups of scholars in the discipline, those interested in Chronicles and the Deuteronomistic History. It also opened for me avenues into related worlds of scholarly investigation as diverse as historical reconstruction and narrative analysis. As a result, I have acquired a greater appreciation for the work of the scholarly community at large than I had in 1985. In preparing the present monograph I made a conscious effort to read widely, and I learned important things from every writer whose work I consulted. In fact, there is little here that is really original. To a large extent I have merely tried to suggest different ways of linking pieces of a puzzle which others have supplied through painstaking research. I may have misplaced some of them, and others are still missing. But I hope that my suggestions will assist other scholars with greater skill and vision some day to complete the puzzle.

It has been my good fortune to become personally acquainted with many of the individuals whose work is cited in this volume. I consider them all friends and mentors. My thinking has been significantly influenced as a result of informal conversations with friends in the field. I hope they will forgive me for altering my views in this volume about some of the points we have discussed. I have particularly profited from conversations and correspondence with Professor Julio Trebolle Barrera of the Universidad Complutense in Madrid. I consulted his studies on the development of the text of Kings frequently in preparing this monograph. He is a perceptive and judicious textual critic who has shown the significance of textual variants as evidence for the compositional process of biblical books. His work offers a measure of vindication for the education of people like me who learned Spanish instead of German in high school and college.

Like my 1985 monograph, this volume began as an effort to peal back redactional layers in Kings and the Deuteronomistic History by means of the "objective" criterion of another document. In 1985 the other document was the book of Chronicles. Here, it was the variant version of the Jeroboam cycle in 3 Reigns 12:24a-z. In the course of the investigation, however, my understanding of the 3 Reigns variant and of the composition of the book of Kings changed. A major influence behind this change was a 1989 Summer Seminar on ancient historiography sponsored by the National Endowment for the Humanities and directed by Professor John Van Seters at the University of North Carolina, Chapel Hill. I am grateful to Professor Van Seters for the careful attention he gave to portions of my manuscript during the Seminar. His comments were always quite insightful and taught me the value of addressing a question from different angles. His interest in seeing this monograph published is also deeply appreciated.

I am especially grateful for the encouragement and assistance that I have received in my academic career from three leading scholars. In his volume on textual criticism Professor P. Kyle McCarter discusses the importance of having a model to follow (1986:22). It is obvious from the names I have already mentioned that I have had several excellent models to emulate. Professor McCarter is one of them. But he, along with Professors J. Maxwell Miller and H. G. M. Williamson have been models in another way. Their work blends rigor with originality and has earned each of them an outstanding reputation. But beyond this, each has shown a generous interest in my work; each has treated me as a colleague, despite the difference between their status in the field and my own. And so to Kyle, Max, and Hugh I owe a special vote of thanks for their inestimable support over the past few years.

Several individuals and institutions have had a hand in bringing this volume to fruition. I am grateful for the use of the libraries of the University of North Carolina at Chapel Hill and Duke Divinity School during the summer of 1989. In Memphis, the library of Harding Graduate School of Religion graciously allows me full use of its facilities. And at Rhodes College, Mrs. Annette Cates of Burrow Library has been remarkably efficient at procuring the materials I needed through interlibrary loan. Finally, I wish to thank Prof. André Lemaire for accepting my manuscript into the Supplements to *Vetus Testamentum* and for his corrections and suggestions which led to improvement at several turns.

Steven L. McKenzie

A HISTORY OF THE HISTORY:
THE THEORY OF THE DEUTERONOMISTIC HISTORY AND THE PROBLEM OF THE BOOK OF KINGS

The story of the theory of the Deuteronomistic History (DH)[1] is itself a telling review (cf. Radjawane 1973; Weippert 1985). It begins with the great biblical scholar, Martin Noth, who established the theory of the DH in the field in the first half of a monograph published in 1943. That monograph, with its inimitably German title, *Überlieferungsgeschichtliche Studien*, has since become a classic in the study of the Hebrew Bible because it forever changed the way that scholars regard the "historical books" of the Bible.

NOTH'S THEORY

Noth proffered a new model in critical scholarship for the composition of biblical literature. Previously, scholars had tended to treat the Former Prophets (Joshua, Judges, Samuel, Kings) either as the continued compilation of the literary sources in the Pentateuch or as independent units which had passed through one or more Deuteronomistic redactions. This was particularly true of the book of Kings. Before the appearance of Noth's groundbreaking monograph, the most widely held view of Kings was that it was compiled first before the exile of 586 B.C.E. and then revised during the exile (Nelson 1981:14-19; Provan 1988:8-11).

Noth posited that the Former Prophets, with the book of Deuteronomy at their head, were originally a unified history of Israel written by a single, exilic author/compiler whom Noth named the Deuteronomist (Dtr). Besides the similarity of language throughout the Former Prophets, Noth pointed to the common chronology and ideology of these books as evidence of an individual hand. He also showed that Dtr's primary structuring device involved the use of programmatic, reflective summaries in common Deuteronomistic style which he inserted at key junctures in the History,

---

[1] The term "Deuteronomic" has been used as a synonym for "Deuteronomistic." For clarity I prefer to use "Deuteronomic" only for matters regarding the book of Deuteronomy and "Deuteronomistic" for matters regarding the DH as a whole. The latter is also a better translation of Noth's adjective, *deuteronomistische*.

mostly in the form of speeches attributed to major characters. Noth dated the DH to the middle of the sixth century B. C. E. and proposed that its purpose was to show that the Babylonian exiles were suffering for centuries of decline in Israel's loyalty to its God, Yahweh.

The novelty of Noth's model was neither in the perception of the continuity of these books nor in the observation of their Deuteronomistic editing. The Deuteronomistic stratum within these books had been recognized long before Noth, but it was understood as editorial overlay(s) on top of the separate books.[2] Noth, in contrast, held it to be the basic level of a work that was only later divided into books.

> The originality of the thesis lies in his combination of these two views for the first time, that is, in his claim that the continuity between the historical books derives solely from Dtr, cannot be explained on any other basis, and is of quite a different nature to that found in the Tetrateuch (Provan 1988:5).

It should be stressed that Noth perceived the Deuteronomistic History to be an <u>original</u> unit beneath the present books of Deuteronomy and the Former Prophets. Noth found plenty of passages in Deuteronomy through Kings which he took to be later additions to the original work of Dtr. Some were quite extensive (e.g., Joshua 13-22). But Noth made no attempt to relate the numerous additions to each other or to contend that they had a common origin. He found no indication, therefore, that Dtr's History had been systematically revised by a later editor. It was fundamentally the work of one person in the middle of the exile who had gathered traditions about Israel's history from a wide variety of sources and organized them into an extended account. Noth summarized the compositional model which he envisioned for Dtr in the following way (Noth 1981:10-11).

> Dtr. was not merely an editor ["nicht nur 'Redaktor'"] but the author of a history which brought together material from highly varied traditions and arranged it according to a carefully conceived plan. In general Dtr. simply reproduced the literary sources available to him and merely provided a connecting narrative for isolated passages. We can prove, however, that in places he made a deliberate selection from the material at his disposal. As far as facts were concerned, the elements were

---

[2] For lists of Deuteronomistic idioms see Weinfeld (1972:320-365) and Cross (1973: 252-254). However, the features of Deuteronomistic language and style in these and other books were well defined long before Noth, and his 1943 study assumed them. While such features continue to be widely recognized as Deuteronomistic, they are not a foolproof indication of Dtr's hand. Even Noth recognized that later additions to the DH imitated Dtr's language and style. Hence, other criteria, particularly theme and ideology, are important indicators of Dtr's presence, as Cross observed (see below).

arranged as given in tradition - e.g, the whole of the history of the kings, or the insertion of the period of the "judges" between the occupation of the land and the period of the monarchy. At times the order is determined by the older tradition, as in the incidents prior to the conquest. Elsewhere, though, Dtr. apparently arranged the material according to his own judgement, as in the details of the history of the "judges". Thus Dtr.'s method of composition is very lucid. The closest parallels are those Hellenistic and Roman historians who use older accounts, mostly unacknowledged, to write a history not of their own time but of the more or less distant past.

On the basis of Noth's arguments, most biblical scholars now consider the books of Deuteronomy through Kings in the Hebrew Bible as an original unit. Noth's perspective on the structure of the DH has also gained wide acceptance.[3] But scholarship, by and large, has moved away from Noth's view that the DH was the composition of a single individual. The related issues of the date, authorship, and purpose of the DH have been vigorously debated since Noth's time, especially in the last three decades. And the arena where the opinions on these matters have jousted has usually been the book of Kings. Noth's own date for the DH and his view of its purpose were in fact based on his interpretation of Kings. The book ended with the elevation of Jehoiachin (2 Kgs 25:27-30), so Noth dated it shortly after 562 B. C. E. Since it offered no explicit expectation of the end of the exile Noth concluded that its purpose was to show that Israel and Judah had been justly punished for centuries of decline in their loyalty to Yahweh.

TWO EARLY REACTIONS

The early reactions of Alfred Jepsen and Gerhard von Rad to Noth's view anticipated and have influenced the direction of scholarly development on these issues since the time of Noth. Both were studies of the book of Kings and set the stage for the central role of Kings in the subsequent scholarly discussion. For these reasons, their reactions are worth summarizing at this point.

Jepsen

Jepsen's 1953 volume on the sources of Kings (= Jepsen 1956) was a precursor to Noth's famous monograph in a way. Jepsen actually completed his study four years before the advent of *Überlieferungsgeschichtliche Studien,* but World War II delayed its publication. Partly as a result of the delay,

---

[3] 2 Samuel 7 and 1 Kings 13 have been proposed as additions to Noth's list of structural texts. On 2 Samuel 7 see McCarthy (1965; 1974) and Cross (1973:241-264). On 1 Kings 13 see Lemke (1976) and the discussion in Chapter Two.

Jepsen's work has not received all the credit it deserves for its contribution to the study of the DH. The complexity of Jepsen's analysis has also kept it from having as much of an impact on the field as Noth's essay.[4] Jepsen concluded that two sources underlay the book of Kings. One was a synchronistic chronicle from the eighth century which contrasted the Davidic dynasty with the turbulent succession of dynasties in the North. This was supplemented by a seventh century annalistic work from Judah. There were two exilic redactions of this material, the first by a priest, the second by a prophet. When his book finally appeared in print, Jepsen stated that his second redactor was essentially the same as Noth's Dtr (Jepsen 1956:100-101, 105).

Jepsen's independent conclusions provided corroboration for elements of Noth's thesis. But Jepsen's belief that complex redactional development could be discerned behind Kings was clearly different from Noth's determination and presented an alternative on the authorship of the DH which would be adopted by later scholars.

von Rad

In 1947, shortly after the appearance of *Überlieferungsgeschichtliche Studien*, von Rad published an important article on the Deuteronomistic theology of history in the book of Kings (= von Rad 1958). He traced a scheme of prophecy and fulfillment throughout Kings. This confirmed the negative purpose which Noth had proposed for the DH. The destruction of Israel and Judah fulfilled the prophetic threats of doom for disobedience. But there was another theme in Kings which Noth had missed -- the promise to David found in 2 Samuel 7 and reiterated throughout the book of Kings. These two themes stood in tension and created a theological quandary for Dtr, since he could neither minimize the severity of God's punishment in the exile nor concede that Yahweh's promise to David had failed. Von Rad saw the account of Jehoiachin's elevation in the final four verses of Kings as Dtr's solution to this dilemma. The continuation of the Davidic line left history open for Yahweh to begin again with his people.

Von Rad's study highlighted the important prophecy - fulfillment motif in Kings and in the DH as a whole. But more importantly, his demonstration of the importance of the Davidic promise in the DH called into question Noth's perception of the purpose of the DH as totally negative.[5]

----

[4] To my knowledge, the only scholar to have followed Jepsen's views in publication is Baena (1973, 1974a, 1974b).

[5] H. W. Wolff's 1961 study followed up on von Rad's and questioned Noth's understanding of the purpose of the DH in the following way (1961:173). "Warum wohl ein Israelit des 6. Jh.s v. Chr. überhaupt noch zur feder griff, wenn er wirklich nur das

REDACTIONAL THEORIES

The observations of Jepsen and von Rad precipitated an erosion of Noth's understanding of the authorship, date, and purpose of the DH. The generations since 1943 have witnessed the emergence of a bewildering number of modifications to Noth's position on these matters. In particular, in the past three decades a variety of alternative reconstructions involving redactional levels have been put forward. Again, these alternative theories are founded primarily on research within the book of Kings where it is felt that the material is simply too uneven to accept its assignment to a single writer (cf. Jones 1984:39).[6] These can be described in the following categories.

A Deuteronomistic School

E. W. Nicholson (1967) and Moshe Weinfeld (1972) have published separate studies focused on Deuteronomy which contend that the DH was produced by a circle of tradents (cf. also Debus 1967:114-115). In Nicholson's view, Northern prophetic circles fled to Judah after the destruction of Israel in 721 B.C.E. with the traditions they had collected. They supported Hezekiah's reform movement. After it failed, they planned their own reform program during Manasseh's reign (1967:101-102). This program was an early form of the book of Deuteronomy. A copy of it was found in the Temple during Josiah's reign and provided a foundation for his reforms. As a result, the Deuteronomistic school revived during Josiah's reign and eventually generated its History. Thus, while the final form of the DH was exilic, its origin should be sought in the late pre-exilic era (1967:113-114).

For Weinfeld, the DH developed in two stages (1972:7-9). The book of Deuteronomy was written in the second half of the seventh century. Then, in the first half of the next century, the Former Prophets were compiled and edited. A third Deuteronomistic stage accounted for the composition of the prose sermons in Jeremiah in the latter half of the sixth century. Thus, like Nicholson, Weinfeld sees the Deuteronomistic literary activity beginning in

---

abschließende Ende der Geschichte Israels als das gerechte Gericht Gottes verständlich machen wollen?"

[6] One should also mention here those few scholars who rejected Noth's theory outright or adopted other reconstructions because of perceived differences in theology or editorial technique between books within the DH. Von Rad's remark in this regard from his 1957 *Theologie* is often quoted (1957:344): "Es ist schwer vorstellbar, daß die dtr Redaktion der Königsbücher und die des Richterbuches in einem Arbeitsgang erfolgt sein sollte." Cf. Fohrer 1968:194-195.

the seventh century and continuing into the exile.[7] He thinks it possible that different literary strands lay behind the DH, but he is convinced that there are no criteria by which to determine the editorial stages of the work (1972:8) In a more recent piece (1985) Weinfeld extends the period of development of the first stage. He describes the book of Deuteronomy as having evolved during the period from Hezekiah to Josiah and consisting of various layers that are difficult to date (1985:91).

The idea that a Deuteronomistic "school" produced the DH is echoed frequently and uncritically in the literature. But it has never been clearly defined and remains too vague to be helpful.[8] It is essentially an *ad hoc* attempt to account for the overall similarity of the DH as well as its inner tensions and inconsistencies. There is no conceptualization of what a "school" was. How was it organized? What was its social function? What parallels are there for the existence of such an organization? Linguistic affinity does not indicate social unity. Also, Nicholson and Weinfeld present no clear evidence for the different production stages of the Deuteronomistic "school" that they posit for the DH. Weinfeld, in fact, believes that no evidence for literary levels exists. But many scholars find sufficient evidence to reconstruct literary strata in the DH. Moreover, the differences in ideology which scholars have perceived between editorial hands in Kings are sometimes so great that one wonders how those hands could possibly reflect the views of the same "school." At the very least the notion of a Deuteronomistic "school" needs to be characterized literarily, historically, socially, and ideologically before it can be taken seriously as an explanation for the origin of the DH.

Pre-Exilic Composition and Exilic Redaction

The idea of a pre-exilic version of Kings was in vogue well before Noth's famous monograph (Cf. Nelson 1981:13-28). However, Frank Moore Cross elevated the argumentation for this position to a new level of importance in regard to the DH.[9] Cross affirmed the validity of some of the older literary

---

[7] The major concern of Weinfeld's first study was to locate the Deuteronomistic school within the Israelite wisdom tradition. His arguments for this position have not convinced many of his peers. He actually spends very little time discussing levels of writing within the DH. However, his volume is unexcelled in its compilation of Deuteronomistic expressions and its citation of parallels to them from Assyrian documents, with which he demonstrates a thorough acquaintance.

[8] Compare the rather nebulous description of Debus (1967:114): "eine festgefügte und über mehrere Generationen hinweg existierende Gruppe von Theologen." Jones (1984:44) also writes loosely about the "unified ideological outlook" of the Deuteronomistic circle. Lemaire (1986:231-234) is more specific in describing the "school" that he envisions behind the DH, but this "school" is not Deuteronomistic in its earlier levels.

[9] 1973:274-289; first published as "The Structure of the Deuteronomic History," *Perspectives in Jewish Learning*, Annual of the College of Jewish Studies 3 (Chicago, 1968) 9-24.

arguments for separate redactions of Kings, such as the one based on the "to this day" formula in texts presuming the existence of the kingdom of Judah (2 Kgs 8:22; 14:7; 16:6).[10] But he then adduced a further, theological argument for this position from two themes which he traced throughout 1 - 2 Kings. One theme was the sin of Jeroboam and the wickedness of the North. This theme climaxed in the peroration on the destruction of Samaria in 2 Kings 17. A second, contrasting theme was the faithfulness of David and the promise to David of an enduring dynasty, as von Rad had noted. The climax of this second theme was the reign of Josiah, the only king of Israel or Judah to escape criticism by Dtr.

The persistence of these two themes and their climaxes suggested to Cross that the original edition of the DH was pre-exilic. He concluded that Dtr[1], as he called the primary editor, wrote to present Josiah as the new David and to promote his reforms. A second redactor (Dtr[2]) updated the work in the exile, with the addition of 2 Kgs 23:25b-25:30, which blamed the exile on Manasseh. Cross also suggested that a series of passages in Kings and earlier in the DH were glosses by Dtr[2] because they conditionalized the promise to David, presupposed the exile, or addressed the exiles and called for their repentance.[11]

A large number of scholars have found Cross's theory attractive. The theory offers thematic arguments in support of literary critical indications of more than one level of composition. It also ties these themes to a concrete historical and political *Sitz im Leben*. A propagandistic function for the material in Kings seems particularly appropriate (but cf. Long 1984:18-19). Still, there are questions which arise concerning this reconstruction. The Northern prophetic stories are problematic. Cross did not treat these, yet it is not clear how they fit with a work promoting a Judahite king. Also, Cross left open the number and extent of texts to be assigned to his Dtr[2]. This aspect of his theory has been the occasion for a good deal of discussion by subsequent scholars. Finally, Cross assumes, because of the unity of the DH established by Noth, that the evidence for a Josianic edition in Kings applies to the entire DH. However, the possibility that the Josianic work pertained only to Kings or to Samuel and Kings and not to the entire DH must be considered.

---

[10] While this argument has some validity, recent studies have pointed out some serious problems with it (Childs 1963; Long 1969; Nelson 1981:23-25). It is not always certain whether the expression comes from the hand of the Deuteronomistic redactor or was in his sources (Childs 1963:292). Dtr seems to have displayed little interest in the etymological aetiologies which he passed on (Long 1969). Also, some of the situations referred to by the expression would have remained true in Palestine during the time of the exile.

[11] These are my categories not Cross's. He simply listed the following as Dtr[2] passages: Deut 4:27-31; 28:36-37, 63-68; 29:27; 30:1-10; Josh 23:11-13, 15-16; 1 Sam 12:25; 1 Kgs 2:4; 6:11-12; 1 Kgs 8:25b, 46-53; 9:4-9; 2 Kgs 17:19; 20:17-18; 21:2-15; 22:15-20. He also described Deut 30:11-20 and 1 Kgs 3:14 as suspect. Cf. 1973:285-287.

A handful of scholars in recent years have published the opinion that there was a version of the DH even earlier than the time of Josiah, during Hezekiah's reign. Helga Weippert's 1972 analysis of the regnal formulas for Northern and Southern kings in the book of Kings led her to conclude that three redactors had produced the DH. Her R^I was from the North but worked in Judah during Hezekiah's reign. The edition of R^{II} incorporated the R^I material and stretched to include Josiah's reign. Then R^{III} finished the DH in the exile. Weippert's analysis has been followed, with variations, by W. B. Barrick (1974), F. Gonçalves (1986:73-76), G. C. Heider (1985:286-289), A. Lemaire (1986), and A. D. H. Mayes (1983:120-124).

H. R. Macy's 1975 dissertation also dealt with changes in the regnal formulas. Macy noticed three such changes for kings of Judah after Hezekiah. The expressions "with his fathers" and "in the city of David" are a regular part of the death and burial formulas for Judahite kings before Hezekiah in the book of Kings. From Hezekiah on both expressions cease to be used. Also, the names of the queen mothers disappear from Chronicles' accession formulas for Judahite kings following Hezekiah, though they continue to be listed in Kings. Macy ascribed all three changes to a variation in Deuteronomistic scribal tradition during Hezekiah's time (1975:139-142). B. Halpern (1981) has accepted Macy's results and suggested that the earliest DH was Hezekian.[12]

Multiple Exilic Redactions

Rudolf Smend sowed the seed for one important redactional theory in a 1971 article. He examined five passages in Joshua (1:7-9; 13:1bβ-6; 23) and Judges (1:1-2:9; 2:17, 20-21; 23) and concluded, on the basis of literary considerations, that they were secondary additions to the basic DH or DtrG (for *Grundschrift*). The five passages shared the view, in contrast to the DtrG, that conquest of the land was contingent on obedience to the law. Smend concluded, therefore, that all five were from the same redactor. Because of the Deuteronomistic character of the five texts and the interest they displayed in the law, Smend designated the redactor responsible for them DtrN (for nomistic).

Walter Dietrich (1972) extended Smend's conclusions by arguing for the presence in Kings of a middle redactor between DtrG and DtrN whom he designated DtrP (for prophetic). Dietrich began by analyzing a series of prophetic speeches and fulfillment notices. He concluded on the basis of

---

[12] Halpern and D. Vanderhooft have graciously shared with me the draft of a lengthy paper in preparation for publication which adds further arguments from the regnal formulas for a three tiered redaction (Hezekiah, Josiah, exile) of the DH. I leaned toward this view in my 1985 monograph (pp. 174-176), but it will become clear in this study that I no longer espouse it. Wilson (1980:157) advocates a first edition of the DH at the time of Hezekiah. Hayes and Hooker (1988:75) end the initial edition in Hezekiah's reign, while dating it under Manasseh. Neither Wilson nor Hayes and Hooker offer ny supporting arguments.

similarities in form and content that these passages came from a common redactor, provisionally designated RedP. Dietrich then argued at length that differences in language and theology indicated that RedP was to be distinguished from DtrN and especially from DtrG. RedP could, therefore, be called DtrP. DtrP added prophetic accounts to his DtrG *Vorlage* and was primarily responsible for the structure of the DH. DtrN added the pro-Davidic references but otherwise remained the most nebulous of the redactors in Dietrich's presentation. Dietrich's basic reconstruction has been applied to Samuel in two monographs by T. Veijola (1975; 1977). This approach has also been adopted in several other recent works, including commentaries by R. Klein (1983) on Samuel and E. Würthwein (1984; 1985) and G. H. Jones (1984) on Kings.

.There are some serious methodological problems with this approach. For one thing, it simply assumes Noth's exilic date for DtrG. The possibility of earlier redactional levels is never broached. This is particularly problematic for Dietrich's treatment of Kings, where critics have argued for a good deal of pre-exilic material. Dietrich's dates for the different redactors lack the concrete historical setting so attractive for other reconstructions. More serious is the unreliable nature of the criteria by which Dietrich assigns material to different redactors. His distinction between DtrG and DtrP in Kings is based more on the content and form of the stories than on actual literary evidence for different hands.[13] Indeed, Dietrich states that the language of DtrG and DtrP is too similar to be separated with any accuracy (1972:110). And DtrN remains an obscure figure throughout Dietrich's treatment of Kings.

Exilic Redaction of Pre-Exilic Sources

A 1981 article by Norbert Lohfink attempted to accomodate aspects of Cross's theory to Lohfink's own version of the Göttingen approach of Smend and Dietrich. On the basis of different theological themes (what Lohfink called *kerygmata*) which he perceived within the DH Lohfink contended that two Josianic documents had been used by Noth's Dtr (Lohfink: DtrG) to build parts of the DH. One of the documents underlay Deuteronomy 1 - Joshua 22 and was concerned to show Israel's right to the land in perpetuity. Lohfink called this document DtrL (for *Landeroberungserzählung*). The other was Cross's first edition of the book of Kings (not the entire DH). Lohfink also found at least two Deuteronomistic writers who retouched the DH after DtrG. One of these was DtrN, though not the same DtrN as Dietrich identified in Kings.

Iain Provan, in a new monograph (1988), is sympathetic to Lohfink's position, although he does not agree with it completely. The centerpiece of Provan's volume is an analysis of the במות theme of the book of Kings.

---

[13] See Provan's critique (1988:24-25).

He detects two distinct understandings of the במות betraying the work of two separate editors. The first, in 1 Kings 3 - 2 Kings 18, took the במות as Yahwistic shrines which were tolerated by the righteous kings of Judah until Hezekiah removed them and centralized the cult. A later editor, who regarded the במות as idolatrous shrines to other gods, interjected material into the account of the first editor and augmented it with the record of the century before Judah's exile, beginning with the end of Hezekiah's reign. Similarly, a reexamination of the David theme in Kings leads Provan to conclude that it originally climaxed in the first account of the deliverance of Jerusalem under Hezekiah (2 Kgs 18:17-19:9a + 19:36-37).

Provan actually dates the pre-exilic edition of Kings not in Hezekiah's reign, but early in Josiah's (1988:153-155) on the basis of the reference to Sennacherib's death in 2 Kgs 19:37 and the comparison in 2 Kgs 18:5 of Hezekiah to the kings of Judah after him. He includes most of Samuel in the pre-exilic work but sees Deuteronomy - Joshua and Judges as the addition of the exilic editor who revised Samuel - Kings. Thus, "the first DH, although influenced by Dtn laws, probably did not contain the books of Deuteronomy and Joshua. It was simply a history of the monarchy from Saul to Hezekiah" (Provan 1988:169).

Lohfink and Provan raise an important *caveat* about drawing conclusions for the entire DH based on the book of Kings. But their proposals leave several important questions unanswered. They do not seem to explain adequately the unity of the DH, accounting for the ties between Samuel - Kings and Deuteronomy - Judges. Provan, in particular, does not clearly distinguish between source and History. How could Samuel and Kings alone be the Deuteronomistic History? His delineation of the במות and David themes may be overly simple (see Chapter Six). His view seems to downplay the unequivocal glorification of Josiah in Kings. One wonders whether Provan has really come to grips with Dtr's linking of the accounts of different kings as observed by Hoffmann (see below). Finally, both Lohfink and Provan fail to explain the place of Northern prophetic stories in a work of Southern royalist propaganda.

EXCURSUS: RECONSTRUCTIONS OF A PRE-DTR PROPHETIC LEVEL IN SAMUEL - KINGS

The contribution of prophetic stories to the make-up of the book of Kings is obvious even to the most casual reader. Yet, we have seen that several redactional theories advanced to explain the formation of the DH ignore altogether the place of the prophetic stories in that work. From the beginning of the book of Kings until 2 Kings 18 all of the prophets mentioned are from Israel except for the young prophet in 1 Kings 13 and perhaps Shemaiah in 1 Kgs 12:21-24. The problem is that the stories about Northern prophets do not always accord well with the Southern royalist interests of redactors in the times of Hezekiah, Josiah, and the exile whom scholars have credited with composing the DH .

Scholars have long recognized this problem, and as a way of resolving it have theorized that Northern prophetic tales come, at least in part, from a separate prophetic source or redaction (cf. Fohrer 1968:232-235; Mayes 1983:106-132). A. Weiser (1964:175-179) is rather unique in this regard because he stressed what he saw to be the diversity and independence of the individual prophetic tales in Kings before they were collected and edited by Dtr. Even Noth (1967: 80) believed the tales in 1 Kings *11, *12, *14, (20), 22, and 2 Kings 9-10 derived from a cycle of stories about prophetic intervention in the succession of Israelite kings.

The idea of a prophetic stratum of editing in the DH has resurfaced in recent years in the study of Samuel and Kings, where the material most amenable to such an explanation is found. A handful of studies in the 1960s argued for a prophetic level in specific portions of Samuel.[14] We have seen that Dietrich found evidence of three hands in Kings, the middle one of which was a writer interested in prophecy, and Veijola followed this reconstruction in Samuel. Whatever its frailties, this approach at least incorporates within it an explanation of the prophetic stories.

Campbell and McCarter

Dietrich and Veijola viewed the prophetic stories as a layer imposed upon the Dtr *Grundschrift*. Bruce Birch (1976), in contrast, discovered a level of prophetic redaction immediately underlying 1 Samuel 7-15. P. Kyle McCarter, in basic agreement with Birch, traced the "Prophetic History," as he called it, through 1 - 2 Samuel in his commentaries on those books (1980b:18-20; 1984:6-8). He agreed, by and large, with Veijola as to the extent of material belonging to the prophetic stage, at least in 2 Samuel. But, like Birch, he characterized the prophetic level as lying behind the Deuteronomistic work rather than as a layer imposed upon it. In a sense he adapted the "Göttingen school's" identification of a prophetic level of redaction to Cross's theory of two Deuteronomistic editions. Antony Campbell (1986) has also reconstructed a pre-Deuteronomistic, prophetic work, which he names the "Prophetic Record," beneath 1 - 2 Samuel and on into Kings, and he has been followed closely by M. O'Brien (1989). It will be worthwhile to compare the views of McCarter and Campbell regarding the

---

[14] Nübel (1959) and Knierim (1968). See also G. C. Macholz ("Untersuchungen zur Geschichte der Samuel Überlieferungen," unpublished dissertation, Heidelberg, 1966), F. Mildenberger ("Die vordeuteronomistische Saul-Davidüberlieferung," unpublished dissertation, Tübingen, 1962), and J. Schüpphaus (*Richter- und Prophetengeschichten als Glieder der Geschichtsdarstellung der Richter- und Königszeit*, Bonn: Rheinische Friedrich-Wilhelms-Universität, 1967). I have been unable to secure copies of these last three works. Nübel actually concluded that the editor (*Bearbeiter*) of the second level, who incorporated much of the prophetic material in Samuel - Kings (especially the Elijah stories), was a priest.

contents of the prophetic layer in order to provide a background for the study of the subsequent chapters.

Both McCarter and Campbell assign the bulk of 1 Samuel 1-3 to the prophetic level and agree that these chapters depict Samuel as the paradigmatic prophet (3:19-21). McCarter thinks that the Prophetic History included most of the Ark Narrative in chapters 4-7. He argues that the goal of the Prophetic Historian in 1 Samuel 1-7 as a whole was to illustrate the efficacy of prophetic leadership as background and contrast to the sinful demand of the people for a king in chapter 8. Campbell, on the other hand, does not believe that the Prophetic Record included the Ark Narrative, although it may have included older traditions behind 1 Samuel 4 and 7 about the loss of the ark and Yahweh's rout of the Philistines at Samuel's intercession. It portrays Samuel as the beginning of a new epoch of prophetic power.

McCarter describes the function of 1 Samuel 8-15 in the Prophetic History as "not only to present the origin of monarchy from a prophetic perspective but also to introduce paradigmatically the relationship between king and prophet and . . . to establish the ongoing role of the prophet" (1980:20). Most of the material in these chapters was in the Prophetic History.[15]

Campbell (1986:68-70) assigns significantly less material in 1 Samuel 8-15 to his Prophetic Record: 9:1-10:16 (minus additions), 11:1-11, 14-15; 14:52; 15:1-35. Other passages (8:1-22; 10:17-25; and the pre-Dtr form of chap. 12) originated with prophetic circles, but these were not the same circles that produced the Prophetic Record, because the two sets of texts reflect different views of monarchy. In the Prophetic Record kingship is the gift of Yahweh and not, as according to 1 Sam 8; 10:17-25; 12, the result of popular demand or the rejection of Yahweh. Chapters 13-14 betray no prophetic concerns and were not, therefore, in the Prophetic Record.[16]

Both McCarter and Campbell conclude that the prophetic writer included the story of David's rise (1 Samuel 16 - 2 Samuel 5). McCarter sees the story of David's anointment in 1 Sam 16:1-13 as the composition of the Prophetic Historian introducing the story of David's rise. Campbell, in contrast, regards 16:1-13 as an original part of the older document about David's rise. McCarter finds additions of the Prophetic Historian in 1 Sam 19:18-24; 25:1; and 28:3-25. Campbell sees 1 Sam 25:1a; 28:17-19a; and 2 Sam 5:2bβ as prophetic additions. 1 Sam 19:18-24 was not in the Prophetic Record but was added by another prophetic hand (Campbell 1986:70-71).

McCarter believes that most of the rest of 2 Samuel was in the Prophetic History. It included a version of the Davidic promise (2 Sam 7:4-9a, 15b, 20-21). The Prophetic Historian borrowed an apology for Solomon (2

---

[15] McCarter finds significant Deuteronomistic retouching in 1 Samuel 12 (vv 6-15, 19b, 20b-22, 24-25). Otherwise, the only Deuteronomistic pluses are 8:8; 13:1-2; 14:47-51. Similarly, Birch (1976) assigns 8:8, 10-22; 12:6-24; 13:1 to Dtr.

[16] Nevertheless, according to O'Brien (1989:130-131), who subscribes to Campbell's theory, the two chapters were added at the pre-Dtr level.

Samuel 13-20 + 1 Kings 1-2) and prefaced it with the account of David's sin and Nathan's parable in 2 Sam 11:2-12:24.[17] In addition, the Prophetic Historian revised the story of David's census in 2 Samuel 24 by the addition of vv 10-14, 16a, and 17-19. Campbell (1986:72-81) also finds in 2 Sam 7:1a, 2-5, *7-10, 11b-12, 14-17 an earlier version of the Davidic covenant in the Prophetic Record.[18] Chapter 8 may also have been in the Prophetic Record. The greatest difference with McCarter relates to the Succession Narrative.   2 Samuel 11-20 may have been in the Prophetic Record, but Campbell thinks not. Only 12:7b-10 shows connections with the material in the Prophetic Record, and those verses could have been added to an independent version of the Succession Narrative.   But the story of Solomon's accession, consisting of 1 Kgs 1:1a, 5-15a, 16-48; 2:1a, 10, 12 was in the Prophetic Record (Campbell 1986:82-84).

McCarter does not extend his reconstruction of the Prophetic History beyond 2 Samuel, but he apparently sees it continuing to underlie much of 1 - 2 Kings, since he dates it, with Birch, around the fall of Samaria in 721 B.C.E. Since much of Campbell's perspective on the Prophetic Record is influenced by his perception of it in Kings, it is worth summarizing that part of his hypothesis before pausing to evaluate his perspective beside that of McCarter.

Campbell (1986:85-87) finds a narrative thread in 1 Kgs 3:1; 9:15-24; 11:7 which linked the stories of Samuel, Saul, and David in the Prophetic Record with those of Ahijah and Jeroboam and the subsequent characters. He then gives to the Prophetic Record a version of Ahijah's oracle to Jeroboam (11:26-31, 37, 38b, 40) and of Jeroboam's return (conflated in the MT with a second version in 12:2-3a) and the division of the kingdom (12:1, 3b-15a, 16-18, 20). Next, the Prophetic Record narrated the erection of Jeroboam's palace and shrines in 12:25, 28-29; 13:33b-34. There followed the story of Jeroboam's sick son (14:1-8a, 9bβ-13, 17-18a, 20b), then an account of Baasha's reign and the subsequent civil war (15:27a, 28b, 29a; 16:6, 9-10aαb, 11, 15b-18, 21-22, 24, 28, 31b-32). The story of the drought brought on through Elijah, including the encounter on Mount Carmel, followed (17:1; 18:2b-3a, 5-12a, 15-18a, 19abα, *20-36a, 37-40, 42b, 45-46). Next came the Naboth story (21:1-7a, 8, 11a, 14-19a, 21-22a, 24; 22:40) and the account of Ahaziah's death (2 Kgs 1:2-8, 17aα). Finally, the Prophetic Record told of Jehu's revolt in 2 Kgs 9:1-7a, 8-9a, 10b-27, 30-35; 10:1-9, 12-28 (Campbell 1986:87-101).

Both McCarter and Campbell, then, argue for an extended Northern prophetic narrative which immediately underlies a relatively light

---

[17] McCarter (1981). For McCarter 2 Samuel 13-20 and 1 Kings 1-2 were originally separate. The apologetic flavor of the latter is clear. The addition of 1 Kings 1-2 to the Succession Narrative in 2 Samuel 13-20 created the extended apologetic work.

[18] For Campbell (cf. O'Brien 1989:132-133) the earliest version of Nathan's oracle is in 2 Sam 7:1a, 2, 4b-5, 7*, 11b, 16.

Deuteronomistic redaction. The composition techniques are similar in both reconstructions. The prophetic writer(s) brought together older documents and shaped them into a running account of the early monarchy from a prophetic perspective. The work presented the ideal roles of prophet and king in which a prophet, as Yahweh's representative, designated the king and then directed his administration or denounced his failures through the divine word.

There are important differences between the reconstructions of McCarter and Campbell. These are due in part to the fact that McCarter was interested only in describing the Prophetic History behind 1 - 2 Samuel and not in characterizing its full extent. McCarter saw the Prophetic History as the work of a single person while Campbell seems to ascribe the Prophetic Record to a "school" of prophets. They also envision different settings for the prophetic writing. McCarter agrees with Birch (1976:83-85, 154), who dated the prophetic level in the second half of the eighth century on the basis of the prophetic forms in the work. Campbell places it earlier, in the reign of Jehu. He develops the motif of prophetic designation of the monarch noticed by R. Knierim (1968) and Birch. Campbell contends that the Prophetic Record sought to legitimize the prophetic anointing of Jehu by describing through older traditions the role of the prophet in relation to the king. The accounts of the anointing of Saul and David were fashioned, in Campbell's view, on the story of Jehu's anointing; hence his assertion that the Prophetic Record viewed kingship as a divine gift.

There are serious questions about this reconstruction which McCarter and Campbell do not address. As with Dietrich's theory of a DtrP much of the evidence for such a document is based on content. But are all stories about prophets written by prophets? This is especially problematic for Campbell who thinks in terms of prophetic schools or circles behind his Prophetic Record. He even sees material emanating from different prophetic circles. As with the idea of a Deuteronomistic school this is a nebulous notion. It does not explain how the stories came to be part of a single work. Surely they did not just gather themselves into collections. The issue of genre is also problematic, especially for Campbell. What kind of work was the Prophetic Record? What was the setting and purpose of the prophetic layer? If it comes from ca. 721 as Birch and McCarter contend, why are there no Northern prophetic tales after the Jehu dynasty?

These questions do not rule out the possibility of a prophetic work behind Kings, but they do raise doubts about its existence at least as formulated by McCarter and Campbell. The analysis in the following chapter will focus on the prophetic materials in the book of Kings to determine whether they form a stratum of composition and what they reveal about the formation of the work as a whole.

A SINGLE EXILIC COMPOSER

With this reconstruction of the DH scholarship would appear to have come full circle to Noth's original thesis. But scholars in this category have proposed important revisions concerning two aspects of Noth's model of composition (see the quotation on pp. 2-3). First, H.-D. Hoffmann (1980) and Brian Peckham (1983; 1985) begin from essentially the same point. Each perceives an inherent tension within Noth's proposal between the ideas of Dtr as author and editor ("Dtr war nicht nur 'Redaktor', sondern der Autor eines Geschichtswerkes," Noth 1967:11). Hoffmann and Peckham seek to resolve this tension, though in very different ways.

Hoffmann

For Hoffmann the DH was essentially a fictional history of Israel's cult by an exilic or post-exilic author (Dtr) who had very few actual sources. Hoffmann's view is based largely on his treatment of the book of Kings. He argues for the literary unity of several passages where previous scholars found evidence of different hands. He also tries to show that Dtr linked the accounts of individual kings in a contrasting pattern of good "reforming" kings with evil "reforming" kings. The climax of Dtr's progression of contrasts was Josiah's reform in 2 Kings 22-23, which had connections with every preceding reform and was designed to serve as the model for a new beginning after the exile. The linking of texts by means of different techniques is the hallmark of Dtr's hand and demonstrates the unity of his work. Dtr was not an editor at all but an inventive author.

Hoffmann's position is intriguing if idiosyncratic.[19] His demonstration of the linking of texts throughout the DH, especially in Kings, is valuable, and the alternation of good and evil "reformers" is suggestive. But he has failed to interact with contemporary scholarship on the DH. He dates the DH to the exile, under the influence of Noth, despite his perception of Josiah as the focus (*Zielpunkt*) of the work, and he never discusses this issue in detail. He does not deal with the arguments of Cross and others for a Josianic date for the DH and does not even cite in his bibliography any works that take this position. He effectively denies the existence of source material, but he is less than successful at explaining what most scholars have perceived as traditional material behind the book of Kings. His assertion that the DH is essentially fiction is also an extreme to which few scholars are willing to go. Hoffmann's perception of Dtr's creativity both in individual passages and in the overall structure of the DH is a refreshing change from the emphasis that scholarship since Noth has tended to place on

---

[19] See Provan (1988:22-24) and Weippert (1985:222-223).

redaction. But his view hardly replaces the model of composition initially posited by Noth.

Peckham

Peckham, in contrast, describes Dtr's role as primarily an editorial one. Noth's error, he believes, was in seeing Dtr's sources as fragmentary and discontinuous (1985:3). He sees the entire historical work from Genesis through Kings as having been formed over centuries in a series of revisions of a running historical tradition (1985:8).[20] Thus, J was expounded by the Josianic editor of the DH (Dtr[1]). An alternative interpretation of J was written by P. E was composed to supplement J and P and to offer a variant to Dtr[1]'s interpretation. The culmination of this process was a thorough rewriting of this traditional material by the exilic editor, Dtr[2].

Peckham shows how the DH may be read but has provided no evidence that it must be read this way. If traces of the earlier sources remain, where are they? If they have been thoroughly revised, how can one know they once existed? It is, in fact, integral to Peckham's theory that no trace of the series of traditions behind the DH remains because Dtr[2] so thoroughly rewrote what he inherited. But this explanation exacerbates the tension between the models of author and redactor for Dtr instead of resolving it. Peckham wants to see Dtr as an author, but he cannot ignore the evidence adduced by other scholars for redactional layers beneath the DH. He cannot escape the tendency of scholarship to explain the composition of the DH on the basis of a redactional model. His theory is even more idiosyncratic than Hoffmann's. This, plus the fact that it cannot be verified, renders it unacceptable.

Van Seters

The second aspect of Noth's statement about his compositional model which has proven significant for continuing research is his reference to parallels to Dtr's method of composition in the work of Hellenistic and Roman historians. Noth did not elaborate further on this set of parallels. But John Van Seters has now substantiated Noth's assertion in an important investigation of the genre of historiography in the Ancient Near Eastern and Mediterranean worlds (1983a; cf. 1981).

Van Seters dubs Dtr "the first known historian in Western civilization," (1983a:362) because he was the first to engage in the intellectual enterprise

---

[20] Freedman (1976) and Hayes and Hooker (1988:75) also take Genesis through Kings as a literary unit. Freedman calls this unit the "Primary History." Hayes and Hooker find the first edition of this work in Genesis - 2 Kings 18:12, minus Deuteronomy, and date it to the reign of Manasseh. Like Peckham, Freedman and Hayes and Hooker also present their ideas in summary fashion without supporting evidence.

of research (*historia*) for the purpose of composing a historical document for posterity. Dtr's *modus operandi* as envisioned by Van Seters is very similar to Noth's understanding. Dtr gathered disparate materials and arranged them paratactically into an extended literary work that rendered to Israel an account of its past (cf. Long 1984:19-21). Dtr was certainly dependent on sources of various kinds, but he also exercised a great deal of freedom in the arrangement and elaboration of those sources. He was the first to forge the sources together into a running account of history; there was no single extended document redacted by Dtr, no one *Vorlage*.

Like Noth, Van Seters believes that Greek historiography, especially Herodotus' *Histories,* furnishes the closest analogue to Dtr's brand of composition. He also believes the Neo-Babylonian chronicles to be the best parallels for the official sources cited in the DH. Partly because of these parallels, Van Seters agrees with Noth's exilic date for the DH. However, again like Noth, Van Seters sees several lengthy passages in the present DH as post-Dtr additions, not the least important of which is the Court History of David in 2 Samuel 2:8-4:12; 9-20 + 1 Kings 1-2 (1983a:277-291).

Van Seters has improved the case for Noth's compositional model in several respects. For one thing, he has revised Noth's understanding of the purpose of the DH, which has always been a drawback. Noth saw Dtr's reason for writing as entirely negative. He offered no hope for the future but simply tried to show that the destructions of Israel and Judah were their just desserts for centuries of sin. Van Seters suggests that Dtr's purpose was historiographic; he sought to render an account of his nation's past, perhaps under the impulse of its disintegration in the exile (cf. Damrosch 1987:163-165). But perhaps the most important facet of Van Seters's comparison with Greek historiography is that it adds concrete reinforcement to one of the most attractive features of Noth's compositional model. It explains how Dtr's History could be an editorial product as well as a work of great literary creativity and imagination. It shows that the dichotomy between Dtr as author and Dtr as editor is false.

Van Seters raises a number of other challenging points about biblical historiography that lie outside of our present concerns. However, his investigation of comparative historiography both supports and corrects Noth's model for the composition of the DH. Still, some of the same questions raised about Noth's initial theory, such as how to explain the literary unevenness or the presence of what appear to be pre-exilic themes, remain and will have to be addressed in a detailed analysis of the material.

SYNTHESIS

It is clear from the preceding survey that many scholars have abandoned Noth's model of composition for the DH in favor of a redactional one. Actually, the current situation in scholarship is even more complicated than this survey indicates. Taking off from the theories of Cross and Smend scholars have posited a series of redactional levels in two directions -- before

the exile and after the primary version of the History.[21] This is illustrated
by the recent dissertations of Rainer Stahl[22] and Mark O'Brien (1989). Stahl
is led to posit a total of nine Deuteronomistic levels of redaction behind the
DH: the fundamental history (DtrH),   a prophetic level (DtrP), three
nomistic levels (DtrN[1,2,3]) and four "theological" levels (DtrTh[1,2,3,4]).
O'Brien, following Campbell, reconstructs several redactional strata, each of
which may reflect more than one hand. He agrees in positing a Prophetic
Record as the basis of Samuel and Kings, which then received a Northern
expansion and the attachment of a corresponding Southern document before
coming into the hands of Dtr. The basic DtrH, written in the reign of
Josiah, was redacted three times in the exile, the final redaction being
nomistic in character.

The treatments of Stahl and O'Brien may be somewhat extreme. Redactional proposals do not all contrast so strongly with Noth's theory. For example, Cross attributed the bulk of the DH to his Dtr[1] and described the
work of Dtr[2] as relatively light glossing. But the results of Stahl and
O'Brien do illustrate what has happened to Noth's original proposition. The
more redactional levels one finds in the DH the more its overall unity is
compromised. Scholarship seems to have lost hold of the real insight of
Noth's theory of the DH, namely, that this History was fundamentally the
creation of a single individual. The emphasis on literary (source) criticism
and the proliferation of redactional levels in the DH are reminiscent of
Pentateuchal scholarship of past generations. The problems with this
approach have been well articulated by J. J. M. Roberts (1984:329) in his
review of H. Spieckermann's complex reconstruction of the Josiah account
(1982).

> It is possible, of course, that the composition of 2 Kings is the result of
> a process as complicated as that envisioned by S., but even if it were,
> one may well question whether it would still be possible for modern
> scholars to disentangle all these strands and supplements with the
> certainty that S. and company suppose. Such criticism runs the risk of
> discrediting the discipline in the same way that the splintering of the
> pentateuchal sources ultimately reached the point of absurdity.

The frustration with literary fragmentation has prompted recent studies
like those of Hoffmann and Peckham which try to return to Noth's view of
the unity of the DH in some form. It may also be part of the motive for

------

[21] For a fuller listing of recent works that follow the basic redactional approaches of
Smend and Cross see O'Brien 1989:7, n. 22 and p. 11, n. 33.

[22] *Aspekte der Geschichte deuteronomistischer Theologie. Zur Traditionsgeschichte
der Terminologie und zur Redaktionsgeschichte der Redekomposition.* Diss. B, Jena,
1982. Stahl's volume has been inaccessible to me. The information here is based on
the summary of it in *TL* 108 (1983) 74-75.

turning away altogether from historical critical approaches to the DH and adopting structural or "newer" literary methods.[23]

At the same time, the literary unevenness in so much of the DH must be satisfactorily explained. This is what Hoffmann and Peckham failed to do. In short, an acceptable reconstruction of the DH's formation must account for both its unity and its diversity -- not an easy task! Here it is important to reiterate that Noth's model for the DH allowed for the presence of later additions, although he did not find sufficient coherence between the additions to indicate redactional levels. As the previous survey suggests, in my view Noth's model for the composition of the DH is still the most useful, although it needs to be retested and perhaps revised in light of work on the DH during the past fifty years. The area for such testing should be the book of Kings. The scholarly debate over composition and related issues has converged on the book of Kings because it raises the most difficulties, literary critical and ideological, for the understanding of a unified DH. Of course, what has happened in Kings may not necessarily be true for the rest of the DH, as Lohfink and Provan observed. This point will have to be considered before drawing conclusions for the entire DH. But a sounding of Kings is still the most fruitful way of approaching the question of composition in the DH. I shall begin that sounding in the next chapter by taking up the suggestion of a separate layer of prophetic editing in Kings.

----

[23] Cf. Polzin 1989:1-17. Many of Polzin's criticisms of the "genetic" approach on these pages are well founded. But his wholesale rejection of historical criticism is unwarranted. Polzin spurns attempts to reconstruct a "pre-text" behind the canonical text. Yet, he accepts and treats the DH, which is not a canonical unit but a reconstruction of historical criticism If "poetic" methods can be used to analyze one scholarly reconstruction why can they not be used for others? The objectives and hence the methods of this monograph are strictly historical-critical. But I believe that both "genetic" and "poetic" methods have value, and I hope that scholars can discover how to use them both as complements for each other in analysis. A clearer understanding of the DH's composition may even help to foster interaction between the approaches.

CHAPTER ONE

THE *READERS DIGEST* ® ACCOUNT OF JEROBOAM: AN ANALYSIS OF 3 REIGNS 12:24A-Z

The first section in Kings that includes material about Northern prophetic activity is the Jeroboam cycle in 1 Kings 11-14. What is particularly interesting and important about this section is the lengthy "supplement" in the LXX at 3 Reigns 12:24a-z.[1] Its text is important enough to reproduce here with a translation.

THE TEXT OF 3 REIGNS 12:24A-Z[2]

24a Και ο βασιλευς Σαλωμων κοιμαται μετα των πατερων αυτου, και θαπτεται μετα των πατερων αυτου εν πολει Δαυειδ· και εβασιλευσεν Ροβοαμ υιος αυτου αντ ' αυτου εν Ιερουσαλημ, υιος ων εκκαιδεκα ετων εν τω βασιλευειν αυτον· και δωδεκα ετη εβασιλευσεν εν Ιερουσαλημ. και ονομα της μητρος αυτου Νααναν, θυγατηρ Ανα υιου Ναας βασιλεως Αμμων· και εποιησεν το πονηρον ενωπιον Κυριου και ουκ επορευθη εν οδω Δαυειδ του πατρος αυτου.

24b Και ην ανθρωπος εξ ορους Εφραιμ δουλος τω Σαλωμων, και ονομα αυτω Ιεροβοαμ, και ονομα της μητρος αυτου Σαρεισα, πορνη· και εδωκεν αυτον Σαλωμων εις αρχοντα σκυταλης επι τας αρσεις οικου

---

[1] The text of Kings which I intend as the subject of this study is an eclectic one, i.e., the text which can be determined to be the most primitive by applying the art of textual criticism to a careful comparison of the textual witnesses. Besides the Masoretic Text of the Hebrew Bible the "Old Greek" translation, best preserved in Codex Vaticanus (LXX^B) and the "Lucianic" minuscules (b,o,c$_2$,e$_2$), are very valuable witnesses. See McCarter (1986) and Trebolle (1980:12-27).

In the discussion to follow I use the term "supplement" (always in quotation marks) merely as a convention without intending thereby to express any judgement about the origin and value of this material. My view of it will become clear in my analysis.

[2] The text reproduced here is that of Codex Vaticanus (LXX^B) as given by Brooke, McLean, and Thackeray (1930) with variants included where they are significant for the subsequent study. The translation in my own.

Ιωσηφ. και ωκοδομησεν τω Σαλωμωντι[3] την Σαρειφα την εν ορει Εφραιμ, και ησαν αυτω αρματα τριακοσια ιππων· ουτος ωκοδομησεν την ακραν εν ταις αρσεσιν οικου Εφραιμ· ουτος συνεκλεισεν την πολιν Δαυειδ, και ην επαιρομενος επι την βασιλειαν. [24c] και εζητει Σαλωμων θανατωσαι αυτον· και εφοβηθη και απεδρα αυτος προς Σουσακειμ βασιλεα Αιγυπτου, και ην μετ᾿ αυτου εως απεθανεν Σαλωμων. [24d] και ηκουσεν Ιεροβοαμ εν Αιγυπτω οτι τεθνηκεν Σαλωμων, και ελαλησεν εις τα ωτα Σουσακειμ βασιλεως Αιγυπτου λεγων Εξαποστειλον με, και απελευσομαι εγω εις την γην μου· και ειπεν αυτω Σουσακειμ Αιτησαι τι αιτημα και δωσω σοι. [24e] και Σουσακειμ εδωκεν τω Ιεροβοαμ την Ανω αδελφην θεκεμεινας την πρεσβυτεραν της γυναικος αυτου αυτω εις γυναικα· αυτη η μεγαλη εν μεσω των θυγατερων του βασιλεως, και ετεκεν τω Ιεροβοαμ τον Αβια υιον αυτου. [24f] και ειπεν Ιεροβοαμ προς Σουσακειμ Οντως εξαποστειλον με, και απελευσομαι. και απεστειλεν αυτον Σουσακειμ.[4] και εξηλθεν Ιεροβοαμ εξ Αιγυπτου, και ηλθεν εις γην Σαρειρα την εν ορει Εφραιμ· και συναγεται εκει παν σκηπτρον Εφραιμ· και ωκοδομησεν Ιεροβοαμ εκει χαρακα.

[24g] Και ηρρωστησε το παιδαριον αυτου αρρωστια κραταια σφοδρα· και επορευθη Ιεροβοαμ επερωτησαι υπερ του παιδαριου· και ειπε προς Ανω την γυναικα αυτου Αναστηθι, πορευου· επερωτησον τον θεον υπερ του παιδαριου, ει ζησεται εκ της αρρωστιας αυτου. [24h] και ανθρωπος ην εν Σηλω και ονομα αυτω Αχεια, και ουτος ην υιος εξηκοντα ετων, και ρημα Κυριου μετ᾿ αυτου. και ειπεν Ιεροβοαμ προς την γυναικα αυτου Αναστηθι και λαβε εις την χειρα σου τω ανθρωπω του θεου αρτους και κολλυρια τοις τεκνοις αυτου και σταφυλην και σταμνον μελιτος. [24i] και ανεστη η γυνη, και ελαβεν εις την χειρα αυτης αρτους και δυο κολλυρια και σταφυλην και σταμνον μελιτος τω Αχεια· και ο ανθρωπος πρεσβυτερος, και οι οφθαλμοι αυτου ημβλυωπουν του

---

[3] The majority of witnesses read τω Σαλωμωντι. B,u: Σαλωμων.
[4] BNhjnua₂ lack και απεστειλεν αυτον Σουσακειμ.

ιδειν. ^{24k} και ανεστη εκ Σαρειρα και πορευεται· και εγενετο ελθουσης αυτης εις την πολιν προς Αχεια τον Σηλωνειτην, και ειπεν Αχεια τω παιδαριω αυτου Εξελθε δη εις απαντην Ανω τη γυναικι Ιεροβοαμ και ερεις αυτη Εισελθε και μη στης, οτι ταδε λεγει Κυριος Σκληρα εγω επαποστελλω επι σε. ^{24l} και εισηλθεν Ανω προς τον ανθρωπον του θεου, και ειπεν αυτη Αχεια Ινα τι μοι ενηνοχας αρτους και σταφυλην και κολλυρια και σταμνον μελιτος, ταδε λεγει Κυριος Ιδου συ απελευση απ ' εμου, και εσται εισελθουσης σου την πυλην εις Σαρειρα, και τα κορασια σου εξελευσονται σοι εις συναντησιν και ερουσιν σοι Το παιδαριον τεθνηκεν. ^{24m} οτι ταδε λεγει Κυριος Ιδου εγω εξολεθρευσω του Ιεροβοαμ ουρουντα προς τοιχον, και εσονται οι τεθνηκοτες του Ιεροβοαμ εν τη πολει, καταφαγονται οι κυνες, και τον τεθνηκοτα εν τω αγρω καταφαγεται τα πετεινα του ουρανου. και το παιδαριον κοψονται^{5} Ουαι κυριε, οτι ευρεθη εν αυτω ρημα καλον περι του κυριου. ^{24n} και απηλθεν η γυνη ως ηκουσεν· και εγενετο ως εισηλθεν εις την Σαρειρα, και το παιδαριον απεθανεν, και εξηλθεν η κραυγη εις απαντην.

Και επορευθη Ιεροβοαμ εις Σικιμα την εν ορει Εφραιμ και συνηθροισεν εκει τας φυλας του Ισραηλ, και ανεβη εκει Ροβοαμ υιος Σαλωμων. ^{24o} και λογος Κυριου εγενετο προς Σαμαιαν τον Ενλαμει λεγων Λαβε σεαυτω ιματιον καινον το ουκ εισεληλυθος εις υδωρ, και ρηξον αυτο δωδεκα ρηγματα· και δωσεις τω Ιεροβοαμ^{6} και ερεις αυτω Ταδε λεγει Κυριος Λαβε σεαυτω δεκα^{7} ρηγματα του περιβαλεσθαι σε. και ελαβεν Ιεροβοαμ· και ειπεν Σαμαιας Ταδε λεγει Κυριος επι τας δεκα φυλας του Ισραηλ βασιλευσεις.^{8} ^{24p} Και ειπεν ο λαος προς Ροβοαμ υιον Σαλωμων Ο πατηρ σου εβαρυνεν τον κλοιον αυτου εφ ' ημας, και εβαρυνεν τα βρωματα της τραπεζης αυτου· και νυνι κουφιεις συ εφ ' ημας, και δουλευσομεν σοι. και

---

^{5} B,u: κοψεται. Most witnesses read the plural.
^{6} The Lucianic witnesses, boc$_2$e$_2$, add δεκα ρηγματα.
^{7} B alone has δωδεκα.
^{8} Reading βασιλευσεις with the Lucianic mss. B ends the verse with Ισραηλ.

ειπεν Ροβοαμ προς τον λαον Ετι τριων ημερων και αποκριθησομαι υμιν ρημα.   ²⁴q και ειπεν Ροβοαμ Εισαγαγετε μοι τους πρεσβυτερους, και συμβουλευσομαι μετ᾽ αυτων τι αποκριθω τω λαω ρημα εν τη ημερα τη τριτη.   και ελαλησεν Ροβοαμ εις τα ωτα αυτων καθως απεστειλεν ο λαος προς αυτον· και ειπον οι πρεσβυτεροι του λαου Ουτως ελαλησεν προς σε ο λαος λαλησεις προς τον λαον αγαθως.⁹ ²⁴r και διεσκεδασεν Ροβοαμ την βουλην αυτων, και ουκ ηρεσεν ενωπιον αυτου· και απεστειλεν και εισηγαγεν τους συντροφους αυτου, και ελαλησεν αυτοις Ταυτα¹⁰ και ταυτα απεστειλεν προς με λεγων ο λαος.   και ειπαν οι συντροφοι αυτου Ουτως λαλησεις προς τον λαον λεγων Η μικροτης μου παχυτερα υπερ την οσφυν του πατρος μου· ο πατηρ μου εμαστιγου υμας μαστιγξιν, εγω δε καταρξω υμας εν σκορπιοις.   ²⁴s και ηρεσεν το ρημα ενωπιον Ροβοαμ· και απεκριθη τω λαω καθως συνεβουλευσαν αυτω οι συντροφοι αυτου τα παιδαρια.   ²⁴t και ειπεν πας ο λαος ως ανηρ εις εκαστος τω πλησιον αυτου, και ανεκραξαν απαντες λεγοντες Ου μερις ημιν εν Δαυειδ ουδε κληρονομια εν υιω Ιεσσαι· εις τα σκηνωματα σου, Ισραηλ, οτι ουτος ο ανθρωπος ουκ εις αρχοντα ουδε εις ηγουμενον.   ²⁴u και διεσπαρη πας ο λαος εκ Σικιμων, και απηλθεν εκαστος εις το σκηνωμα αυτου.   και κατεκρατησεν Ροβοαμ, και απηλθεν και ανεβη επι το αρμα αυτου και εισηλθεν εις Ιερουσαλημ· και πορευονται οπισω αυτου παν σκηπτρον Ιουδα και παν σκηπτρον Βενιαμειν.

²⁴x Και εγενετο ενισταμενου του ενιαυτου και συνηθροισεν Ροβοαμ παντα ανδρα Ιουδα και Βενιαμειν, και ανεβη του πολεμειν προς Ιεροβοαμ εις Σικιμα.   ²⁴y και εγενετο ρημα Κυριου προς Σαμαιαν ανθρωπον του Θεου Ειπον τω Ροβοαμ βασιλει Ιουδα και προς παντα οικον Ιουδα και Βενιαμειν και προς το καταλειμμα του λαου

---

⁹ B,a₂ end the verse with λαος, but most mss. continue with λαλησεις προς τον λαον αγαθως or the like.   Similarly, also the Old Latin: *et sic dices ad populum.*
¹⁰ B,a₂:τα αυτα.

λεγων Ταδε λεγει Κυριος Ουκ αναβησεσθε ουδε
πολεμησετε προς τους αδελφους υμων υιους Ισραηλ·
αναστρεφετε εκαστος εις τον οικον αυτου, οτι παρ ᾿ εμου
γεγονεν το ρημα τουτο. ²⁴ᶻ και ηκουσαν του λογου Κυριου,
και ανεσχον του πορευθηναι, κατα το ρημα Κυριου.

TRANSLATION OF 3 REIGNS 12:24A-Z

²⁴ᵃ King Solomon slept with his fathers and was buried with his fathers in the city of David. Rehoboam, his son, became king in his stead in Jerusalem. He was sixteen years old when he became king, and he reigned twelve years in Jerusalem. The name of his mother was Naanan, daughter of Ana, son of Naas, king of Ammon. He did what was evil before the Lord and did not walk in the way of David his father.

²⁴ᵇ There was a man from the hill country of Ephraim, a servant of Solomon, whose name was Jeroboam. The name of his mother was Sareisa. She was a harlot. Solomon made him head of the levy of the house of Joseph. Jeroboam rebuilt Sareira, which is in the hill country of Ephraim, for Solomon. He had 300 horse-drawn chariots. He it was who built the *millo* with the levies of the house of Ephraim. It was he who closed in the city of David, and he exalted himself to the kingship. ²⁴ᶜ So Solomon sought to kill him. Then he was afraid and fled to Shishak king of Egypt. And he was with him until Solomon died. ²⁴ᵈ When Jeroboam heard in Egypt that Solomon had died he spoke to Shishak king of Egypt saying, "Send me away and let me go to my country." Shishak said to him, "Ask what you wish and I will give it to you." ²⁴ᵉ So Shishak gave to Jeroboam, as his wife, Ano the older sister of Thekemeinas, his wife. She was the oldest among the daughters of the king. She bore to Jeroboam Abijah his son. ²⁴ᶠ And Jeroboam said to Shishak, "Now send me away and let me depart. So Shishak sent him away. And Jeroboam left Egypt and went to the land of Sareira, which is in the hill country of Ephraim. All the tribe of Ephraim gathered there, and Jeroboam built a fortification there.

²⁴ᵍ Now his child became ill with a very serious illness. So Jeroboam went to inquire about the child. And he said to Ano his wife, "Arise, go. Inquire of God about the child, whether he will recover from his illness." ²⁴ʰ There was a man in Shiloh whose name was Ahijah and who was sixty years old, and the word of the Lord was with him. So Jeroboam said to his wife, "Arise and take in your hand loaves of bread for the man of God and cakes for his children and a bunch of grapes and a jar of honey." ²⁴ⁱ So the woman arose and took in her hand loaves of bread, two cakes, a bunch of grapes, and a jar of honey for Ahijah. Now the man was old and his eyes were dim so that he could not see. ²⁴ᵏ She departed from Sareira and went. And when she came to the city, to Ahijah the Shilonite, Ahijah said to his servant, "Go out to meet Ano the wife Jeroboam and you shall say to her, 'Come in. Do not stand still, for thus says the Lord, "I am sending harsh

tidings about you."'" ^{24l} Then Ano came to the man of God, and Ahijah said to her, "Why have you brought to me loaves of bread, a bunch of grapes, cakes, and a jar of honey? Thus says the Lord, 'When you depart from me and come to the gate of Sareira your maidservants will come out to meet you and they will say to you, "The child has died."' ^{24m} For thus says the Lord, 'I will destroy all those belonging to Jeroboam who urinate on a wall. Those belonging to Jeroboam who die in the city the dogs will eat, and he who dies in the country the birds of the sky will eat. They will mourn the child, 'Alas, Lord,' for in him was found something good concerning the Lord."'" ^{24n} So the woman left when she heard this. And when she came to Sareira the child died, and the cry went out to meet her.

Jeroboam went to Shechem which is in the hill country of Ephraim, and he gathered there the tribes of Israel. Then Rehoboam, son of Solomon, went up there. ^{24o} The word of the Lord came to Shemaiah the Enlamite saying, "Take a new garment that has never been washed and tear it into twelve pieces. You shall give them to Jeroboam and you shall say to him, 'Thus says the Lord, "Take ten pieces to dress yourself."'" So Jeroboam took them. Then Shemaiah said, "Thus says the Lord, 'You shall reign over the ten tribes of Israel.'" ^{24p} The people said to Rehoboam son of Solomon, "Your father made his yoke heavy upon us and increased the food on his table. Now you lighten [the yoke] upon us, and we will serve you." Rehoboam said to the people, "Wait three days, and I will answer you." ^{24q} Rehoboam said, "Gather the elders to me so that I may take counsel with them how I should answer the people on the third day." Rehoboam spoke to them (the elders) as the people had sent to him. The elders of the people said, "As the people spoke to you so should you speak kindly to the people." ^{24r} But Rehoboam rejected their advice, and it did not please him. He sent and gathered those who had been brought up with him and told them, "The people sent to me saying thus and so." Those who had been brought up with him said, "Thus you shall say to the people, 'My little finger is thicker than my father's loins. My father beat you with whips, but I will rule you with scorpions.'" ^{24s} The saying pleased Rehoboam. He answered the people as the youths, who had been brought up with him, advised him. ^{24t} All the people spoke as one man, each to his neighbor, and they all cried out saying, "We have no part in David nor inheritance in the son of Jesse. To your tents, Israel! For this man shall not be leader or ruler. ^{24u} All the people were dispersed from Shechem and went, each to his tent. Rehoboam strengthened himself and entered his chariot and went to Jerusalem. All the tribe of Judah and all the tribe of Benjamin followed him.

^{24x} At the beginning of the year Rehoboam gathered all the men of Judah and Benjamin and went up to fight Jeroboam at Shechem. ^{24y} But the word of the Lord came to Shemaiah the man of God, "Say to Rehoboam king of Judah and to all the house of Judah and Benjamin and to the rest of the people, 'Thus says the Lord, "Do not go up or fight against your brothers, the children of Israel. Each of you return to his house, for this matter has come from me."'" ^{24z} Then they listened to the word of the Lord and refrained from going up according to the word of the Lord.

Summary

As indicated in the translation, the "supplement" account divides neatly into five sections. It begins in v 24a with the concluding formula for Solomon and the initial formula for Rehoboam. This is followed by three extended narratives. The first in vv 24b-f introduces Jeroboam and describes his relationship to Solomon. Next, it relates Jeroboam's flight to Egypt out of fear of Solomon. Its notice of Jeroboam's return to Israel after the death of Solomon includes an account of Jeroboam's marriage to Ano, daughter of Shishak (vv 24d-f). The second narrative in vv 24g-nα recounts the story, familiar from 1 Kgs 14:1-18, of the illness and resulting death of Jeroboam's son. A part of that story is the oracle of Ahijah to Jeroboam's wife predicting the boy's death. That oracle includes a condemnation of Jeroboam's entire house in v 24m. The third narrative in the "supplement" (vv 24nβ-u) is an account of the convocation at Shechem and the division of Israel. Its MT parallel is in 1 Kings 12. However, the "supplement" version also includes in v 24o the prophetic sign of the torn garment and the accompanying oracle announcing the division of the kingdom, whose counterpart in the MT is in 1 Kgs 11:29-39. The "supplement" concludes in vv 24x-z with Shemaiah's oracle to Rehoboam, warning him against waging war with Israel since the division is Yahweh's doing.

PREVIOUS EVALUATIONS OF THE "SUPPLEMENT"

Two very different opinions about the "supplement" have arisen over the years.[11] My own analysis will draw on work from both camps, so it is worthwhile to review them briefly here. One view characterizes the "supplement" as "midrash" or even a "jumble" of midrashes (Montgomery 1951:254). D. W. Gooding has been the primary advocate of this view. He sees the "supplement" as a kind of midrash on the MT whose purpose was to vilify Jeroboam, in deliberate contrast to the other LXX account, which sought to whitewash Jeroboam's character (1967a:187-188).[12] R. P. Gordon has assumed Gooding's position in his article (1975) contending that the "supplement" is untrustworthy as a historical source.

---

[11] The *Forschungsbericht* in Debus (1967:68-80) is the fullest as far as it goes. For more recent bibliography see Gordon (1975:368-369, 377). Skinner's (n.d.:443-446) brief summary of the content of the "supplement" and scholarly opinions about it is very judicious and still quite useful despite its age.

[12] This is typical of Gooding's overall perspective (1964; 1965a; 1965b; 1967b; 1968; 1969a; 1969b; 1972; 1976) that the LXX in Kings is a witness not to a variant text type but to ancient exegesis of the MT.

Debus (1967:80) rightly criticizes the use of the term "midrash" for the "supplement," since its accounts are generally shorter than the MT's. This view also does not give sufficient consideration to the fact that the "supplement" is in the Old Greek, one of the earliest and best textual witnesses for the text of Kings.[13] But the greatest shortcoming of this view is its lack of an adequate explanation for the most startling feature of the "supplement" - its paucity of Deuteronomistic language *vis-à-vis* the MT. The absence from 3 Reigns 12:24g-nα of the searing Deuteronomistic condemnations of its MT (14:1-18) counterpart poses an especially serious problem for the idea that the "supplement" is out to vilify Jeroboam. There are a variety of reasons for the many differences between the "supplement" and the MT. This view of the "supplement" helps to explain some of them, but its interpretation of others is forced. In a word, it is simplistic.

The other opinion about the "supplement" is that it is a genuine variant to the Jeroboam cycle in the MT. Those who favor this view cite its overall lack of Deuteronomistic language and argue that its variations with the MT are not tendentious. J. Trebolle (1980) has recently championed this perspective. He contends that the "supplement" material is pre-Dtr and that it illustrates both redactional and recensional activity behind the book of Kings. His detailed literary critical analysis concludes that several important passages, above all its prophetic oracles, are insertions. His work shows that "lower" (textual) and "higher" (literary, form, redaction) criticism cannot be done in isolation from each other.

Trebolle's literary critical observations are valuable. His determination that the oracles in the "supplement" are insertions suggests that a pre-Dtr, prophetic redaction lies behind the MT and makes the "supplement" of particular interest for the present study. At the same time, there are important questions about the "supplement" that Trebolle has not addressed. These concern especially the nature of the "supplement" as a whole. What kind of document is it, and who is responsible for it? Trebolle points out signs of editing, especially the use of narrative resumption or *Wiederaufnahme*,[14] throughout the "supplement." But this technique can be used by authors to organize narratives as well as by editors to make insertions. Trebolle needs to show how the various editorial additions relate to each other and to the

---

[13] Gordon himself (1975:370-371) lists the following Old Greek features of the "supplement" (cf. Debus, 1967:55-56; Shenkel 1968:32-33). 1. The occurrence of the historical present in vv 24a (κοιμαται and θαπτεται), 24f (συναγεται), and 24u (πορευονται) where the καιγε recension would use the aorist. 2. The use of ενωπιον Κυριου in v 24a where καιγε would use εν οφθαλμοις Κυριου to translate בעיני יהוה. 3. The word εκαστος in v 24y for MT אישׁ. καιγε typically uses ανηρ for אישׁ when it means "each." Shenkel (1968:32-33) observes that the "supplement" was omitted by texts exhibiting the hexaplaric recension (Codex Alexandrinus, the Syrohexapla, and the Armenian) and other late Greek witnesses which correct to the MT.

[14] For an introduction to this technique see Kuhl (1952).

"supplement" at large.   Also, there are variants and tensions in the
"supplement" which Trebolle does not discuss but which need to be treated
in conjunction with the other signs of editing in order to understand the entire composition. Trebolle's volume, then, paves the way for a more cogent
assessment of the "supplement."

THE COMPOSITION OF 3 REIGNS 12:24A-Z

24g-nα

I begin my analysis of the "supplement" with its version of Jeroboam's sick
son (cf. 1 Kgs 14:1-18), because, as Shenkel (1968:32) suggests, it is probably the reason that the "supplement" has been preserved. It is the only parallel in the major Greek witnesses to the MT episode. It was added to the
LXX *Vorlage* and retained there in order to fill a void in comparison with
the MT.[15]
The focus of this story in both the MT and "supplement" is the oracle
against the house of Jeroboam (1 Kgs 14:7-11; 3 Reigns 12:24m). The
MT's version of this oracle has a long Deuteronomistic section before the
deprecating judgement on the house of Jeroboam in 14:10-11.   The
"supplement" has only the curse. In the MT the oracle is logical, since it
comes after Jeroboam has been made king. But the oracle's placement in the
"supplement" makes no sense, because it curses Jeroboam's dynasty before
he even becomes king. This misplacement is significant because it suggests
that the "supplement" story or some feature of it is secondary *vis-à-vis* the
Jeroboam cycle in the MT.
Trebolle (1980:152-153) argues that the "supplement" version of the oracle (v 24m - up to και το παιδαριον) is an insertion which interrupted
Ahijah's prediction about how Ano will learn of her son's death. In his view
the narrative originally read:

> When you depart from me and come to the gate of Sareira your
> maidservants will come out to meet you, and they will say to you, "The
> child has died." [insertion] They will mourn the child, 'Alas, Lord," for
> in him was found something good concerning the Lord.

---

[15] Or, more precisely, the text type represented by the MT but before it became the
received text and reached its final form as we know it today. The term "proto-rabbinic"
is perhaps the most accurate way of referring to the text at this stage (cf. McKenzie
1985a:76, n. 18). Of course, the MT as we have it is the only way we have of
knowing what the proto-rabbinic text looked like. Hence, with this *caveat* in mind I
shall continue to refer to the MT for comparison with the "supplement" in this chapter.

Trebolle believes that the insertion separated the verb κοψονται ("they will mourn") in v 24m from its subject, τα κορασια σου ("your maidservants"), in v 24l. The inserted oracle forecast the demise of Jeroboam's house but did not relate to the boy's death. Hence, Trebolle finds three levels of writing behind 1 Kgs 14:1-18. The original story was a "consultation of a prophet in a case of illness" (Trebolle 1980:159-162). This story had affinities with other prophetic legends especially in the Elijah and Elisha cycles. At this level the oracle simply announced the death of the boy. The insertion in v 24m changed the focus of the oracle so that the boy's death became a symbol of Yahweh's animosity toward Jeroboam. Finally, the Deuteronomistic speech in 1 Kgs 14:7-9, 14-16 brought the story to its present condition as in the MT.

A major problem with Trebolle's reconstruction is that the "supplement" oracle is form critically incomplete. The judgement stands by itself and is therefore groundless. One must look to the MT (14:7-9) for the basis of the judgement oracle and for its complete form. Also, Trebolle has misunderstood the significance of the last sentence of v 24m, "One will mourn the child, 'Alas, Lord,' for in him was found something good concerning the Lord." This sentence is very similar to 1 Kgs 14:13:

3 Reigns 12:24m	1 Kgs 14:13
και το παιδαριον κοψονται ουαι κυριε	וספדו לו כל ישראל
	וקברו אתו כי זה לבדו
	יבא לירבעם אל קבר
οτι ευρεθη εν αυτω ρημα	יען נמצא בו דבר
καλον περι κυριου	טוב אל יהוה
	אלהי ישראל בבית ירבעם

One must know the MT version in order to make sense of the "supplement" reading here. The MT refers to the preceding curse of non-burial. The boy, who is the only one in Jeroboam's family pleasing to Yahweh, will be rewarded by being the only one to receive burial. But the "supplement" parallel does not mention burial and therefore lacks the connection between the curse and the mourning for the lad. The "supplement" sentence presupposes the MT.

The "supplement" version of the oracle, then, has come from the MT. The writer who borrowed it drew only from the judgement (14:10-11) and its explanation (14:13), hence the lack of obvious Deuteronomistic language. It is not that he deliberately excluded that language, but he was interested in giving an abbreviated account and thus included only a skeleton version of the oracle.

There are also form critical problems with Trebolle's view that most of v 24m is an insertion. Again, if one removes it or the part of it that Trebolle regards as an addition, there is no reason for the boy's death. The parallels that Trebolle adduces for the "consultation in a case of illness" speak to this matter. Where healing or recovery takes place an accompanying oracle is unnecessary, though it may occur (2 Kgs 20:5-6). But where the result is negative one expects a reason to be given by way of a judgement oracle (2 Kgs 1:3-4). Again, the entire "supplement" account in vv 24g-nα appears to be an abbreviated borrowing of the MT version in 1 Kgs 14:1-18. This is the cause for the absence from 3 Reigns 12:24m of Yahweh's revelation to Ahijah that Jeroboam's wife is coming to see him and the commission to deliver a certain message to her (14:5)

Most of the differences between the MT and "supplement" in this story are the result of the attachment to the latter of motifs from other tales about prophets that do not fit well in this story. Both the MT and "supplement" attest this phenomenon in the motif of Ahijah's blindness due to old age (cf. Eli, 1 Sam 4:15). In the MT (14:4) this motif is in tension with the disguise theme. Why should Jeroboam's wife disguise herself if Ahijah is blind? Both motifs have the same function. They show that one cannot deceive a prophet, for he has vision in another dimension of reality (cf. 2 Kgs 6:15-20). But the disguise motif is integral to the story in 1 Kings 14 (vv 2, 5, 6), while the single mention of the blindness motif appears to be secondary.

Similarly, Ahijah's blindness serves no purpose in the "supplement" version of this story. One cannot argue for the priority of its account on this point. It is not integral to the story like the disguise motif in the MT (14:5-6). Its single mention (v 24i) is, so to speak, a blind motif. It also causes a doublet with the note about Ahijah's age in v 24h. The "supplement" contains several other motifs drawn from stories about prophets that are absent from the MT. These include Jeroboam's going himself to inquire (v 24g; cf. Saul - 1 Sam 9:5-10), Ahijah's sending his servant (v 24k; cf. Elisha - 2 Kgs 4:25), his question to Ano about her gift (v 24l; cf. his question in 1 Kgs 14:6), and Ano's encounter with the maid-servants who inform her of her son's death (v 24l; cf. 1 Sam 10:2-7).

But if the "supplement" version of this story presumes the MT and reflects frequent borrowing of prophetic motifs why does it not include the disguise motif? The desire to avoid tension with Ahijah's blindness is not an adequate reason. Ahijah's question to Ano about her gift (v 24l) instead of her disguise (1 Kgs 14:6) indicates that the disguise theme has been studiously avoided. It is evident from Jeroboam's mandate to his wife in 1 Kgs 14:2 that the disguise motif in the MT presumes the story of Ahijah's designation of Jeroboam as king (1 Kgs 11:26-40). The "supplement" counterparts to that story are in its other two narratives which we must examine before explaining its lack of the disguise theme.

24b-f

A good deal of the case for the vilification of Jeroboam in the "supplement" is based on the identification of his mother as a harlot in v 24b. Some (Olmstead 1913:21; Aberbach and Smolar 1969:69-70) have observed that the similar reference to Jephthah's mother (Judg 11:1) does not seem meant to vilify him. But if the "supplement" presupposes the MT, as I have argued for vv 24g-na, the reference to Jeroboam's mother can hardly be just a variant tradition. It is best regarded as a motif along the lines of Judg 8:31; 11:1 placing a future leader in the lowest possible social status. Whether or not it is meant to vilify Jeroboam it certainly does not allow one to dismiss the "supplement" as character assassination.

Jeroboam is further identified in v 24b as a servant of Solomon (cf. 1 Kgs 11:26) whom he appointed over the levy of the house of Joseph. The latter expression occurs in 1 Kgs 11:28. But the "supplement" lacks the explanation, given by the MT in that verse, for why Solomon chose Jeroboam.

The report of Jeroboam's building activity at Sareira[16] is an adaptation from the account of his building at Shechem (1 Kgs 12:25; Gordon 1975: 380) in the MT:

v 24b	12:25
και ωκοδομησεν	ויבן ירבעם
τω Σαλωμωντι	
την Σαρειφα την εν ορει Εφραψ	את שכם בהר אפרים

Benzinger (1899:82), following (Winckler 1892:11, n. 3), contends that Solomon's name is a gloss and that the verse actually describes Jeroboam building a fortress at Sareira. But this is unlikely, since the writer specifically mentions a fortress as the object of Jeroboam's building in v 24f. In v 24b it is Sareira itself that he builds, or more likely, rebuilds (cf. Gordon 1975:380). The "supplement" writer has simply combined the information about Jeroboam's position over the labor force with the knowledge of Solomon's building activity.

The building projects on the *millo* and the city of David which v 24b attributes to Jeroboam are described in the MT (1 Kgs 11:27) as Solomon's work.[17]

---

[16] The difference between Sareira and Zeredah (MT 11:26) is the result of ר/ד confusion in the *Vorlage* of the "supplement" (cf. Gordon 1975:379n; Wallace 1986:26n).

[17] It is tempting to suggest that the "supplement" writer attributed the building activity in Jerusalem to Jeroboam and not to Solomon as a result of dividing 1 Kgs 11:27 differently than in the MT. The MT has "This is the way he raised his hand against the king. Solomon built the *millo* ...." The "supplement" writer could have read the same verse as "This is the way he raised his hand against King Solomon. He

3 Reigns 12:24b	1 Kgs 11:27
αυτος ωκοδομησεν την ακραν	שלמה בנה את המלוא
εν ταις αρσεσεν οικου Εφραιμ	
ουτος συνεκλεισεν	סגר
την πολιν Δαυειδ	את פרץ עיר דוד אביו

The two verses are very similar. The major difference between them is the additional line in the "supplement" which is drawn from the earlier statement that Solomon appointed Jeroboam εις αρχοντα σκυταλης επι τας αρσεις οικου Ιωσηφ. The expression, "the house of Ephraim," is unusual. It occurs elsewhere only in Judg 10:9 and is a further indication of the imitative nature of this verse.

Gooding (1967:187; 1969:12) and Gordon (1975:380-382) argue that the verb συνεκλεισεν here means "lay siege to" and that Jeroboam did not just "close in" the city of David but actually besieged it with his army of 300 chariots. Trebolle (1980:194-195) has shown that their interpretation is forced. Similar passages in 3 Reigns (2:35e; 10:23; 11:27) refer to Solomon's construction works. Furthermore, the interpretation of Gooding only works in Greek, since the Hebrew verb סגר is never used for besieging a city. Of course, this fits with Gooding's view that the LXX translators exegeted the MT. But we will see evidence that the "supplement" was originally written in Hebrew and was already in place when the book of Kings was translated into Greek.

The claim that Jeroboam's 300 chariots are mentioned simply to enhance his reputation (Evans 1983:117-118) seems as forced as Gooding's view. Trebolle (1980:194-195) sees the chariots not in the context of Jeroboam's rebel activity but in that of Solomon's administration over the district of the Ephraimite hill country and perhaps (n. 364) as a reference to one of Solomon's chariot cities (1 Kgs 9:19; 10:26). This understanding fits well after the reference to Jeroboam building Sareira. In 2 Sam 15:1; 1 Kgs 1:5 chariotry is a motif for the declaration of kingship, but the reference to 300 chariots is unprecedented and suggests that a different origin and meaning than political revolt lies behind it. Trebolle's allusion to 1 Kgs 10:27, which refers to Solomon's chariot force as 1400 strong, suggests another explanation for the number in the "supplement." Its writer referred to Sareira as one of Solomon's chariot cities and placed approximately one-fourth of his chariot force there.

(i.e., Jeroboam) built the *millo*." The problem with this suggestion is that the final word of the verse, אביו, "his father," is attested by all witnesses and makes it clear that Solomon is the subject of the second sentence.

Verse 24b, then, is not an account of Jeroboam's revolt. It is not an interpretation of the MT story that seeks to vilify him. It is not even a narrative. It is best characterized as a collection of statements drawn from the
MT to introduce Jeroboam.

Trebolle argues that the story of Jeroboam's marriage to Shishak's daughter (vv 24d-e) is an addition whose borders are marked by the reiteration of
Jeroboam's request to be sent home:

v 24d	v 24f
και ελαλησεν	και ειπεν Ιεροβοαμ
εις τα ωτα Σουσακειμ	προς Σουσακειμ
βασιλευς Αιγυπτου λεγων	
Εξαποστειλον με	Οντως εξαποστειλον με
και απελευσομαι	και απελευσομαι
εγω εις την γην μου	

Trebolle's conclusion is supported by form critical considerations. Verses
24c-f remind one of the Moses story in Exod 2:15-23 + 4:18-20. Pharaoh
seeks to kill Moses who flees in fear to Midian where he lives with Reuel
who gives him his daughter, Zipporah, in marriage. She bears him a son,
Gershom. Then Moses learns that the king who sought his life has died.
He asks Jethro to let him go home. Jethro agrees, and Moses returns to
Egypt. The account in 3 Reigns 12:24d-e confuses the elements of this motif. It reports Jeroboam's marriage and children after the news of Solomon's
death and Jeroboam's request to be allowed to go home. This suggests that
vv 24d-e are an imitation of the motif of the fugitive in a foreign land, visible in the Moses story, that has been inserted here.

The source for this insertion was Hadad's marriage in 1 Kgs 11:19-22.
That story follows the same basic motif of the fugitive in a foreign land but
does not interrupt its context as does the account of Jeroboam's marriage in
the "supplement" (cf. Debus 1967:91). The use of this motif also explains
the odd description in v 24e of Ano[18] both as the older sister of Thekemeinas
and the oldest daughter of the king. The second description is standard in the
motif described above; the fugitive always marries the oldest daughter of his
sponsor. But the first description is unusual and must come from the story
of Hadad in 1 Kgs 11:19. The motivation for adding 3 Reigns 12:24d-e is
tied to the story of Jeroboam's sick son. That story presupposed that Jeroboam had a wife, so the "supplement" writer "improved" the Jeroboam
cycle by providing an account of his marriage. The placement of the

---

[18] The name Ano (אהנה) probably arose as a corruption of אחות which occurs twice
in 1 Kgs 11:19. See the discussion of Gordon (1975:385-386).

marriage account after Jeroboam's request of Shishak may have been motivated by Shishak's question in 1 Kgs 11:22, imitated in 3 Reigns 12:24d (cf Gen 30:31): "What have you lacked with me that you seek to return home?" The "supplement" gives a marvelous answer -- a family -- never mind that it substantially delayed Jeroboam's return and the subsequent history of Israel and Judah.

For the ending to his account in v 24f the "supplement" writer returned to the building motif which he had used earlier. Jeroboam came back from Egypt to "the land of Sareira" (another curious expression which signals imitation) where he gathered his fellow Ephraimites and built a fortification. The other major change in vv 24b-f of the "supplement" *vis-à-vis* the MT is the omission of Ahijah's oracle to Jeroboam in 1 Kgs 11:29-39. That episode is recounted in the third narrative of the "supplement" (vv 24nβ-u) in the context of the division at Shechem.

24nβ-u

The story of the schism at Shechem begins with a notice that is very similar to the one at the end of v 24f:

v 24f		v 24nβ	
και	ηλθεν	και	επορευθη Ιεροβοαμ
εις	γην Σαρειφα	εις	Σικιμα
την	εν ορει Εφραιμ	την	εν ορει Εφραιμ
και	συναγεται εκει	και	συνηθροισεν εκει
παν	σκηπτρον Εφραιμ	τας	φυλας του Ισραηλ

This similarity suggests that v 24nβ is a kind of *Wiederaufnahme*. This possibility is further supported when one notices that Jeroboam is not mentioned again in this section (vv 24nβ-u) except for the insertion in v 24o (see below). This does not automatically mean, however, that the material between the two notices (vv 24g-nα) is an insertion. This device can be used by authors as well as editors as a way of organizing narratives. This case is a good example. The two notices are not exactly alike. In v 24nβ Jeroboam goes to Shechem not to Sareira as in v 24f. Also, in the latter he gathers only the tribe of Ephraim, but all the tribes of Israel in v 24nβ. The notice of Jeroboam's journey to Shechem moves the narrative along. It sets the stage for the oracle to Jeroboam in v 24o. Its references to Shechem and the tribes of Israel also prepare the reader for the story in vv 24nβ-u. The notice thus displays an interest in more than inserting the material in vv 24g-nα. It indicates that all three narratives in vv 24b-u of the "supplement" were the work of one person.

Like the other "supplement" narratives, the one in vv 24nβ-u has also been abbreviated from the MT. The MT (12:1) explains the purpose behind the meeting at Shechem. The "supplement" does not. It lacks the MT's notice of the people's departure (12:5), the statement that the elders had also advised Solomon (12:6), and Rehoboam's question to the elders (12:6). The elders' response to Rehoboam is much abbreviated (12:7; v 24q). Rehoboam's question to the younger advisers (v 24r) does not repeat the popular request as in the MT (12:9) and uses the abbreviating formula ταυτα και ταυτα (= כזה וכזה, Debus 1967:63). The younger advisers' response in v 24r also does not repeat the people's demand as in 12:10. The statement about the yoke in 12:11 is omitted; only the more colorful response about whips and scorpions is given. The return of the people (12:12) is not reported in v 24s. Rehoboam's forsaking of the elders' counsel and his speech to the people (12:13-14) are not in v 24s. The theological explanation in 12:15 is absent from v 24s. The people's acknowledgement of the king's response (12:16aα) is not in v 24t, and their cry in that verse is shortened from the MT's.

This sketch shows how the "supplement" writer has abbreviated the MT account throughout. The connectives in the MT -- its organizational rubrics, repetitions of speeches, and theological explanations are omitted. An especially significant omission from the "supplement" is the story of the stoning of Adoram in 12:17-20:

v 24u	12:18
και κατεκρατησεν Ροβοαμ	והמלך רחבעם התאמץ
και απηλθεν και ανεβη	לעלות
επι το αρμα αυτου	במרכבה לנוס
και εισηλθεν εις Ιερουσαλημ	ירושלם

The meaning of the passage in the MT is clear. Rehoboam is frightened by the stoning of Adoram and beats a hasty (התאמץ) retreat to Jerusalem. This meaning of the verb התאמץ is unusual. Except for the Chronicles parallel to this verse (2 Chr 10:18) it does not occur in this sense elsewhere. The Greek versions of Kings and Chronicles render התאמץ with verbs that mean "hasten, hurry."[19] The "supplement," in contrast, says that Rehoboam "strengthened (himself)," a very literal translation of התאמץ. Without the story of Adoram's death the "supplement" makes no sense. Why should Rehoboam strengthen himself for a ride home in his chariot? This reading

---

[19]In 1 Kgs 12:18 LXX uses εφθασεν, from φθανω, which can mean "make haste" (Liddell and Scott 1968:1927), and 2 Chr 10:18 has εσπευσεν, from σπευδω, which most often translates מהר or בהל.

only fits in the MT's context. It also shows (against Gooding) that the "supplement" was originally composed in Hebrew. Its author knew the MT as we have seen. If he were working from a translation he would have used a verb meaning "to hurry." The presence of κατεκρατησεν can only be understood as the translation of הִתְאַמֵּץ already removed at the Hebrew stage from its context in the story of Adoram.

If the "supplement" narrative as a whole presumes the MT, so must the oracle in v 24o. It seems to have been inserted into the narrative since it separates the notice of Rehoboam's journey to Shechem (και ανεβη εκει Ροβοαμ υιος Σαλωμων) in v 24nβ from the Israelites' demands to him in v 24p (cf. Trebolle 1980:147-148). The insertion need not be assigned to another hand. It reflects the same techniques of borrowing and abbreviation as in the "supplement" as a whole. It lacks the MT's references to the sin and punishment of Solomon (11:29-39); it gives no justification for the division. Again, it is not that the writer intentionally deletes the Deuteronomistic language, but he abbreviates, as in v 24m, by giving the judgement of the oracle and leaving out the theological justification. Jeroboam is told that he will rule over ten tribes, but the garment is torn into twelve pieces. No explanation for the other two tribes is offered. Verse 24u takes them to be Judah and Benjamin, but this seems to be based on v 24x which is part of the *Wiederaufnahme* in vv 24x-z that has been copied almost verbatim from the MT. Thus, the "supplement" has abbreviated the story in 1 Kgs 12:1-20 at the same time bringing into it a shortened version of the oracle from 1 Kgs 11:29-39.

In addition to locating this oracle (v 24o) in the context of the division the "supplement" attributes it to Shemaiah instead of Ahijah. The "supplement" writer has made this change under the influence of the other oracle in this context already attributed to Shemaiah (1 Kgs 12:22-24). This puts us in a position to address the question raised about the absence of the disguise motif from the "supplement" in vv 24g-na. As noted, that motif is closely tied in the MT (1 Kgs 14:1) to Ahijah's designation of Jeroboam as king. Since the "supplement" writer moved that story to the context of the division at Shechem and assigned its oracle to Shemaiah, he left out of vv 24g-na the disguise motif which depended on the MT's order and identification of the prophet.[20]

---

[20] The "supplement" version of this story draws on motifs from other prophetic stories. The "supplement" description of the garment as not having gone into water is a motif like the one in Jer 13:1. Van Seters suggests (personal communication) that Shemaiah's reference to Jeroboam dressing himself with the torn garment is based on some sort of investiture motif.

24a

We have seen that the "supplement" narratives deal primarily with Jeroboam and the history of the North and contain no obvious Deuteronomistic language. Hence, this verse with its regnal formulas for Solomon and Rehoboam and its evaluation for Rehoboam in Deuteronomistic terms demands an explanation. A serious shortcoming of Trebolle's reconstruction is that it does not adequately explain this Deuteronomistic formula.

The standard practice in the book of Kings is to integrate narrative materials into a king's reign by placing them between his initial and concluding formulas (cf. Trebolle 1980:94). Thus, the stories about Jeroboam in 1 Kings 11-14 fall within the literary boundaries for his reign since he is the main character.[21] But the "supplement" stories about Jeroboam are encased by v 24a within Rehoboam's reign! Verse 24a is certainly out of sync with Dtr's regular schema.

Verse 24a gives Rehoboam's age at accession as sixteen, but this can hardly be historical. If Solomon reigned forty years (1 Kgs 11:42) and had many children, the son who succeeded him would certainly have been older than sixteen. The narratives about Rehoboam in Kings nowhere hint that he was so young. This figure shares the interpretation in 2 Chr 13:7, probably based on the story about Rehoboam and his advisors in 1 Kgs 12:6-11, that he was a youth when he became king (cf. Montgomery 1951:267; Gray 1963: 310). Similarly, the tracing of Rehoboam's maternal lineage back to Nahash (Naas) king of the Ammonites is unique to this verse. If it were historical one would expect to find it elsewhere in Kings. It seems to reflect the remark in 2 Sam 10:2 that Nahash and David were friends or treaty partners.

Rehoboam's accession formula in the "supplement" is coupled with the death and burial formula for Solomon. Trebolle (1980:84-109) argues that this order is more primitive than the MT's separation of the formulas (11:41-43; 14:21-22), so that the "supplement" must preserve the original formula for Rehoboam. But Trebolle himself shows that the MT's separation of the formulas for Solomon and Rehoboam is unusual, and the sentence in 14:21a רחבעם בן שלמה מלך ביהודה is anomolous. It would be very easy for a writer to compose the formulas in v 24a from the regular, ubiquitous pattern.

The same is true of the first part of Rehoboam's evaluation in v 24a: "he did evil in Yahweh's eyes." This language is very common in Kings. This exact evaluation occurs for all the kings of Judah from Manasseh on with the exception of Josiah. Any writer could imitate it with ease. The second part of the evaluation, "he did not walk in the way of David his father," is more telling. It is not in the MT's evaluation for Rehoboam (1 Kgs 14:22).

---

[21] Actually, there is no accession formula for Jeroboam, but his elevation to kingship is narrated in 1 Kings 11-12. His closing formulas are in 14:19-20.

In fact, it never occurs for any king of Judah. This suggests strongly that it is an imitation of the Deuteronomistic evaluation. Thus, 3 Reigns 12:24a is not the pristine version of Rehoboam's accession formula but an imitation of the formulas for kings of Judah throughout the book of Kings. The figure for Rehoboam's tenure as king remains unexplained, but in light of the other imitative features of the verse it is best regarded as an invention.

24x-z

The final section of the "supplement" stands out like v 24a in that it also focuses on Rehoboam and Judah. It contains the only oracle in the "supplement" not addressed to Jeroboam (24y-z). This oracle from Shemaiah warns Rehoboam against going to war with Jeroboam. Debus (1967:90n) and Trebolle (1980:148-149) have observed that vv 24y-z were inserted into the "supplement" from 1 Kgs 12:22-24. The two texts are nearly word for word the same. Verse 24x has also been borrowed from the MT. It abbreviates 1 Kgs 12:21, reporting that Rehoboam came to fight at Shechem. The only part of it that needs explanation is its dating of the event "at the beginning of the year." This is a common rubric introducing battle accounts in the DH (cf. 2 Sam 11:1; 1 Kgs 20:26). The oracle in 12:24y-z, then, was reproduced from the MT in order to resume the narrative which the MT and LXX have in common after the "supplement."

CONCLUSIONS

The foregoing analysis of the "supplement" in 3 Reigns 12:24a-z suggests both an understanding of its purpose and the way in which it was composed. It was written on the basis of the MT to provide the story of Jeroboam's sick son for the *Vorlage* of the Old Greek. It is not clear why that text of Kings lacked this story, but there can be no doubt that it was part of Dtr's History originally. The author of the "supplement" wrote a condensed version of the story. He also included a number of motifs drawn from other stories about prophets in the DH.

In addition to the story of Jeroboam's sick son this author also rewrote the other episodes of the Jeroboam cycle in Kings. Because of the important role of Jeroboam's wife in the 1 Kings 14 story the "supplement" writer added an account of Jeroboam's marriage to his version of Jeroboam's flight to Egypt. He borrowed that account from the story of Hadad's marriage in 1 Kgs 11:19-20. He further "improved" the Jeroboam cycle by moving Ahijah's designation of Jeroboam as king to the beginning of the narrative about division. He condensed the story of division but included Shemaiah's oracle from that story almost verbatim as a way of resuming the account into which he inserted his composition. Because Shemaiah was already present in the narrative, he attributed the designation oracle which he had transferred also to Shemaiah. He prefaced his version of the Jeroboam cycle with an imitation of the regnal formula for Rehoboam.

Since the "supplement" is based on Dtr's account of Jeroboam it cannot be used as evidence for a pre-Dtr, prophetic redaction of the book of Kings. Of course, that does not rule out the possibility of such a level of editing, but the case for it in the Jeroboam cycle must be made purely on the basis of the MT. The next chapter will examine the Jeroboam cycle in the MT more closely.

CHAPTER TWO

TEARING THE KINGDOM:
THE JEROBOAM CYCLE IN 1 KINGS 11-14

The Jeroboam cycle in the MT contains several difficult passages which are crucial for any understanding of the composition of the book of Kings and the DH. This chapter will focus on three key passages in the cycle in an effort to characterize the role of the Jeroboam cycle in the book of Kings.

AHIJAH'S ORACLE (1 KINGS 11:29-39)

Noth's treatments of this text illustrate its difficulty. In *Überlieferungs-geschichtliche Studien* (1967:72) he argued that it contained an earlier prophetic story about Ahijah's encounter with Jeroboam which Dtr had revised for inclusion in his History. But in his later commentary on Kings (1968: 245-246, 258-262) Noth took all of vv 29-39 as Dtr's work based on 1 Sam 15:27b-28.

It is widely agreed that Deuteronomistic language abounds in this oracle: v 32a - "for the sake of my servant David and for the sake of Jerusalem, the city which I chose from all the tribes of Israel;" v 33b - "they (*sic*, see below) did not walk in my ways doing what is right in my sight, my statutes and ordinances, like David his father;" v 34b - "for the sake of David my servant whom I chose because he kept my commandments and statutes;" v 36b - "so that David my servant will always have a fiefdom[1] before me in Jerusalem, the city which I chose for myself, to place my name there;" v 38 - "if you listen to all that I command you, walk in my ways, and do what is right in my sight, keeping my statutes and my commandments as did David my servant, I will be with you and will build a sure house for you just as I built for David, and I will give Israel to you."

At the same time, these verses present some obvious difficulties.[2] There are a few widely recognized glosses (cf. Debus 1967:11): the plural verbs in v 33a, (cf. Plein 1966:18; Provan 1988: 99 and n. 18), the reference to "ten tribes" at the end of v 35b, and v 39 (see below). In addition, vv 32 and 34 are problematic and have frequently been taken, in whole or in part, as addi-

---

[1] See Hanson (1968) for this meaning of נִיר.

[2] See Provan (1988:100-105), Nelson (1981:109-116), and Trebolle (1989:129-131) for bibliography and the range of scholarly opinion.

tions. The most common way of explaining the literary unevenness of the oracle in the light of its Deuteronomistic nature is to posit redactional levels behind it. This has been done in two ways. As mentioned, Noth argued in *Überlieferungsgeschichtliche Studien* that Dtr edited an earlier prophetic story (cf. Nelson 1981:109-116). Others (e.g., Provan 1988:101-105; Würthwein 1985:139-144) have found multiple Deuteronomistic editions within the passage.

The most obvious difficulty in the passage concerns the number of fragments of Ahijah's robe (12) in v 30 compared with the number of tribes accounted for (11) in vv 31-32. But this problem is not solved by positing an earlier "prophetic" version of this oracle. It pervades the entire oracle. Dtr could easily have changed the numbers, but he evidently understood the relationship of the tribes of Israel in such a way that he did not see a contradiction here.

Scholars have proposed a number of explanations along these lines (cf. Nelson 1981:110-111). Noth's view, for example, was that the oracle assumed Judah's continuation with the Davidic house and that Benjamin was the "one tribe" to go with Rehoboam (1967:72, n. 7; cf. Grønbaek 1965:425).[3] Another explanation (Gordon 1963:90) is that Levi is the "missing tribe" because of its dispersement in both Israel and Judah. Finally, Van Seters has pointed out (private communication) that the DH elsewhere indicates that Simeon was understood to be assimilated within Judah (Josh 19:1-9; 21:4, 9; Judg 1:3-21 - but note the reference to Benjamin in v 21). Whatever the correct explanation, this difference does not require and is not smoothed by the reconstruction of an underlying prophetic source for the oracle.

In addition to the problem of numbers, other disturbances are evident in this oracle and have led scholars to argue for levels of Dtr redaction. Most recently, Provan (1988:99-105) has contended that additions in vv 32, 34b-35, and 38bβ-39 come from a later, exilic redaction of Kings with a "Messianic" interpretation of the Davidic promise. Provan's literary evaluation is well founded. On both literary and form critical grounds v 32 is problematic. It breaks the connection between Ahijah's announcement in v 31 and the basis for it in v 33. Similarly, the judgement that vv 38bβ-39 are secondary is supported by their absence from the Old Greek (cf. Debus 1967:11n).[4]

---

[3] The references to Benjamin in 12:21-24 cannot be used to support this view, since those verses are a later addition to the account of the division, as Noth recognized (1968:269; cf. Debus 1967:34). The statement in 12:20 that only the tribe of Judah followed the house of David seems to preclude this interpretation. Also, the explanation that Rehoboam gets one tribe so that David may retain a fiefdom in Jerusalem (11:32, 36) indicates that Judah is meant as the "one tribe."

[4] Nelson's explanation that the OG translator was motivated by pedantic logic and piety to omit these verses is not convincing (1981:115).

However, the situation with vv 34-35 is more complicated. Provan (1988:102-103) correctly observes that vv 34b-35 currently separate the promise in v 34a about not taking away <u>all</u> the kingdom from its natural conclusion in v 36.[5] He cites the use of נשיא for Solomon in v 34b and מלוכה in v 35 instead of ממלכה (cf. vv 31, 34) as further evidence for his judgement.

These problems are best explained by text critical means. Some comentators have recognized that the solution to these verses is at least partly text critical (especially Noth 1968:243, 261; cf. Gray 1963:270n, 275). But Trebolle (1989:129-135) has now given a more detailed explanation for the textual shape of these verses. He contends that the MT in 11:34 contains the fusion of a double reading, both elements of which remain independent in the Lucianic witnesses to the LXX:

αντιτασσομενος αντιταξομαι αυτω πασας τας ημερας
της ζωης αυτου
και ου μη λαβω την βασιλειαν εκ χειρος αυτου εν ταις
ημεραις της ζωης αυτου

The first sentence, "I will oppose him *all his lifetime* " (=כל ימי חייו), fits perfectly with the preceding context which details Solomon's idolatries.[6] The second sentence, "I will not take the kingdom from him *during his lifetime* " (בימי חייו), fits equally well with the reference to the Davidic promise which follows (δια Δαυιδ τον δουλον μου ον εξελεξαμεν αυτον = למען דוד עבדי אשר בחרתי אתו). The LXX[L] reading is protolucianic and not the result of late recensional work as shown by the support it receives from the Old Latin.[7]

Trebolle uses the readings of both the MT and LXX[L] to reconstruct an original reading. The first sentence. "I will oppose him all his lifetime," has come into the MT secondarily as כי נשיא אשתנו כל ימי חייו where it interrupts the continuity between v 34a and v 34bβ. Trebolle also argues that it has occasioned the loss of the original complement to the second sentence, "during his lifetime." On the other hand, the fact that the first

---

[5] Actually, he takes the first אשר clause in v 34bβ (אשר בחרתי אתו) and the final three words of v 35 (את עשרת שבטים), as noted, as even later additions (1988:102n).

[6] αντιτασσομενος αντιταξομαι αυτω apparently translates נָשָׂא אֶשָּׂא לוֹ as in Hos 1:6 (cf. Gray 1963:270n; Noth1968:243). The same meaning, "I will oppose" fits well in Hos 1:6.

[7] Trebolle (1989:132-133). The Old Latin reads: *et non accipiam regnum totum de manu eius in diebus vitae eius propter David servum meum quem elegi quoniam contra faciam illi per omnes dies vitae eius.*

sentence (v 34bα)[8] appears in a different place in the two forms of the text
(MT, LXX[L], and Old Latin) indicates that it is secondary. Hence, v 34 originally contained the following reading: ולא אקח את הממלכה מידו
ביטי חייו למען דוד עבדי אשר בחרתי אתו = "I will not take the
kingdom[9] from his hand[10] during his lifetime for the sake of David my
servant whom I chose."[11]

Trebolle's text critical solution to v 34 shows the difficulty of trying to
explain this passage as the result of systematic later redaction. The passage
has clearly been glossed in several places, probably because of the importance of Ahijah's oracle. The glosses are not all from the same hand, as
Provan recognizes (see n. 5). Moreover, it is hard to find convincing criteria
by which to isolate individuals levels, because the glosses make use of Dtr's
language and ideology regarding the Davidic promise.[12]

Provan's ascription of the glosses in 11:32 and 11:38bβ-39 to the same
late "Messianic" editor may be correct, but the narrow base of evidence calls
for a good deal of caution. Provan (1988:113) proposes that the Davidic
promise in 11:36 is from the pre-exilic Dtr because it uses the expression
"forever" (כל הימים), while the promise in v 32, which lacks כל הימים,
is from the late, "messianic" Dtr. Given that v 32 is a gloss anticipating
and imitating Dtr's oracle, especially v 36, it is hard to know how much to
make of the absence of כל הימים. It may have been omitted unintention-
ally or for purposes of abbreviation. The last four words of v 39, אך לא
כל הימים , do seem to betray a hope in the Davidic house, but they also
appear attached as an afterthought to what precedes; they may be even later
than vv 38bβ-39. The inconsistencies within 1 Kgs 11:29-39, then, come
from glosses and corruption in the transmission of its text. There is not

---

[8] Trebolle's statement to this effect (1989:134) contains a crucial error, identifying v
34bβ as the addition instead of v 34bα. "El hecho de que la frase de 34bβ (sic)
aparezca en cada una de las dos formas del texto (TM, LXX[L], VL) en un emplazamiento
deferente, viene a significar que tal frase constituye una glosa secundaria."

[9] Minus כל as in LXX[L].

[10] Trebolle (1989:134), without explanation, omits מידו from his reconstruction.

[11] The second אשר clause in the MT is secondary as suggested by its absence from
LXX[B].

[12] 11:9-13 are also widely regarded as a later addition because they anticipate and
even summarize Ahijah's oracle. Their language and ideology are virtually identical
with those of 11:29-39. Provan notes the similarity of 11:32 (למען ירושלם
העיר אשר בחרתי בה מכל שבטי ישראל ולמען עבדי דוד) to 11:13
(למען ירושלם אשר בחרתי ולמען דוד עבדי) and assigns both to his second
editor. But both verses are similar to 14:21 (העיר אשר בחר מלך בירושלם
יהוה לשום את שמו שם מכל שבטי ישראל), which Provan assigns to his first
redactor (Dtr). Both are dependent on Dtr for their language and theology.

enough evidence to decide whether the glosses come from one or two hands, much less to describe the ideological motivation of the glossators.

The possibility of a prophetic story underlying 11:29-39 is also dubious because Dtr's shaping of the account has been so strong. He may have had sources for some of the biographical information about Jeroboam in 11:26-28. The narrative in these verses is somewhat choppy and may indicate the presence of source material.[13] But he connected this material with the oracle itself by setting it near Jerusalem where Jeroboam was working (v 29a) on Solomon's building projects (v 27b). Many scholars think that the encounter of Ahijah and Jeroboam displaced an earlier account of Jeroboam's revolt. They contend that v 27a (וזה הדבר אשר הרים יד במלך) leads the reader to expect a story, which never occurs, detailing how Jeroboam used his leadership qualities and position over the labor force to revolt against Solomon.[14] But in the present narrative v 27a anticipates Ahijah's oracle and is probably from Dtr. The oracle motivates Jeroboam's revolt (v 27a) and Solomon's efforts to kill him (v 40). Yahweh condones the revolt because of Solomon's unfaithfulness.

The account of Ahijah's encounter with Jeroboam contains several motifs found in other prophetic stories. But these do not necessarily mean that Dtr had a prophetic source. For example, he may have imported the motif of the prophet and the king designate from anointment narratives such as those for Saul (1 Sam 9:27-10:1) and Jehu (2 Kgs 9:1-6).[15] Dtr's creativity in this account is suggested by the language in 11:31b about tearing (קרע) the kingdom. This expression elsewhere in Samuel and Kings always refers to tearing the kingdom __away__ from the offending king: 1 Sam 15:27-28; 28:17;

_____

[13] Noth (1968:255-256) believed that an independent narrative in vv 26, 27b-28, 40 was interrupted by the story in vv 29-39. Debus (1967:4-5) and Mayes (1983:117) hold that vv 26 and 40 alone comprised the old narrative, vv 27-28 and 29-39 being later expansions and additions.

[14] See Dietrich (1972:54-55) and the bibliography he cites. Cf. Benzinger (1899:82) and Würthwein (1985:143).

[15] Weippert (1983:347-348) contends that the original story of Ahijah's meeting with Jeroboam (11:29-31, 37, 38bαβ, 40abα) was an example of a genre which she calls _Legitimationslegende_. She finds other examples of this genre in the narratives concerning the anointings of Saul, David (1 Sam 16:1-13), and Jehu. According to Weippert, this genre supports kings, such as usurpers, who do not possess a hereditary claim to the throne. The attraction of this proposal is the propagandistic function which it ascribes to these texts. Yet, there are important differences between the Jeroboam episode and the other passages in the alleged genre. Ahijah does not anoint Jeroboam as the prophets in the other stories do to the future kings. Weippert's main argument for associating the Jeroboam episode with this genre is the motif of the isolation of the prophet and the future king when the anointing does take place. But this motif is not consistent in the anointing stories. David and Samuel are not alone in 1 Kings 16; David's father and brothers at least are present. The same criticisms apply to Campbell's attempt to trace an anointment motif in his Prophetic Record. In addition, the text in 2 Kgs 9:7-10a is essential for Campbell's reconstruction of this motif. But 2 Kgs 9:7-10a is probably Dtr's insertion into the Jehu story (see Chapter Three).

1 Kgs 11:11, 12, 13; 14:8; 2 Kgs 17:21.[16]   Thus, in 1 Sam 15:27-28,
reiterated in 28:17, Saul tears away part of Samuel's robe and is told that
Yahweh will tear the kingdom away from him. The symbol corresponds to
the interpretation.

But that symbol would be inadequate for the message of 1 Kgs 11:29-39,
where there are two points: Yahweh is taking the kingdom away from
Solomon, but not all of it; the kingdom will be divided.   Trebolle
(1980:146) has pointed out that v 31b contains a subtle play on the mean-
ings of the verb קרע.   In vv 30-31a קרע means "tear apart, in pieces,"
while in v 31b it means "tear away." He cites this word play as evidence
that Dtr rewrote the oracle from his *Vorlage* so that its point was no longer
the division ("tearing apart") of the kingdom but its removal ("tearing
away") from the house of David.[17] But the reverse is more likely, i.e., that
the oracle depends on the message Dtr wishes to communicate. In other
words, it looks like Dtr is responsible for writing Ahijah's oracle.

In Ahijah's oracle Dtr provided the motivation for Jeroboam's rebellion
and the theological explanation for the divison. The kingdom is taken from
the Davidids because of Solomon's sins but Rehoboam retains a part of it
because of Yahweh's promise that David would have an eternal ניר in
Jerusalem (11:36). Dtr's emphasis on this promise is very significant because it suggests that his History was composed before the end of the Davidic monarchy in the Exile. Ahijah tells Jeroboam that he too can have a
"sure house" (בית נאמן) like David's if, like David, he is obedient. This
verse has sometimes been taken as secondary because the offer to Jeroboam
of a dynasty like David's "would be remarkable coming from the pen of
DTR" (Campbell 1986:26; cf. O'Brien 1989:163; Noth 1968:262).[18] But
different scholars have recently pointed out ways in which this verse still
implies or incorporates Dtr's contrast between David and Jeroboam. The dynasty (בית נאמן) promised to Jeroboam in 11:38 is never called "eternal"
(עולם, contrast 2 Sam 7:16). It is extended only because of Solomon's
disobedience and is conditioned upon Jeroboam's obedience, while the
promise to David in 2 Samuel 7 is a reward for his faithfulness and is un-
conditional (Holder 1988:28-29). Like David, Jeroboam has the opportunity

---

[16] The passages in Kings all occur in Deuteronomistic contexts. The origin of the
Samuel passages is debated. They have been assigned to both an earlier prophetic layer
(Birch 1976:98-103; McCarter 1980:270, 423; Campbell 1986:43, 46, 69) and to a
post-Deuteronomistic level (Van Seters 1983:258-264).

[17] Trebolle, of course, assumes the priority of the "supplement" account. However,
"tearing apart" the kingdom could hardly be a common prophetic motif since it only
happened once. On the other hand, the kingdom was "torn away" from several ruling
dynasties.   Again, this suggests that the word play was made specifically for this
account.

[18] The tension between vv 38 and 39 is sometimes cited in support of the idea that v
38 is secondary. But our removal of v 39 on text critical grounds resolves that
tension.

for a dynasty. But unlike David, Jeroboam is disobedient to Yahweh (Barré 1988:104; Provan 1988:103-104; Wallace 1986:36-40), as Dtr makes quite clear in 14:7-9. Thus, the verse does not detract from the Deuteronomistic portrait of Jeroboam as the paradigmatic villain. One may even perceive in the promise to Jeroboam an implicit threat (Dietrich 1972:19). Both writer and reader know that Jeroboam will fail to secure a dynasty because of his apostasy.

In sum, Ahijah's oracle in 1 Kgs 11:29-39 (minus later glosses) is best understood as Dtr's composition. It announces the division of the kingdom as the result of two factors that are Dtr themes. Yahweh will tear the kingdom away because of Solomon's sins, but his son will retain part because of the legacy of David. There is no clear indication that the later glosses in the oracle came from the same writer or were motivated by a common ideology.

JEROBOAM'S ROLE AT SHECHEM (1 KINGS 11:41-12:3, 12)

This passage is notorious for its inconsistencies regarding Jeroboam's role in the convocation at Shechem.[19] According to 12:2-3a, 12 (MT) Jeroboam was summoned to Shechem to lead the Israelites in revolt against Rehoboam. But according to 12:20 the Israelites became aware that Jeroboam had returned only after they had rejected Rehoboam. Then, they summoned Jeroboam and made him their king. In addition, the explanation about Jeroboam's flight to Egypt in 12:2 repeats information just given in 11:40, and the language of 12:3a recounting the people's summons of Jeroboam is reproduced in 12:20. Finally, as it now stands, 12:2 says that when Jeroboam heard of Rehoboam's trip to Shechem he stayed in Egypt (וַיֵּשֶׁב בְּמִצְרָיִם). This contradicts the inference of 11:40 that Jeroboam returned upon Solomon's death as well as the subsequent account, which assumes that Jeroboam returned to Israel.

The obvious confusion in this chapter over the role played by Jeroboam in the Shechem assembly has often led scholars to posit that Dtr had two different versions of the event (usually a Northern one and a Southern one) which he combined to form the present narrative (Debus 1967:19-27; Jones 1984:247-249; Nielsen 1959:171-208; Noth 1968:268ff). Trebolle's 1980 volume argues that problems in the passage have been caused by both redactional activity and textual corruption and that its problems cannot be solved by text critical methods alone. He may be correct in this last point, but the different view which I have taken of the "supplement" requires a reexamination of the textual evidence.

---

[19] See the bibliography and summary of positions in Trebolle (1980:51-62). Add to his list McKenzie (1985a:142-143; 1987).

A close comparison of the MT and LXX^B in 11:43-12:3a will help to locate the source of the problem.

LXX^B	MT
και εκοιμηθη Σαλωμων (11:43)	(11:43a) וישכב שלמה
μετα των πατερων αυτου	עם־אבתיו
και εθαψαν αυτον	ויקבר
εν πολει Δαυειδ του πατρος αυτου	בעיר דויד אביו
και εγενηθη ως ηκουσεν	(12:2) ויהי כשמע
Ιεροβοαμ υιος Ναβατ	ירבעם בן נבט
και αυτου ετι οντος εν Αιγυπτω	והוא עודנו במצרים
ως εφυγεν εκ προσωπου Σαλωμων	אשר ברח מפני שלמה המלך
και εκαθητο εν Αιγυπτω	וישב ירבעם במצרים
κατευθυνει[20] και ερχεται	
εις την πολιν αυτου	
εις την γην Σαρειρα	
την εν ορει Εφραμ	
και ο βασιλευς Σαλωμων εκοιμηθη	
μετα των πατερων αυτου	
και εβασιλευσεν Ροβοαμ (11:43b)	(11:43b) וימלך רחבעם
υιος αυτου αντ᾽ αυτου	בנו תחתיו
και πορευεται βασιλευς Ροβοαμ (12:1)	(12:1) וילך רחבעם
εις Σικιμα οτι εις Σικιμα ηρχοντο	שכם כי שכם בא
πας Ισραηλ βασιλευσαι αυτον	כל ישראל להמליך אתו
	וישלחו ויקראו־לו
	יבאו ירבעם וכל־קהל ישראל
και ελαλησεν ο λαος	(12:3) וידברו
προς τον βασιλεα Ροβοαμ λεγοντες	אל רחבעם לאמר

The MT reading in 12:2 is clarified by the LXX^B parallel at 11:43. The statement that Jeroboam stayed in Egypt (וַיֵּשֶׁב בְּמִצְרָיִם) was not originally the main clause as it is now in the MT but was part of a parenthesis detailing Jeroboam's flight to Egypt as in LXX^B: και αυτου ετι οντος εν Αιγυπτω ως εφυγεν εκ προσωπου Σαλωμων και εκαθητο εν

---

[20] Reading the third singular, κατευθυνει, instead of the infinitive, κατευθυνειν, as in LXX^B. A form of the verb צלח, "to rush," is presupposed, and the meaning of the sentence is clear: "when Jeroboam heard ... he came immediately to his city."

<u>Αιγυπτ</u>ω‎ = ‏והוא עודנו במצרים אשר ברח מפני שלמה וישב‎
‏במצרים‎. The original main clause is preserved in LXX[B] (11:43):
κατευθυνει και ερχεται εις την πολιν αυτου εις την γην
Σαρειρα την εν ορει Εφραιμ = ‏צלח ויבא אל עירו אל ארץ‎
‏צררה אשר בהר אפרים‎. The presence of this clause in a variety of
Greek witnesses (Ndefhmptvwyz) and the Syriac, which otherwise follow the
MT in its reading and placement, shows that this clause was once in the
MT's textual tradition. Its loss by haplography from the MT was occasioned by the similarity of ‏מצרים‎ and ‏אפרים‎. After the haplography,
‏וַיֵּשֶׁב בְּמִצְרָיִם‎ had to be read as the main clause in the MT, even though
it made no sense. Later witnesses, including LXX[A] and Chronicles (MT),
reflect a correction to ‏וַיָּשָׁב מִמִּצְרָיִם‎ for the sake of sense. The fact that
LXX[A] (Kings) agrees with Chronicles (MT) in reading "returned from
Egypt" instead of "remained in Egypt" is very important, because it indicates
that the Chronicler found the correction already in his Kings *Vorlage* and did
not make it himself. The text of 1 Kgs 12:2-3a has not been borrowed from
Chronicles as has sometimes been asserted.[21] LXX[B]'s reading for 1 Kgs
12:2, then, is more primitive than that of the MT, which has suffered an ac-
cidental omission.

   The comparison above also shows that the entire notice of Jeroboam's return ("when Jeroboam heard ... hill country of Ephraim") is secondary in
both the MT (12:2*) and LXX[B] (11:43). In the MT it contradicts the surrounding narrative. In LXX[B] it is marked as an insertion by the repetition
of the formulaic element, "Solomon slept with his fathers" (Trebolle,
1980:73-74; cf. Klein, 1970:217; 1973:583). The parenthetical statement in
both the MT 12:2* and LXX[B] 11:43 notices of Jeroboam's return also indicates the secondary nature of those notices. It simply restates the information about Jeroboam's presence in Egypt.

   Once the secondary nature of the notice of Jeroboam's return in the MT
12:2 is recognized the other problems in its narrative are easily explained.
12:3a has no parallel in LXX[B]. It obviously depends on 12:2 and makes an
explicit connection between Jeroboam's return and the gathering at Shechem.
It was probably added to accomodate the insertion of v 2 to the following
narrative.[22] Thus, it already had the understanding that Jeroboam was in-

---

[21] Montgomery (1951:248) and Klein (1970:218). The Chronicler also omitted 1
Kgs 12:20 in line with his practice of ignoring the history of the North. As a result,
there is no ambiguity in Chronicles about Jeroboam's involvement at Shechem as there
is in the MT of Kings.

[22] Trebolle (1980:67-71) contends that the *Qere* in 12:3a, ‏ויבא ירבעם‎, is a
remnant of the main clause which originally completed the temporal clause in v 2:
"When Jeroboam heard . . . <u>Jeroboam came</u>." However, Trebolle does not notice the
evidence for the loss of the main clause from the MT by haplography.

volved in the Shechem assembly.[23] Its mention of Jeroboam occasioned the further addition of his name in the MT (but not in LXX[B]) at 12:12.

How, then, did two similar notices about Jeroboam's return come to be inserted secondarily into both the MT and LXX[B]? The source for the inserted notice in MT *12:2/LXX[B] 11:43 is suggested by the expression "the land of Sareira which is in the hill country of Ephraim" (την γην Σαρειρα την εν ορει Εφραιμ). One expects to find Jeroboam's home referred to as "the city of Sareira" or "the land (or hill country) of Ephraim." But the reference to Sareira as a land is odd. The same expression occurs in the "supplement" account of Jeroboam's return from Egypt (v 24f), which is undoubtedly its place of origin. Thus, it appears that the MT, which was the basis for the "supplement," was itself later glossed on the basis of the "supplement" notice of Jeroboam's return. Dtr's original narrative contained no notice of Jeroboam's return. It stated only that Jeroboam stayed in Egypt until the death of Solomon (11:40). The need was later felt for a notice of Jeroboam's return after the mention of Solomon's death and perhaps in view of the division. That notice was borrowed from the "supplement" into the MT and LXX. This, in turn, led to the addition of other material in MT 12:2//LXX[B] to recap the story about how Jeroboam came to be in Egypt.

The earlier statement in 11:40 that Jeroboam stayed in Egypt until Solomon's death (עד מות שלמה), originally closed Dtr's account of Ahijah's oracle and its effect on the relationship of Solomon and Jeroboam. To this account Dtr attached the concluding formulas for Solomon in 11:41-43 before proceeding to the story of the Shechem assembly in chapter *12. The notice of Jeroboam's return in LXX[B] 11:43//MT 12:2 was inserted into these witnesses at a later point in time under the influence of the "supplement" narrative.

Dtr's narrative of the division in 1 Kings 12 did not include 12:2-3a or Jeroboam's name in v 12. Verses 2-3a are a late scribal gloss based on the

---

[23] It is commonly proposed that the reading of v 3a and the placement of vv 2-3a were borrowed from the parallel in 2 Chr 10:3a (Klein 1970:218; Montgomery 1951:248; cf. Gray 1963:278-279). However, there are several considerations which militate against this possibility. First, as shown above, the textual evidence in v 2 indicates that the influence was in the opposite direction, i.e., that the Chronicles reading borrowed from a text of Kings in the MT tradition. The strongest point in favor of 1 Kgs 12:2-3a being borrowed from 2 Chr 10:2-3a is R. Klein's argument (1970:218) that וכל קהל ישראל in 1 Kgs 12:3a (so also LXX[A] of Chronicles) is a conflation of variants found only in the textual tradition of Chronicles: וכל הקהל reflected in LXX[B] and וכל ישראל in the MT. However, it is possible, as Gooding argues (1972:532), that קהל in Kings is an independent expansion influenced by כל קהל ישראל in 1 Kgs 8:14, 22, 55. Secondly, wider analysis of parallels between Kings and Chronicles shows that the direction of borrowing is consistently Kings to Chronicles; there is no clear example to the contrary (McKenzie, 1985a:119-158; 1986). Thirdly, the Chronicler's work attests no particular zeal on his part to vilify Jeroboam, so that he has no clear motive to add vv 2-3a (McKenzie, 1985a:86; 1987:298).

notice of Jeroboam's return in the "supplement." The name in v 12 is also secondary. These verses are not the remnants of an earlier source nor the sign of a second Deuteronomistic redaction of the chapter. That chapter is essentially Dtr's composition, probably based on an earlier source about the Shechem assembly. Signs of his hand are especially clear in the explanation in 12:15b of the division as Yahweh's doing and the reference in v 19 to Israel being in rebellion against the house of David. [24]

THE LEGEND OF THE MAN OF GOD FROM JUDAH (1 KINGS 13)

The intriguing legend about the young man of God from Judah and the old prophet from Israel in 1 Kings 13 (MT) stands apart from the other narratives about Jeroboam in that it has no Old Greek counterpart either in the "supplement" or elsewhere in LXX[B] or the Lucianic tradition. The tale has received a good deal of fruitful discussion by scholars, beginning with Karl Barth's classic exposition (1957:393-409).

It is widely recognized that 1 Kings 13 is an insertion by *Wiederaufnahme*.[25] There has been disagreement about the precise limits of the insertion, but that issue can now be resolved thanks to recent literary critical treatments of the passage. Dietrich (1972:116) has pointed out that 12:33 reiterates most of 12:32:

12:32	12:33
1. ויעש ירבעם חג	5. ויעל על המזבח
2. בחדש השמיני	6. אשר עשה בבית אל
3. בחמשה עשר יום לחדש	3. בחמשה עשר יום
4. כחג אשר ביהודה	2. בחדש השמיני
5. ויעל על המזבח	בחדש אשר בדא מלבו
6. כן עשה בבית אל	1. ויעש חג לבני ישראל
7. לזבח לעגלים אשר עשה	5. ויעל על המזבח להקטיר
8. והעמיד בבית אל	
9. את כהני הבמות אשר עשה	

---

[24] Dtr's Southern perspective is evident here. For those present at Shechem it would have been ludicrous to speak of Israel being in rebellion against the house of David. The bulk of the kingdom sided with Jeroboam! It was Judah who would have been seen as the splinter faction.

[25] The "supplement" offers confirmation for this literary critical conclusion. I have argued that the "supplement" is an abbreviated rewriting of the MT's version of the Jeroboam cycle. Its lack of a counterpart to MT 1 Kings 13 suggests that the "supplement" writer did not have that chapter in the version of Kings which he used as the basis for his abbreviation of the Jeroboam cycle.

Dtr's original diatribe continued through 12:32. Dtr condemned Jeroboam
for setting up the golden calves with their accompanying shrines at Dan and
Bethel and for appointing non-Levitical priests to officiate at those shrines.
The doublet in 12:33 subtly shifts the topic of the narrative from Jeroboam's
institution of a permanent festival in 12:32 to the role of Jeroboam in the
initiation of the altar at Bethel. But since no elements of 12:33 are repeated
in the resumption in 13:33 Dietrich concludes that 12:33 was not part of the
insertion in chapter 13 but an even later gloss on 12:32. The gloss prepares
for the story in chapter 13 and anticipates Jeroboam's ascension to the altar
in 13:1. The additional line in v 33, בחדש אשר בדא מלבו, adds another item to Dtr's list of Jeroboam's offenses -- Jeroboam changed the religious calendar.[26]

     At the other end of the insertion, 13:33 resumes Dtr's language and
themes from 12:32. 12:32b and 13:33b both describe Jeroboam's appoint-
ment of priests. The language of 13:33b (וישב ויעש מקצות העם
כהני במות החפץ ימלא את ידו ויהי כהני במות) strongly resembles
that of 12:31 (ויעש כהנים מקצות העם אשר לא היו מבני לוי), and
the stress of both verses on the non-Levitical origin of Jeroboam's priesthood is identical. The sentence, "this thing became a sin" in 13:34 is a reiteration of one of Dtr's major themes -- the sin of Jeroboam (12:30). It once
followed directly after 12:32. 13:32b requires special comment. The expressions "cities of Samaria" and "shrines of the high places" both occur in that
half verse. In 13:32a the old prophet confesses that the word of the young
prophet against the altar at Bethel (13:2) will come true. But 13:32b goes
on to say that the young prophet's word was also against "the shrines of the
high places which are in the cities of Samaria." Yet, the word in 13:2 is
only against the altar in Bethel and mentions nothing about shrines of the
high places or cities of Samaria. This half verse is obviously dependent on
Deuteronomistic material, especially 12:31. It extends the old prophet's
words, linking the inserted story in chapter 13 with the framework (13:33-
34). It was probably added by the writer who inserted 1 Kings 13. The
story in 13:1-32a, then, has been inserted by a post-Dtr writer into Dtr's diatribe against Jeroboam which is preserved in 12:25-32 + 13:34 (cf. Van
Seters 1981:171).

     In addition to the presence of בדא A. Rofé (1974:163) has pointed to
several late idioms in the story which indicate that its present form is post-
exilic. These include the use in v 7 of מתת instead of משאת and of סעד
instead of סעד לב and the reference to the "word of Yahweh" instead of
"Yahweh" as the source for the prophetic message. Rofé describes 1 Kings
13 as the combination of an aetiology (vv 1-10), also reflected in 2 Kgs
23:16-18, and a prophetic parable (vv 11-32). On the basis of the language

---

[26] The presence of the late verb בדא in v 33 also indicates its late, secondary nature.

in the aetiology and the parable form which he believes to be late, Rofé dates this chapter to the fifth century B.C.E.

W. E. Lemke (1976) has argued that Deuteronomistic influence pervades 1 Kings 13. He concludes that the chapter was composed and added by a second Deuteronomist. Indeed, he goes so far as to nominate this chapter as one of the key structural passages for the DH (p. 317). His argument is based on six expressions in the chapter which are used predominately in the DH: 1. "cities of Samaria" (עָרֵי שֹׁמְרוֹן 13:32), 2. "priests of the high places" (כֹּהֲנֵי הַבָּמוֹת 12:32; 13:2, 33), 3. "shrines of the high places" (בָּתֵי הַבָּמוֹת 12:31 [emended]; 13:32), 4. "to rebel against the command of Yahweh" (לַמְרוֹת [אֶת] פִּי יהוה 13:21, 26), 5. "to keep the commandment" (לִשְׁמֹר אֶת הַמִּצְוָה 13:21), and 6. "to turn from/return by the way" (לָשׁוּב בְּ/מִן הַדֶּרֶךְ 13:9, 10, 17, 26, 33).

Lemke also argues that the two key motifs in 1 Kings 13 signal its Deuteronomistic composition. The encounter between the nameless prophet and the king in 13:1-10 is "a polemic against the cultic establishment of Jeroboam," and the deception by the old prophet of the young prophet in vv 11-32 is "a discursive narrative about the importance of obedience to the divine word" (p. 306). These two themes, the apostasy of Jeroboam and the importance of obedience to the divine word, are among the most important aspects of Dtr's theology.

Lemke's arguments for the Deuteronomistic nature of 1 Kings 13 are very weak. The first three expressions he cites as evidence occur only or predominately in the verses that frame the inserted story. They do not indicate a Deuteronomistic presence in the story itself.[27]

Expression 4. occurs twice in this chapter in vv 21 and 26, and expression 5. occurs in v 21. Both expressions occur outside of this chapter predominately, but not exclusively, in Deuteronomistic contexts. Lemke's argument in both cases is that the non-Deuteronomistic occurrences of these expressions are later than Dtr and therefore probably dependent on Deuteronomistic usage (1976:309 and nn. 43 and 50). The same point can certainly be made for the occurrences of expressions 4. and 5. in 1 Kings 13. The basic story in this chapter may be older than Dtr, but the editor who inserted was certainly familiar with Dtr's work.

The final expression (6.) has two variations, one with מִן and the other with בְּ. Lemke (p. 310-11) contends that the three occurrences of the expression with בְּ refer to the command to the young prophet not to return by

---

[27] Stipp (1987:403-407) also uses these three expressions to argue for the common authorship of 1 Kings 13 and 2 Kgs 17:24-33 (34a). Like Lemke, he fails to recognize that these expressions predominate in the framework around 1 Kings 13 which is, of course, based on Dtr's work. Dtr may have written 2 Kgs 17:24-33(34a) (see Chapter Seven). But he is not responsible for 1 Kgs 13:1-32a, which was inserted into his work.

the way in which he came, while the two uses of the expression with בֶֿ (vv 26, 33) are Deuteronomistic metaphors for changes in behavior. This is true of the instance in v 33 which is part of the framework constructed from Dtr's language by the editor who inserted chapter 13. The instance in v 26 is usually understood in the sense of the young prophet's physical return. But even if the expression in v 26 is metaphorical, it is not necessarily Deuteronomistic. Lemke concludes only that "the idiom in question was characteristic of the late pre-exilic or exilic prose tradition" (p. 310).

The sin of Jeroboam is certainly one of Dtr's major themes (Cross 1973:279), as is apparent from his diatribe in 12:31 and 13:34. But this theme is not at work in the intervening story. The word of the young prophet contains no direct condemnation of Jeroboam or the golden calf at Bethel. It is a simple prediction of Josiah's desecration of the altar at Bethel. The mention of Josiah in 13:2 is certainly *vaticinium ex eventu*, but it is not necessarily a mark of Dtr's intervention (against Cross 1973:279-280). It just means that the editor responsible for the insertion lived after Josiah's reform (cf. Rofé 1974:163). This same editor added the notice in 2 Kgs 23:15bβ-18, which relates to the story in 1 Kings 13.

Likewise, the theme of obedience is a major theme of Dtr's. But Dtr had no monopoly on the doctrine of obedience. Obedience to the word of God was also emphasized in prophetic circles. Indeed, T. Dozeman (1982) has suggested that the story in 13:11-32 originated in prophetic circles as a catechism,[28] and Rofé (1974:163) calls it a prophetic parable. Moreover, the object of obedience in 13:11-32a is slightly different from the one in Dtr's theology. Dtr's theme involves obedience to Deuteronomic law, while our passage is concerned with a prophet's obedience to Yahweh's command to him (cf. Lemke 1976:312). Thus, the theme of obedience in 1 Kings 13, like the language of the chapter and the references to Jeroboam and Josiah, differs from Dtr's use of it.

The two parts of 1 Kings 13 (vv 1-10; 11-32a) seem to derive from two separate prophetic legends that have been linked by Yahweh's command to the young prophet not to eat, drink, or return by the same way (vv 9-10, 16-17) and by his oracle against the altar at Bethel (vv 2, 32).[29] The content of

---

[28] Dozeman described the central theme of the catechism as the contrast between true and false prophecy. But Stipp (1987:467n) rightly observed that obedience to the prophetically mitigated word is the real concern of the text.

[29] Cf. Jepsen 1971:172. Würthwein (1973) has a much more complex reconstruction. One legend (vv 1, 4, 6) originally described the conflict between a man of God and a king. It ended with the man of God healing the king's withered hand. A second legend, behind vv 11-32 contained the grave tradition of a man of God from Judah and an Israelite prophet. It illustrated the universal esteem in which prophets are held (the lion did not eat the Judahite man of God) and the fraternal relationship of Northern and Southern prophets. The two legends were bound together by the addition of vv 7-9a and 16-18 which deal with the order to the man of God not to eat, drink, or return to Bethel. A third level added vv 9b, 20-22, which misunderstood the injunction against returning to Bethel as an order to return to Judah by a different route and which interpreted the young man's death as punishment for disobedience. At a final stage the

the young prophet's original oracle is unknown. It has been replaced by the prophecy against the Bethel altar in 13:2 which has yet to be fulfilled, according to 13:32a (Dozeman 1982:383). The destruction of the altar at Bethel was originally a "sign that Yahweh has spoken" (vv 3, 5). Thus, the editor who inserted the prophecy in 13:2 in anticipation of Josiah's reform was probably also responsible for linking the two legends in chapter 13.

The narrative in 1 Kings 13 has striking similarities to other prophetic stories, especially the ones in 1 Kings 20 (cf. Lemke 1976:313-315). Both 1 Kings 13 and 1 Kgs 20:35-43 deal with obedience to the prophetic word. As in 1 Kings 20, the old and young prophets in 1 Kings 13 are nameless. The title "man of God" is used for the young prophet in 1 Kings 13, the prophet in 1 Kgs 20:26-30a, and Elijah and Elisha. There is a strong element of miracle working in 1 Kings 13, as in 1 Kings 20 and the Elisha stories. In 1 Kings 13, as in 20:35-36, a prophet is killed by a lion for failing to heed Yahweh's word. Finally, as in 1 Kings 20 and many of the Elisha stories, the king who is condemned in 13:1-10 was originally nameless. The name, Jeroboam, in 13:1b is part of an addition. It is also secondary in 13:4, as indicated by its absence from the Old Greek (cf. Dietrich, 1972:115).

These similarities suggest that at least the story in 1 Kgs 13:11-32a likely derives from Northern prophetic legends like those of Elijah and Elisha and 1 Kings 20.[30] It may have served as instruction for young prophets regarding obedience to the divine word (cf. Dozeman 1982). It was linked with 13:1-10 and inserted into Dtr's account of Jeroboam at a late date. They were further tied with Josiah's reform by the insertion of 2 Kgs 23:15bβ-18. The sign in 13:3, 5 involving the destruction of the Bethel altar may have attracted the editor's attention to the possibilities of using these legends in connection with both Jeroboam and Josiah. The Judahite editing of the story in 13:11-34 also seeps through, as noticed by Barth (1957:353-409), in the story's distrust for Northern officials.

A number of scholars have argued for the identity of the man of God from Judah with Amos. This idea was first proposed by Wellhausen (1963:277-278) and has been accepted and elaborated by various writers (Morgenstern 1941:164-179; Eissfeldt 1968; Crenshaw 1971:41-42). There are indeed some striking similarities between the episode about the young prophet and

---

word of the man of God against the king was redirected to the altar by the addition of v 2 and later of vv 3, 5. Some of Würthwein's ideas are intriguing, but it is difficult to believe that the young man's death by a lion was not initially intended as punishment (cf. 1 Kgs 20:35-36). Also, Würthwein's explanation of 13:5 is weak. This verse appears secondary and contradicts the other references to the altar in vv 2, 3, and 32.

[30] Stipp (1987:399-403, 464-465) emphasizes the similarities between 1 Kings 13 and 2 Kgs 20:35-43 and concludes that both were written by the same author who also edited 1 Kgs 20:1-34 and 22* and inserted all of them into Dtr's History. He assigns 2 Kgs 23:15-20 and the Elijah and Elisha legends to other levels of editing. (See Chapter Four).

the work of Amos. Among the more meaningful of these, both come from Judah and prophesy in Bethel, both predict the destruction of the sanctuary there, and both work under a king named Jeroboam. But there are also some important differences which make the identification of the "man of God" in 1 Kings 13 with Amos tenuous. Notably, Amos worked in the monarchy of Jeroboam II not Jeroboam I, Amos has no direct encounter with Jeroboam such as the one in 1 Kings 13 when the king's hand is withered, and there is nothing in Amos like the story of the young prophet's death in 1 Kgs 13:11-32a (see further Crenshaw 1971:41-42; Lemke 1976:315-316; Wolff 1970:292-293). Although the legend in 1 Kings 13 was probably not originally about Amos it may have been influenced by traditions about him, particularly as it was transmitted in Judah.

DTR'S PORTRAIT OF JEROBOAM[31]

The Jeroboam cycle serves as a fountainhead for several of the most important themes in the DH, especially the Davidic promise and the sin of Jeroboam. Both themes are closely bound together and begin with Dtr's previous presentation of Solomon's reign in 1 Kings 3-11. Dtr is forced to periodize Solomon's reign. Solomon's incomparable wisdom and wealth (3:3-14) are the results of his early piety. His construction of the Temple in chapters 5-7 is a sign of his piety as is the prayer in chapter 8 which Dtr composed for him. Because of his piety Yahweh reaffirms with him the promise to David (9:1-5). But here the promise is that Solomon will retain the throne of Israel, and it is conditionalized upon Solomon keeping Yahweh's commandments.[32] Dtr's negative orientation on Solomon begins with 11:1-8 where he details Solomon's idolatries.[33]

The stories about Solomon's three adversaries followed next in Dtr's original account.[34] They are presented as Yahweh's agents for punishing Solomon's apostasy. The language introducing Jeroboam in v 26 (וירם יד במלך) is different from the language introducing Hadad and Rezon in vv 14 and 23 (ויקם שטן), suggesting that the story of Jeroboam was originally

---

[31] I owe several points in the following discussion to Dr. Gary Knoppers whose forthcoming monograph on this section of Kings will highlight these themes in more detail.

[32] Both 1 Kings 8 and 9:1-9 will be discussed in more detail in Chapter Seven.

[33] Cf. Nelson (1981:109); Weippert (1983:372). Campbell (1986:87, n. 51) sees 11:7 as an old tradition which was in his Prophetic Record. He also sees v 8 as post-Dtr, though his only reason for this judgement is that the verse is a generalization. O'Brien (1989:161) also sees v 3a as source material. While older traditions may lie behind 11:1-8, its language indicates that it is now completely the work of Dtr.

[34] Yahweh's announcement to Solomon in 11:9-13 regarding the division of the kingdom anticipates Ahijah's oracle in 11:29-39* and is best considered a later addition as mentioned earlier (n. 12).

independent from the other two and from this setting. But Dtr placed it here as part of his scheme showing the consequences of Solomon's sins. In the context of the description of Jeroboam as the third adversary comes Ahijah's oracle (vv 29-39*) announcing that the ensuing division of the kingdom is Yahweh's response to Solomon's sins, in case the reader has failed to discern that relationship from the order of the stories. In Dtr's presentation the oracle was "the reason that [Jeroboam] raised his hand against the king" (11:27).

After Ahijah's oracle Dtr gives the concluding formula for Solomon in 11:41-43, which he separated from the initial formula for Rehoboam (14:21) in order to include the narratives in chapters 12 and 14 (cf. Trebolle 1980:94). The story of division at Shechem in 1 Kings 12:1-20 was retold by Dtr as the fulfillment of Ahijah's prediction. The coronation motif in 12:1b ("for all Israel went to Shechem to make him king" -- כי שכם בא כל ישראל להמליך אתו) and 12:20, where all Israel summons Jeroboam to Shechem to crown him king (וימליכו אתו על כל ישראל) frames the story of the division. Thus, Dtr's retelling of the story contrasts the rejection by "all Israel" of Rehoboam with the coronation of Jeroboam according to Ahijah's oracle. The explanation in v 15 that the division was Yahweh's doing is Dtr's. Whatever historical reasons may be adduced for the schism -- Jeroboam's leadership qualities, Solomon's oppression of the Northern tribes, etc. -- take a back seat to Dtr's theological explanation that the division was the work of Yahweh as punishment for Solomon's sins.

Dtr's original narrative resumes in 12:25, since vv 21-24 are widely recognized as a later addition.[35] Verse 25 serves to link the story of the schism with the next topic which Dtr takes up -- Jeroboam's rival cultus (vv 26-32). At the end of Ahijah's oracle (11:38) Dtr makes it clear that Jeroboam had the opportunity to receive a "sure house," like David's if, like David, he remained faithful to Yahweh. In 12:26-32 + 13:34 Dtr tells of the shrines built by Jeroboam at Dan and Bethel which kept him from receiving Yahweh's promise. The concern in the passage for cultic centralization is a clear sign of Dtr's writing. The references to the "house of David" in v 26 (cf. Trebolle, 1980:132) and the sin of Jeroboam in v 30 mark those verses in particular as Dtr's work. In fact, it is best characterized as a diatribe by Dtr against "the sin of Jeroboam."

---

[35] Dietrich (1972:114n) collects the arguments. Grønbaek (1965) contends that v 21 is original, and Trebolle (1980:124, 164) accepts Grønbaek's position, arguing that vv 21 and 25 were originally connected, the latter describing Jeroboam's construction projects in defense against Rehoboam's military activity. But Jeroboam's building at Penuel (v 25), in Transjordan, could hardly have been a defensive measure against Judah, and v 21 seems closely tied to vv 22-24 as a prelude to Shemaiah's oracle. One indication of the secondary nature of vv 21-24 is that they contradict the statement in Dtr's formula (14:30) that Rehoboam and Jeroboam were continually at war.

The final installment in Dtr's account of Jeroboam is the story of his sick son in 14:1-18. Dtr placed this story toward the end of Jeroboam's reign, after the account of his apostasy in chapters 12-13. The point of the story accords with the message of Ahijah's oracle; because of Jeroboam's cultic sins at Dan and Bethel his dynasty is cursed and will not endure. Dtr followed the story immediately with the closing formulas for Jeroboam (14:19-20) and then for Rehoboam (14:21-24) so that he could move on quickly to show how Ahijah's oracle against Jeroboam's house came to be fulfilled.[36]

Both Solomon and Jeroboam, then, are guilty of idolatry. Dtr narrates the stories of both kings according to his theological requirement that cultic sin receive prompt punishment. But Yahweh's response to Solomon's sin differs from his response to Jeroboam because of his promise to David. These two topics, the sin of Jeroboam and the faithfulness of David, in Dtr's presentation of the Jeroboam cycle now become themes which he will carry through the rest of his History. They form the basis for his polemic against the Northern kingdom and his generally positive view of Judah.

CONCLUSIONS

Dtr likely had sources for parts of the Jeroboam cycle, especially information like the introduction of Jeroboam in 11:26-28, his building activities in 12:25, and the regnal formulas and other information in 14:19-31.[37] He may also have had an account of the division which now underlies 12:1-20. However, Dtr's overwriting has been so thorough in the rest of the Jeroboam cycle that sources for other parts of it are highly questionable. For example, some (Cross 1973:199; Halpern 1976) have suggested that an old polemic against the Aaronids on the part of an old Mushite priesthood underlies the account of Jeroboam's apostasy in 12:26-32. But Dtr's hand pervades this passage to such an extent that the literary evidence for an underlying, written polemic must be considered very tenuous.

The extent of Dtr's influence in the Jeroboam cycle raises serious doubts about the existence of a pre-Dtr, prophetic work. This is especially true if

---

[36] The regnal formula for Rehoboam in 14:21-24 attests retouching by a later hand. The description of Jerusalem in v 21 as "the city which Yahweh chose from all the tribes of Israel to place his name there" is Dtr's. It draws on the theme of the Davidic promise which already surfaced in 1 Kgs 11:26-40 and plays such an important role in the book of Kings. But the reference to "Judah" instead of "Rehoboam" in v 22 is anomolous in the regnal formulas and seems to reflect a desire to condemn the entire nation of Judah for sins which led to its exile. Therefore, vv 22b-24 and the name "Judah" in v 22a are probably an exilic addition. Cf. Provan (1988:74-77).

[37] While it is widely agreed that these formulas draw on an official source of some kind, the nature of that source is uncertain. Van Seters (1983:292-302) has shown the inaccuracy of the usual term "annals" for it. He believes that this kind of information was drawn from king lists.

Ahijah's oracle is Dtr's composition, since it is focal to his account of Jeroboam. It explains the reason for the loss of Israel to the Davidids and alludes to the demise of Jeroboam's house if he is faithless. The ties that bind the oracle in 11:29-39 with the one in 14:7-16 are all Dtr's. In fact, there is no indication of any pre-Dtr relationship among any of the Jeroboam stories. Still, it is possible that elements of the oracle in 14:7-16 were derived from a prophetic source used by Dtr, and some scholars (especially Campbell) have reconstructed their pre-Dtr, prophetic account on the basis of the oracles against the Northern dynasties. In the next chapter I shall examine that series of oracles.

CHAPTER THREE

DOG FOOD AND BIRD FOOD:
THE ORACLES AGAINST THE DYNASTIES IN THE BOOK OF
KINGS

The book of Kings contains a series of oracles against the first three Israelite
royal houses (1 Kgs 14:7-16; 16:1-4; 21:21-24; 2 Kgs 9:6-10). Each of the
oracles is accompanied by one or more fulfillment notices (cf. 1 Kgs 15:27-
30; 16:11-13; 2 Kings 9:25-26, 36-37; 10:10, 17).

AGAINST THE HOUSE OF JEROBOAM (1 KINGS 14:7-18; 15:27-30)

Ahijah's oracle against Jeroboam's house in the context of the consultation
concerning his sick son is the first of these anti-dynastic oracles. The
judgement portion of the oracle (14:10-11) utilizes a gruesome curse that is
also found in the oracles in 16:1-4 and 21:21-24: "The one belonging to
Jeroboam who dies in the city the dogs will eat, and the one who dies in the
open country the birds of the sky will eat." The curse is leveled against every male (משתין בקיר), "bond or free" (עצור ועזוב) of the house of
Jeroboam (cf. 1 Kgs 16:11; 21:21; 2 Kgs 9:8).

The uniqueness of the curse and the rarity of the expressions משתין
בקיר and עצור ועזוב have led some scholars to contend that the language of these verses is not typical of Dtr and therefore betrays the existence
of a pre-Dtr version of the oracle (cf. Campbell 1986:24-25; O'Brien
1989:187). This is an idea that requires examination.

The idiom for males, משתין בקיר, occurs outside of the oracles against
the dynasties only in the Abigail story in 1 Samuel 25 (vv 22, 34). There
also it is used in the context of the annihilation of a (royal?) household and
could be Dtr's addition or inherent to an older story. The enigmatic expression, עצור ועזוב, occurs outside of the oracles against the dynasties only
in Deut 32:36 and 2 Kgs 14:26.[1] The latter passage is clearly from Dtr's
hand. Thus, while the possibility that both expressions are pre-Dtr cannot

---

[1] The exact meaning of the expression remains uncertain in spite of many attempts to
solve it. The most recent treatment is that of Talmon and Fields (1989). See also Gray
(1963:307-308), Noth (1968:316), Saydon (1952), and Würthwein (1985:177).

be ruled out there is no concrete evidence that this is the case. Since their
few occurrences are all in the DH, it is fair to conclude that Dtr at least
imported both expressions and adapted them to his account and that he may
have coined them.

The curse itself, in precisely this form, is unique to the oracles against the
royal houses in Kings. But similar curses involving unburied corpses are
found in Deut 28:16, 26 and in vassal treaties from the ancient Near East
(Hillers 1964:68-69; Wallace 1986:34-35). It is, then, specifically a curse
of non-burial that is drawn from or based on a curse for treaty violations.
But in 1 Kgs 14:11 its thrust has been altered. There it is used as part of a
prophecy of the annihilation of a royal family or at least of its male members; hence its connection with משתין בקיר. The reference to the boy's
burial in vv 13, 18a also serves to connect the curse of non-burial with the
real focus of the oracle -- the demise of Jeroboam's house. The same is true
of this series of oracles in general. Except for the association of the curse
with the story of Jezebel's death in 2 Kings 9, there is no real concern in
these narratives with the burial or non-burial of the royal family. The real
interest is in the end of the current dynasty.

It is the downfall of Jeroboam's dynasty, of course, that is exactly Dtr's
concern in 14:1-18. The language surrounding the judgement in vv 7-16 is
Deuteronomistic, as H. Wallace (1986:23) has shown.[2] Indeed, the basis in
vv 7-9 for the judgement in vv 10-11 comes from the same ideology presented by Dtr in the earlier oracle by Ahijah (11:29-39*). Yahweh tore the
kingdom from the Davidids and gave it to Jeroboam. But unlike David,
Jeroboam was faithless and committed idolatry. There does not appear, then,
to be an earlier oracle underlying 14:7-11. Dtr had an older treaty curse of
non-burial, but he used it to describe the obliteration of Jeroboam's house
because of his failure to be faithful to Yahweh as was David.

It is possible that Dtr used an older prophetic legend, a "consultation of a
prophet in the case of illness," as the basis for the story in 14:1-18. Again,
Wallace (1986:22-23) points to the lack of Deuteronomistic language in vv
1-6 and suggests that those verses plus vv 12, 17, and 18a formed the original legend. He may be correct, but a word of caution is in order. As mentioned in the Chapter One, the original story of the boy's death must have
been accompanied by an oracle explaining the reason for it. That reason is
now supplied by Dtr's oracle in vv 7-16 which has displaced any earlier ex-

---

[2] The passage in 14:14-16 deserves special comment. Verse 14 accords with the
foregoing oracle from Ahijah and seems appropriate as it looks forward to Baasha's
demolition of Jeroboam's house. Verse 16 also fits well with Dtr's theme concerning
the sin of Jeroboam. Along with 2 Kgs 17:21-23 it forms an *inclusio* for Dtr's scheme
tracing the downfall of Israel as the result of Jeroboam's sin. However, v 15 may be a
later gloss. It undercuts the case which Dtr builds against Israel in the series of oracle
against the dynasties. It ascribes the fall of Israel to the idolatry of its citizens (cf. 2
Kgs 17:7-18). But this accusation is unprecedented in the previous treatment of
Jeroboam.

planation. Hence, if an earlier prophetic story does underlie 1 Kings 14 it can no longer be recovered.

There are three fulfillment notices for the oracle in 14:7-16. The first in 14:18 tells of the death of Jeroboam's son as predicted by Ahijah. The reference to Ahijah the prophet as Yahweh's servant is a Deuteronomistic expression. This verse and the similar one in v 13 serve as Dtr's link between the curse of non-burial and the destruction of Jeroboam's house as punishment for his sins. The boy is blessed with a peaceful death and burial. But the other members of Jeroboam's dynasty are slated for violent overthrow without burial because they were not pleasing to Yahweh.

The notice concerning the fulfillment of Ahijah's words against the dynasty is found in 15:27-30. Dietrich (1972:59-60) shows that the accounts of conspiracy and succession for Northern kings, based on official records, regularly consist of the elements in 15:27-28. But, 15:29 is an editorial addition giving the fulfillment of Ahijah's word against the house of Jeroboam in MT 14:10-11. It describes the violent end of Jeroboam's family members and points out that this fulfilled Ahijah's prophecy. Dietrich assigns it to his DtrP. He also argues (1972:37) that one expects the fulfillment notice to conclude, like v 29, with a clause beginning כדבר יהוה referring back to the prophecy which it fulfills. This is the case with other fulfillment notices (1 Kgs 12:15; 22:38; 2 Kgs 10:17). Verse 30 then specifies the theological reason for the destruction of Jeroboam's house. Its language, especially its use of כעס is Deuteronomistic: "the sins of Jeroboam which he both sinned and caused Israel to sin in his provocation with which he provoked Yahweh." Hence, Dietrich assigns 15:30 to another Deuteronomist, his DtrN.

Dietrich's literary case is well founded. Verses 27-28 contain source material from official records.[3] Verse 29 is Dtr's fulfillment notice. But I see no need to take v 30 as a later addition, as does Dietrich. The notice in 15:30 is very similar to the notice for Zimri in 16:19, which is from Dtr. The language and thought of 15:30 were drawn from Dtr's condemnation of Jeroboam for provoking Yahweh with idolatry in Ahijah's oracle (1 Kgs 14:7-9, 10b, 14-16). A similar comment also occurs in regard to the fall of Baasha in 16:13.

In sum, Ahijah's oracle against the dynasty of Jeroboam is the work of Dtr. He used an older treaty curse as the basis for the judgement oracle. But he completely changed the *Sitz im Leben* of the curse to refer to the demise of the Northern royal house. Dtr may have had a prophetic legend about the consultation of Ahijah for Jeroboam's sick son which he used as the setting for his oracle. But that legend cannot be recovered. Dtr composed the fulfillment notices regarding the boy's death in 14:18 and the fall of Jeroboam's

---

[3] On the nature of such official records see n. 37 in Chapter Two.

house in 15:29. The additional theological explanation in 15:30 is also
Dtr's addition.

AGAINST BAASHA (1 KINGS 16:1-4, 11-13)

Noth (1967:82) saw Jehu's oracle in 16:1-4 as Dtr's composition drawn on
the "annalistic" reference to Jehu (16:12) and elements of Ahijah's oracle
(14:7, 10-11). Analysis of this passage confirms Noth's basic position.
This oracle follows the same structure as the one by Dtr in 14:7-11 (cf.
Wallace 1985:24). A causal clause beginning with יען אשר (v 2; cf.
14:7) introduces the oracle. Then judgement is announced with a non-verbal
clause, הנני plus participle (v 3; cf. 14:10), although the לכן before הנני as
in 14:10 is lacking.

Campbell (1986:39-41) observes several differences between Jehu's oracle
against Baasha's house and the oracles against the houses of Jeroboam and
Ahab. 1. Unlike the oracles in 1 Kings 14 and 21, the passage in 1 Kgs
16:1-4 is simply a report of Jehu's oracle without an accompanying narrative. 2. There is no story illustrating how Baasha was "exhalted out of the
dust" (16:2) and no parallel for the use of that expression in such a context.
Campbell calls the expression a "rhetorical flourish" designed to compensate
for the lack of an associated story. 3. The accusation in 16:2b consists of
elements from judgement formulas which are not represented in the material
Campbell assigns to his Prophetic Record. 4. The threat to "cut off every
male bond or free in Israel" (הכרתי משתין בקיר ועצור ועזוב
בישראל), found in the oracles against Jeroboam and Ahab, is lacking in
16:1-4. 5. There is no general statement ("I will bring evil upon ... ")
following "behold" as there is in the oracles against other dynasties. Rather,
the "behold" in 16:3 introduces a particular aspect of judgment. Also, the
stereotypical curse in 16:4 has לו in its second half, which may betray Dtr's
pleonastic style. 6. Baasha's would have been the only Northern dynasty not
explicitly rejected by Yahweh in 1 Kings 14 - 2 Kings 9.[4]

These differences lead Campbell to conclude that Dtr composed the oracle
in 16:1-4. He had no oracle against Baasha in his *Vorlage*. He was forced,
therefore, to write one in order to balance the tradition in 16:11 about the destruction of Baasha's house and to conform to the pattern for the other dynasties. He wrote Jehu's oracle in imitation of the oracles of Ahijah and Elijah
against Jeroboam and Ahab respectively.

Campbell's conclusion that 16:1-4 is Dtr's composition is certainly correct. His sense that 16:2 reflects Dtr's "rhetorical flourish" to compensate

---

[4] Another difference not noticed by Campbell is the use in 16:3 of the hiphil
participle (מבעיר אחרי) in the expression where 14:10 and 21:21 have the piel
perfect,   ובערתי אחרי.

for the lack of a story is attractive. The second half of that verse consists entirely of favorite Dtr expressions: "you have walked in the way of Jeroboam," "you have caused my people Israel to sin," and "provoking me to anger with their sins."

But the differences cited by Campbell between the oracles against Jeroboam and Ahab and the one in 16:1-4 are not very significant and do not support his conclusion that only the latter is Dtr's composition. The lack of an accompanying story for 16:1-4 does suggest that Dtr had no *Vorlage* for Jehu's oracle. But our treatment of 14:7-18 indicates that even where he may have had an earlier story he still composed the oracle. Indeed, the similarities between 14:7-11; 16:1-4; and 21:21-24 are more striking than the minor differences that Campbell notices. Only the absence of the expression, "I will cut off every male bond or free in Israel," from 16:1-4 is noteworthy. Even so, a very similar expression, משתין בקיר ועזוב ועצור, occurs in the fulfillment notice in 16:11.

The fulfillment notices for Jehu's oracle in 16:11-13 match perfectly the fulfillment notices in 15:29-30 for Ahijah's oracle against Jeroboam. Just as 15:27-28 seem to derive from an official record of Baasha's usurpation, so 16:9-10 contain an official report of Zimri's *coup* . Then vv 11-12 are Dtr's addition. We have seen that the idiom משתין בקיר in 14:10 reflects Dtr's use of the curse of non-burial (14:11) against Jeroboam's house. Its occurrence in 16:11 also betrays Dtr's hand. As in 15:29, 16:11-12 tell of the destruction of the royal house in accord with a prophetic oracle and end with a כדבר יהוה clause. Finally, the theological explanation in 16:13, like the one in 15:30, is also probably Dtr's addition. The two verses are nearly identical.[5]

15:30	16:13
על חטאות ירבעם	אל כל חטאות בעשא
	וחטאות אלה בנו
אשר חטא	אשר חטאו
ואשר החטיא את ישראל	ואשר החטיאו את ישראל
בכעסו אשר הכעיס	להכעיס
את יהוה אלהי ישראל	את יהוה אלהי ישראל
	בהבליהם

Since 16:1-4 is so clearly Dtr's composition there can be no question of an underlying, prophetic oracle matched by a fulfillment notice in 16:11-12. Both must be Dtr's. This poses a difficulty for Campbell's reconstruction of

---

[5] The line "and the sins of Elah his son" in 16:13 is superfluous and may be an even later gloss. The same thing may also be true of the reference to "their idols" at the end of the verse.

a Prophetic Record in the book of Kings. He never explains why his Prophetic Record had a gap in its treatment of the house of Baasha. It is hard to imagine a running prophetic account of the Israelite monarchy that would not include an oracle against one of its dynasties.[6]

A further illustration of Dtr's use of these fulfillment notices can be seen in the account of Zimri's death (1 Kgs 16:18-19). The account of Omri's victory over Zimri and Tibni in 16:15b-18, 21-24 seems to draw on official Israelite records. Verses 15a, 19-20, 25-28 are evident Deuteronomistic additions. The addition of v 19 is particularly significant. The story of Zimri's rebellion and brief reign ends perfectly appropriately with his death in v 18. Verse 19 is Dtr's theological explanation for Zimri's demise. Zimri fell because of the sins he commited and because he walked in the way of Jeroboam and in "the sin which he caused Israel to sin," even though he only reigned seven days. This explanation is similar to those used for the destruction of the houses of Jeroboam and Baasha, and may have motivated them. In addition to his own sins, however, Dtr explains that Zimri "walked in the way of Jeroboam and in his [Jeroboam's] sin which he did to make Israel sin." Dtr composed no oracle regarding Zimri's death as he had for Baasha's house, perhaps because of the brevity of Zimri's reign. Consequently, there is no fulfillment notice, and Dtr's theological remark in 16:19 is added directly to his official source.

AGAINST AHAB (1 KINGS 21:20-24; 2 KINGS 9:1-10:17)

The oracle against the "house of Ahab" occurs in the context of the story of Naboth's murder (1 Kings 21) and is fulfilled in Jehu's rebellion (2 Kings 9-10). The two stories were originally unrelated but have been linked by secondary additions. The signs of literary reworking that abound in both passages have exercised scholars considerably for years.[7]

---

[6] The doublet in 16:7, as Dietrich (1972:10, n. 2) puts it, "hat viel Kopfzerbrechen gemacht." Most scholars have discounted the verse as a late corruption of vv 1-4 (Dietrich 1972:10, n. 2). However, Seebass (1975:175-179) has argued for taking v 7 as the original report of Jehu's word and seeing vv 1-4 as a secondary interpretation of it. The location of v 7 is secondary, of course, because it lies outside of the regnal formulas for Baasha. But, Seebass contends that a brief notice like 16:7 would fit much better between 15:34 and 16:5 than does the more detailed version in 16:1-4. He posits that Jehu's oracle against Baasha originally consisted of 16:7 plus 16:3a but that it was displaced with 16:1-4. O'Brien (1989:193) describes 16:7 as an addition in two stages to emphasize that Jehu's oracle was against Baasha and his house and to clarify the nature of Baasha's sin. I find O'Brien's explanation more attractive than Seebass's.

[7] For a review of the literature see Bohlen (1978:23-31).

1 Kings 21:20-24

The Naboth narrative proper in 21:1-16 is markedly different in some respects from the report of Elijah's oracle in vv 17-29. Jezebel is primarily responsible for Naboth's death in vv 1-16, but Ahab is the one condemned in vv 17-29. This and other tensions have led scholars to see in vv 1-16 a distinct and usually later level of composition or redaction from the original word of Elijah beginning in v 17.[8] A. Rofé (1988b) has recently buttressed this viewpoint by observing late linguistic features within the narrative in vv 1-16.

Our focus here is on Elijah's encounter with Ahab in 21:17-29. There is wide agreement that these verses betray more than one hand but very little agreement when it comes to separating various levels of writing within them. I would hazard the opinion that the oldest remaining segment of chapter 21, is in vv 17, *18, 19a, and perhaps 20abα.[9] These verses introduce an individual condemnation of Ahab. The original content of this condemnation has been supplanted by insertions in v 19b and vv 20bβ-29. A portion of the original condemnation may be preserved in 2 Kgs 9:25-26 (see below).

A new level of editing is found in vv 20bβ-24. Here there is more unanimity among scholars. There is a break in v 20b beginning with יען, and the יען clause is a doublet to the introduction of the oracle in v 19a. Deuteronomistic language is present in the rest of v 20b, "you sold yourself to do what is evil in Yahweh's sight," and in v 22, "because of the anger to which you provoked (הכעס אשר הכעסת) Yahweh, causing Israel to sin" (cf. Bohlen 1978:202-205). The structure of this oracle parallels that of the oracles against the houses of Jeroboam (14:7-11) and Baasha (16:2-4), which we determined to be Dtr's work. A causal clause beginning with יען introduces the oracle and is followed by the announcement of punishment, which starts with הנני plus hiphil participle (מביא) in v 21 (cf. Wallace 1986:31). Most scholars agree, therefore, in assigning vv 20bβ-22, 24 to Dtr (Bohlen 1978:25). As with the previous oracles against the Northern dynasties Dtr has utilized the treaty curse of non-burial in the composition of an oracle detailing his theological reasons for the demise of the royal house.

---

[8] E.g., Steck (1968:40-43); Würthwein (1978:376-377). Otherwise, Baltzer (1965:76-77); Welten (1973:24-26). For further bibliography see Campbell (1986:96, n. 77).

[9] Cf. Steck (1968:43). Others, such as Noth (1967:83n), contend that v 20 is secondary because it interrupts the speech of God.

Verses 21b, 24 contain the same judgement as the oracle against Jeroboam
in 1 Kgs 14:10-11: והכרתי לאחאב משתין בקיר ועצור ועזוב
בישראל and the same curse leveled against the royal houses of Jeroboam
and Baasha: המת לאחאב בעיר יאכלו הכלבים והמת בשדה
יאכלו עוף השמים. But two important differences in Elijah's oracle surface in comparison to the other oracles against the royal houses. First,
Elijah's oracle is not directed against the founder of the dynasty, Omri, as are
the oracles against Jeroboam and Baasha, but against the "house of Ahab."
Noth's explanation is that Dtr changed an individual word against Ahab into
an oracle against the royal house in accord with 1 Kgs 14:10-11 (and 16:3-
4). But this does not adequately explain why Dtr broke the pattern of the
previous oracles against royal houses. The anomaly is best explained with
T. Ishida (1977:177-178) as tendentious, reflecting the view that Ahab's
iniquity was the cause of the dynasty's fall, although he was not its founder.
Ishida finds a parallel in Amos' designation of the Jehu dynasty as the
"house of Jeroboam" (Amos 7:9).[10] Thus, Dtr directed the curse against
Ahab because he viewed Ahab as the worst king of Israel.

Secondly, the oracle against Ahab contains the prediction of Jezebel's
grisly death in 21:23. Such a prediction is anomolous in the oracles against
the dynasties, and v 23 has evidently been inserted, in rather clumsy fashion
with וגם, into the oracle against Ahab's house. Again, scholars are nearly
unanimous in taking v 23 as a post-Dtr insertion (e.g., Barré 1988:10-11;
Dietrich 1972:27; Minokami 1989:53).

Noth (1967:83) assigned 21:25-26 to Dtr, and most scholars have continued to affirm their Deuteronomistic origin (Bohlen 1978:28). Verse 25a repeats the expression of v 20b about Ahab selling himself to do what was
evil in Yahweh's eyes, and v 26, following Dtr's introduction to Ahab's
reign (16:29-34), describes Ahab as the worst of Israel's kings. However, the
two verses appear intrusive, and it is striking that they do not mention
Naboth but focus instead on Ahab's idolatry. They are, therefore, best seen
as a late summary of Ahab's reign based on Dtr's account (cf. O'Brien
1989:203; Würthwein 1984:252).

The postponement of the judgement against Ahab's house in vv 27-29 is
odd. The contrast between the description of Ahab as Israel's worst king in
vv 25-26 and that of his piety in vv 27-29 jars the reader. These verses also
do not fit the pattern of the oracles against the royal houses. The curses

---

[10] Miller (1967:320-324) saw the condemnation of the "house of Ahab" as the result
of a conflict over royal ideology in which the prophetic tradition subscribed to the
amphyctionic ideal of charismatic leaders and, thus, condemned the "house of Ahab,"
because Ahab and his sons were the first to succeed at dynastic monarchy. This view is
undercut, however, by recent studies showing the dynastic nature of the Northern
monarchy (Buccellati 1967:200-208; Ishida 1977:171-182; Wallace 1986:37).

leveled at the houses of Jeroboam and Baasha are both enacted against their sons. Why, then, is this delay specifically noted for the curse against Ahab? Some (e.g., Eissfeldt 1967:51, n. 2; Fohrer 1957:26, 42; Hentschel 1977:18-20; O'Brien 1989:203-204; Steck 1968:45) have tried to explain this anomoly by finding a pre-Dtr tradition, which linked the Naboth episode with the account of Jehu's revolt, behind these verses. But the deferment in v 29 of "the evil" (cf. v 21) until the days of Ahab's son presumes the oracle which Dtr placed in Elijah's mouth in vv 20bβ-22, 24 (Kittel 1900:158; Jepsen 1970:147-148). Also, as Jepsen (1970:150-152) in particular has observed (cf. Minokami 1989:35-36) the humbling of oneself, expressed with the verb נכנע is a late theological *topos* which appears elsewhere in the Bible primarily in Chronicles and P (Lev 26:41; 2 Chr 7:14; 12:6, 7, 12; 30:11; 32:26; 33:12, 19, 23; 34:27; 36:12; cf. 2 Kgs 22:19).[11] Therefore, 2 Kgs 21:27-29, are best taken as a post-Dtr addition to this passage by an editor who is already aware of the claim that Elijah's oracle against Ahab was fulfilled in Jehu's revolt.

Two other post-Dtr glosses in Elijah's oracle are worthy of note (cf. Miller 1967:312-313). The first is the reference to Samaria (אשר בשמרון) in v 18, which stands in tension with the references throughout 1 Kings 21 and 2 Kings 9-10 to Naboth and his property being from Jezreel.[12] The second is the prophecy in v 19b that the dogs would lick Ahab's blood in the same place where they had licked Naboth's blood. The latter is signaled as an addition by the repetition of the command, "and you shall say to him, 'Thus says Yahweh . . . .'" The purpose of both of these glosses was to set the scene for the story of Ahab's death in the following chapter: "And they washed the chariot by the pool of Samaria, and the dogs licked up his blood, ... according to the word of the Lord which he had spoken" (22:38). But, Dtr was unaware of the account of Ahab's death in battle in 1 Kings 22. In his account Ahab died in peace (22:40). Both of these glosses in chapter 21 probably came from the editor who added the story of Ahab's death in 1 Kings 22 to the DH (cf. O'Brien 1989:201-202).

---

[11] O'Brien's response that the focus of these verses is not upon Ahab as an individual but upon his house (1989:203) misses the point of the argument regarding the late use נכנע.

[12] All the references to Samaria in chapter 21 are probably glosses. Napier (1959:366-369) has shown that Jezreel was the original setting for the narrative about Naboth. As he points out, Naboth's "inheritance from his fathers" could hardly have been in Samaria which Omri purchased and built (1 Kgs 16:24). Jezreel is also the setting for the original narrative of Jehu's revolt in 2 Kings 9-10. For a different view see Timm 1982:118-121.

2 Kings 9-10

In the present account, Elijah's word against Ahab's house is fulfilled in
Jehu's revolt (2 Kings 9-10). There is general agreement that the narrative
upon which these two chapters are based was a straightforward "historical"
account, written close to Jehu's reign, later used to justify Jehu's bloodlet-
ting.[13] The narrative in 2 Kings 9-10 is sprinkled with references which link
it to 1 Kings 21. These references are all secondary additions to the story of
Jehu's revolt and provide important hints about the composition of the MT's
accounts of that story and the one about Naboth. The recent studies by L.
Barré (1988) and Y. Minokami (1989) are particularly helpful for isolating
and evaluating these secondary additions.

9:7-10a

Jehu's actions are impelled by a prophetic envoy sent by Elisha to anoint
Jehu (9:1-13). The prophet follows his instructions to the letter, as the narrative makes clear:

v 4 - וילך ...רמת גלעד	v 1 - לך רמת גלעד
v 5 - ויבא ... ויאמר דבר	v 2 - ובאת שמה וראה שם יהוא
לי אליך השר	
v 6 - ויקם ויבא	v 2 - ובאת והקמתו מתוך אחיו
	והביאת אתו חדר בחדר
v 6 - ויצק השמן אל ראשו	v 3 - ויצקת על ראשו
v 10 - ויפתח הדלת וינס	v 3 - ופתחת הדלת ונסתה

The gap between notices of the prophet's execution of his instructions in vv
6 and 10 indicates that the extended oracle in vv 7-10a is secondary, and this
has been widely accepted among scholars (cf. Barré 1988:9). There is nothing about this oracle in Elisha's instructions, and the prophet's elaboration
violates Elisha's order not to delay (ולא תחכה v 3). Dietrich (1972:48;
also Barré 1988:10; Bohlen 1978:293) notes a further indication of the secondary nature of vv 7-10a in v 12b where Jehu reports to his companions
what the prophet said to him. He reports verbatim the instructions given by

---

[13] Wellhausen (1963:285-287) derived 9:1-10:27 from a literary source which also
included 1 Kings 20; 22; 2 Kgs 3:4-27; 6:24-7:20. We have already observed that Noth
(1967:80) derived 2 Kings 9-10 from a cycle of stories, including 1 Kings *11; *12; *14;
(20); and 22, which dealt with prophetic intervention in the succession of Israelite kings.
However, Noth recognized that these stories were simply similar in subject matter and were
not specifically linked: "aber zu beweisen ist das nicht, da es an speziellen Beziehungen
dieser Geschichten untereinander fehlt und nur das Thema und die Vorstellung vom
Prophetenwort und seiner Wirkung ihnen gemeinsam sind."

Elisha to the prophetic messenger in v 3: כה אמר יהוה משחתיך
למלך אל ישראל but says nothing about the speech in vv 7-10a.

This passage has obvious affinities with Dtr's oracles against the royal
houses. In vv 8b-9 it forecasts the destruction of Ahab's house in the same
terms as those earlier oracles: והכרתי לאחאב משתין בקיר ועצור
ועזוב בישראל ונתתי את בית אחאב כבית ירבעם בן נבט וכבית
בעשא בן אחיה. At the same time, 2 Kgs 9:7-10a differs from the previous oracles against the dynasties in form and purpose. Unlike the oracles in
1 Kings 14, 16, and 21, 2 Kgs 9:7-10a is not a judgement oracle. The
structure common to the oracles against Jeroboam, Baasha, and Ahab --
(לכן) הנני + יען (אשר) + hiphil active participle is absent from the
prophet's word in 2 Kgs 9:7-10a. The previous oracles against the dynasties
are all delivered to the king whose house is condemned years before the dynasty actually falls. But the prophet in 2 Kgs 9:7-10a addresses the usurper,
Jehu, and impels him to lead his revolt. The word of the prophet in 2 Kings
9 is intended not as a prophecy against the royal house but as a commission
for Jehu to begin his revolution (cf. Barré 1988:109).

The two references to Jezebel within 2 Kgs 9:7-10a are probably later additions. Barré (1988:11) perceives v 7bβ (ודמי כל עבדי יהוה מיד
איזבל) as an expansive gloss and prefers to read on the basis of the LXX in
v 8a "And I will avenge the blood of my servants the prophets ... [which
was shed] at the hand of the whole house of Ahab." But v 7bα may also be
an addition. The only previous references to the murder of Yahwistic
prophets under Ahab are in 1 Kgs 18:12; 19:10, which I believe to be parts
of post-Dtr additions (see next chapter). While the expression "my servants
the prophets" is Deuteronomistic it could be an imitation in this instance.

The prophecy in v 10a that "the dogs shall eat Jezebel in the territory of
Jezreel, and none shall bury her" also occurs in 1 Kgs 21:23 and 2 Kgs 9:36.
In both of these other cases it is secondary. All three passages, therefore,
appear to be the work of an "anti-Jezebel" editor (so Barré 1988:10-11 and
Minokami 1989:59) who may also be the one responsible for revising the
story in 1 Kgs 21:1-16.

Thus, the oracle in 2 Kgs 9:7a, 8-9 is Dtr's composition. It draws on the
oracles against the royal houses but serves a different purpose, that of com-
missioning Jehu. It is one of the links that Dtr provides in his prophecy -
fulfillment scheme between Elijah's oracle against Ahab in the Naboth incident and the narrative of Jehu's revolt. However, the reference in v 7b to
Jezebel killing all of Yahweh's servants, which alludes in part to the murder
of Naboth, is a later addition, along with v 10a, to the commission composed by Dtr.

9:14-16

Another recent monograph by Trebolle (1984) focuses on these difficult
verses and helps to clarify their origin. Trebolle argues (1984:especially

110-125) that the "plus" in the LXX[L] and the Old Latin at 10:36 preserves an Old Greek reading and represents the original form and placement of the notice of Jehu's conspiracy against Ahaziah:[14]

LXX[L]: και επορευθη   Οχοζιας επι   Αζαηλ βασιλεα Συριας
εις πολεμον τοτε συνηψεν   Ιου υιος Ναμεσσει επι   Ιωραμ
υιον   Αχααβ βασιλεα   Ισραηλ και   επαταξεν αυτον εν
Ιεζραηλ και απεθανεν   και ετοξευσεν   Ιου και τον   Οχο-
ζιαν βασιλεα   Ιουδα επι το αρμα   και απεθανεν και
ανεβιβασαν αυτον οι   παιδες αυτου εν Ιερουσαλημ και
θαπτουσιν αυτον μετα των πατερων εν πολει Δαυιδ

OLD LATIN: *Cum enim abiisset Ocazias conuictus dolore regis Israel in pugna aduersus Azahel regem Syriae et in uerbo Domini comprehendisset Ieu filium Namessi Hyoram regem Israel filium Ahab et interfecisset eum factum est ut in eodem bello sagittaret Ochoziam regem Iuda in curru quem cum retulissent mortuum pueri eius in Hyerusalem et sepelissent eum cum patribus eius*

The notice has been fragmented in the MT and the pieces dispersed in the narrative in 8:28-29 and 9:14-15a, which are, in part, duplicates. Since it is unlikely that a later redactor or translator would have reassembled the dispersed elements into a conspiracy notice in its original form, the original conspiracy notice for Ahaziah was probably broken up when it was fused with the narrative about Jehu's revolt in the process of the composition of the MT book of Kings. The original conspiracy notice was a continuation of the formula for Ahaziah begun in 8:25-27. Another "plus" in the LXX[B,L] at 9:16a represents the original placement of the material about Joram's return to Jezreel now paralleled in the MT at 8:29a; 9:15a, which has once again been displaced as a result of the addition of the narrative about Jehu's revolt in this chapter.

Hence, Trebolle identifies the following two insertions relating to 2 Kgs 9:14-16 (cf. 1984:122-125, 185-189). First, part of the original conspiracy notice (now in LXX[L], VL 10:36*) was transferred to 8:28 and used to introduce the narrative about Jehu's revolt. The editor responsible for this trans-

---

[14] The LXX[B] at this point reflects the καιγε recension. However, the Lucianic family of manuscripts and the Old Latin preserve the earlier level. Whether this level is a proto-Lucianic recension, as Cross argued, or the OG as Barthélemy contended, it is the closest extant witness to the OG and frequently preserves OG readings. On this issue and the Greek recensions in general see Shenkel (1968:5-21) and the bibliography that he cites.

fer also added two statements in 8:28 which are not paralleled in the "plus": את יורם בן אחאב and ברמת גלעד. The same editor also took the reference to Joram's wounding from 9:16a (LXX^B,L), moved it to 8:29aβ, and composed 8:28b. This juxtaposition created the contradiction currently in the MT regarding the location (Ramot or Jerusalem) from which Ahaziah went to visit Joram. Secondly, the reference to Jehu's conspiracy against Joram was transferred from its original place (LXX^L, VL 10:36+) to 9:14a. In order to fit this statement into its context, the composer added 9:14b and moved 9:16a (as in LXX^B,L) to 9:15a. Then, 9:16aβ ("for Joram lay there") was added to provide a transition.

Thus, in Trebolle's view, the text behind 9:14-16 originally read, "Now King Joram had returned to be healed in Jezreel of the wounds which the Aramaeans gave him when he fought with Hazael, king of Aram. Then Jehu mounted his chariot and went to Jerusalem." The present text in the MT is the work of a later editor who segmented and dispersed the original conspiracy notice throughout the narrative of Jehu's revolt.

9:25-26

In v 26 Jehu asks Bidkar to recall a threat from Yahweh in response to the murder of Naboth. However, Jehu's recollection differs in several ways from the Naboth story in 1 Kings 21 (Bohlen 1978:288, 300; Hentschel 1977:36-37; Miller 1967:307-317; Rofé 1988b:95-97; Steck 1968:33-34). Jehu does not mention Elijah, who bore the oracle in 1 Kings 21. There is no reference to the presence of Jehu and Bidkar at the encounter between Elijah and Ahab in 1 Kings 21. Also, 1 Kings 21 contains no reference to the execution of Naboth's sons as implied in 2 Kgs 9:26. According to the latter verse, Naboth was killed the day before (אמש) Yahweh delivered the oracle against Ahab,[15] but 1 Kgs 21:17 does not tell how much time elapsed between Naboth's death and Yahweh's word to Elijah. The oracle attributed to Yahweh in 2 Kgs 9:25-26 sounds nothing like any of 1 Kgs 21:17-29.

The two verses contain inserted material, as a large number of scholars have observed (Barré 1988:13-14; Bohlen 1978:282-284; Minokami 1989:

---

[15] Miller (1966:308-311) contends that the word אמש ("yesterday") in 2 Kgs 9:25 indicates that Naboth was killed immediately before the end of Joram's reign and not years before in Ahab's reign. This proposal is ingenious, but Miller does not provide enough evidence to prove it. The word אמש occurs within Jehu's quotation of Yahweh's word when he and Bidkar "were riding behind Ahab." The editor who inserted Jehu's recollection of this word of Yahweh clearly has Ahab's reign and not Jehoram's in mind. Miller needs to show that Yahweh's oath ("As certainly as I saw the blood of Naboth and his sons yesterday") was once completely separate from its present context recalling Ahab's day or to produce independent evidence of a connection between Joram and Naboth.

34-39; Schmitt 1972:26-27; Schmoldt 1985:42; Timm 1982:140-141; Trebolle 1984:163). Verse 25 disrupts the link between vv 24 and 27. Ahaziah
is impelled to flee (v 27) by his observation of Joram's assassination (v 24).
The narrative's depiction of the quickness and secrecy of Jehu's revolt would
hardly allow Jehu pause to give instructions regarding Joram's corpse while
Ahaziah flees (Barré 1988:14). The secondary nature of these verses is also
indicated by the repetition of Jehu's instruction to cast Joram's corpse into
Naboth's field:

v 25a	v 26b
שא השלכהו חלקת	ועתה שא השלכהו בחלקה
שדה נבות היזרעאלי	כדבר יהוה

Some scholars (Bohlen 1978:282-284; De Vries 1978:90n; Schmitt
1972:26-27; Steck 1968:33-34, 44-45) suggest that Yahweh's oath in v 26
was an early prophetic oracle against Ahab (v 26). They believe that it was
applied to the situation under Joram by an apologist for Jehu. This would
explain the variation between the references to Naboth in 9:25-26 and the account in 1 Kgs 21:17-26. S. Olyan (1984:658n) believes that v 26 was the
original word to Ahab following Naboth's murder. It would be appropriate
after 1 Kgs 21:17-19a, and we have already observed that 21:19b is a secondary interpolation anticipating the story of Ahab's death in 1 Kings 22.
Barré (1988:14), on the other hand, attributes 9:25-26 to Dtr. He argues that
they display Dtr's tendency throughout 2 Kings 9-10 to relate Jehu's deeds to
Elijah's oracle against Ahab. Both Olyan and Barré may be correct. Perhaps
Dtr appropriated Elijah's word to Ahab from the original Naboth story and
inserted it in 9:25-26 as a fulfillment notice. This would account for the differences between 9:25-26 and the Naboth story in 1 Kings 21 as well as the
lack of Deuteronomistic language in vv 25-26.

9:27b-29

Verse 29 contains a variant version (cf. 8:25) of Ahaziah's initial formula.
It follows the OG chronology and may come from the same portion of the
text reproduced in the LXX^L and Old Latin at 10:36+ (Trebolle 1984:124),
but it is clearly out of place here. What is more interesting is the account of
Ahaziah's death and burial in vv 27b-28. Trebolle shows that the reference
to the transfer and burial of Ahaziah's body in v 28 is a third insertion of information from the original conspiracy notice in 10:36+ (see under *9:14-16*
above). But Barré (1988:15) also points out that 9:27bβ-28 are dependent on
the account in 2 Kgs 23:30 of Josiah's death at Megiddo and transfer to
Jerusalem and burial there:

9:28abα	23:30a
וירכבו אתו עבדיו	וירכבהו עבדיו מת ממגדו
ירושלמה	ויבאהו ירושלם
ויקברו אתו בקברתו	ויקברהו בקברתו

Since he dates Dtr to the reign of Josiah, Barré sees both passages as the work of a post-Dtr editor.

On the basis of the observations by Trebolle and Barré we may conclude that a late editor inserted 9:27bβ-28. This insertion borrowed partly from the original conspiracy notice for Ahaziah preserved in the Old Latin and LXX[L] at 10:36+ and partly from the account of Josiah's death and burial in 23:30. This editor was probably the same one who inserted most of 9:14-16 into the MT.

9:36-37

These two verses are the fulfillment notice for the prediction against Jezebel in 1 Kgs 21:23. They have been secondarily attached to the story of Jezebel's death. That story climaxes in 9:35, so that vv 36-37 are anticlimactic (cf Dietrich 1972:60).

Verse 36a (up to לאמר) belongs to Dtr (cf. Dietrich 1972:37-38). The expression in 9:36a, "it was the word of Yahweh which he spoke by his servant Elijah the Tishbite" (הוא דבר יהוה אשר דבר ביד עבדו אליהו התשבי), is similar to the notice in 2 Kgs 15:12, which is certainly Deuteronomistic (הוא דבר יהוה אשר דבר אל יהוא). Verse 37 is also Dtr's, as Barré (1988:15) and Rofé (1988a:84) have recently contended. The skatological image in v 37, "like dung upon the surface of the ground" (כדמן על פני השדה) is Deuteronomistic. It occurs elsewhere only in Jer 9:21, with a similar expression, לדמן על פני האדמה, found in Deuteronomistic portions of Jeremiah (8:2; 16:4; 25:33; Bohlen 1978:299; cf. Schmitt 1972:22). This verse accords both with the curse of non-burial leveled by Dtr against the house of Ahab and with the account of Jezebel's death in vv 33-35. "These animals crushed Jezebel's corpse until it became unidentifiable, thus fulfilling the prophecy" (Rofé 1988a:84).

However, v 36b (+ לאמר in v 36aβ) is a post-Dtr insertion, since it presupposes Elijah's prediction in 1 Kgs 21:23. That verse, as we have seen, was inserted into the oracle composed by Dtr for Elijah in 21:20bβ-22, 24. The details concerning Jezebel's death in 9:36b do not correspond with those of the narrative that precedes. Verses 33-35 mention only that Jezebel's body was trampled by horses; they do not refer to the dogs that ate her corpse according to v 36b (Steck 1968:36; Bohlen 1978:297). The addition in 2 Kgs 9:36b fulfills the prediction of 1 Kgs 21:23 that is reiterated in 2

Kgs 9:10a. The three verses, along with 2 Kgs 9:7b and perhaps the current
Naboth story in 1 Kgs 21:1-16, form a late, "anti-Jezebel" retouching to
these stories. The addition in 2 Kgs 9:36b is the strongest expression of
this anti-Jezebel sentiment. It gives a grotesque change of meaning to Dtr's
skatological image in 9:37. Because her corpse is eaten by dogs, what is
left of Jezebel is not simply like dung on the ground but actually is dung.

10:1a

Recent commentators (Barré 1988:17; Minokami 1989:55-56) have observed
that this half verse is a tendentious gloss. It is a doublet of v 6b except that
the king with seventy sons in the latter is Joram. The attribution of the
seventy sons to Ahab in 10:1a reflects Dtr's programmatic effort to describe
Jehu's complete destruction of Ahab's house (with Barré).

10:10-17

Long ago B. Stade (1885:276-278) advanced the view that 10:17 represented
the original continuation of 10:12 and that the intervening material was secondary. Stade was on the right track but did not go far enough. There is
good reason to believe that all of vv 10-17 are a secondary addition to the
narrative.

Most scholars agree that 10:10 is typically Dtr (Barré 1988:17). Dietrich
(1972:24) says that the verse is "im typisch dtr Predigtstil." The verse interprets Jehu's massacre of the seventy princes (10:1-9) as an act of piety on
his part as he sees to it that Yahweh's condemnation of Ahab's house is fulfilled in detail.

Verses 11 and 17 are very much alike and are best treated together.

10:11	10:17
ויך יהוא את כל הנשראים	ויך את כל הנשארים
לבית אחאב ביזרעאל	לאחאב בשמרון
וכל גדליו ומידעיו וכהניו	עד בלתי השאיר לו שריד
עד השמדו	

These two verses form an *inclusio* and suggest that the intervening materials, Jehu's murder of Ahaziah's kinsmen (10:12-14) and Jehu's encounter
with Jehonadab (10:15-16), are secondary additions to the Jehu narrative.
Other considerations confirm this indication. According to 10:1-9, Jehu sent
to Samaria to have Ahab's seventy sons killed. There was no need for him
to go there in v 17. Also, a group of princes from Judah would hardly be
found, unsuspecting, a day's journey north of Samaria two days after the revolt began in Jezreel (chapter 9) and one day after the massacre in Samaria
(10:1-11; Benzinger 1899:149).

Verses 11 and 17 both share the perspective of v 10 that Yahweh is fulfilling his word against the house of Ahab through Jehu. In fact, the statements in vv 11 and 17 regarding Jehu's destruction of the members of Ahab's house are very similar to the fulfillment notices for the oracles against the previous two dynasties.

1 Kgs 15:29	1 Kgs 16:11-12	2 Kgs 10:11, 17
ויהי כמלכו	ויהי כמלכו	ויך (יהוא)
	כשבתו על כסאו	
הכה	הכה	את כל הנשארים
את כל בית ירבעם	את כל בית בעשא	ל(בית) אחאב
לא השאיר	לא השאיר לו	
כל נשמה	משתין בקיר	
		(בשמרון)
		ביזרעאל
לירבעם	וגאליו ורעהו	וכל גדליו ומידעיו
		וכהניו
		(עד בלתי השאיר
		לו שריד)
עד השמדו	וישמד זמרי	עד השמדו
	את כל בית בעשא	
כדבר יהוה	כדבר יהוה	כדבר יהוה
אשר דבר	אשר דבר	אשר דבר
	אל בעשא	אל אליהו
ביד עבדו אחיה	ביד יהוא הנביא	
השלני		

Since the fulfillment notices in 1 Kgs 15:29 and 16:11-12 are Dtr's, 2 Kgs 10:11, 17 should also be assigned to him. The perspective on Jehu shared by 10:11, 17 with v 10 also indicates this. The concern of vv 12-14 for the fate of members of the Southern royal house betrays the hand of a writer from Judah, likely the writer who situated the story of Jehu's revolt within the literary boundaries for Azariah's reign, namely Dtr.

Barré (1988:18-19) has pointed to indications within the stories in vv 12-16 that Dtr did not compose them but drew them from sources available to him. The statement in v 14b that Jehu's men slaughtered the party from Judah seems to contradict his order in v 14a to take them alive. It betrays the editorial concern expressed in v 11 to have Jehu kill all who are in any way related to Ahab. Also, the story in vv 15-16 presupposes the previous acquaintance of Jehu and Jehonadab. But since no word about their former acquaintance is forthcoming the episode here is probably a fragment.

Dtr edited the story of Jehu's revolt to describe how he annihilated the royal family in fulfillment of Elijah's oracle against Ahab's house (v 11). He then had Jehu move to Samaria so that he could include the stories in vv

12-16 as encounters between Jezreel and Samaria, and he enclosed those stories within another fulfillment notice (v 18) after Jehu reached Samaria.

10:18-28

The account of Jehu's destruction of Baal worship from Israel is very different from the foregoing narrative, as several scholars in recent years have noticed (Minokami 1989:96-97; Würthwein 1984:242). The section from 9:1-10:17 is concerned solely with Jehu's overthrow of the royal house in fulfillment of Elijah's prophecy and ends perfectly appropriately with 10:17. It says nothing about Baal worship, but that becomes the focus in 10:18-27. In 10:18-27 Jehu acts essentially alone. He does not have the army with him as in the chapter's previous narrative.

The remark in v 19b and the mention of Jehonadab in v 23 are editorial (Barré 1988:20-21). The entire account has been attached by v 28 to the Dtr summary of Jehu's reign beginning in v 29. The editor responsible for 10:18-27 may have been Dtr, but a post-Dtr editor seems more likely. The story in 10:18-27 bears similarities to the one in 1 Kings 18, which I believe to be part of a post-Dtr addition to Kings. For instance, the prophets of Baal, who play a large role in 1 Kings 18, are mentioned in 2 Kgs 10:19. It is also striking that the Deuteronomistic summary of Jehu's reign in 10:29-31 says nothing about Jehu's destruction of the Baal cult. What is more, while 10:26-27 detail the destruction of the temple of Baal and the מצבות, they say nothing about him destroying the altar of Baal or the Asherah mentioned in Dtr's introduction to Ahab in 1 Kgs 16:32-33 (against Barré 1988:120).

10:29-36

These verses are widely held to be Dtr's work. Despite Jehu's faithful execution, in Dtr's portrayal, of Yahweh's wrath against the house of Ahab, he was still an Israelite king. As such, he received the same judgement as Dtr gave to every other Israelite king -- he persisted in the sin of Jeroboam. But Dtr included something extra in the evaluation of Jehu. Because of his actions against the house of Ahab his dynasty would last to the fourth generation (v 30). This obvious *vaticinium ex eventu* fits very well with Dtr's interpretation of Jehu's revolt as a whole. Jehu's bloodshed was the faithful execution of Yahweh's word against the evil house of Ahab (Barré 1988:119-120).

Synthesis

In sum, I assign the following verses from the passages just surveyed in 2 Kings 9-10, at least in their present placement, to Dtr: 9:7a, 8-9, 15a,

16aα, 25-26, 36a, 37; 10:1a, 10-17; 29-36. Other additions to the story appear to be from post-Dtr writers: 9:7b, 10a, 14, 15a, 16aβ, 27b-29, 36b; 10:18-28. There is little in the Jehu story outside of these additions to indicate a prophetic origin or editing in the Jehu story. The additions make it clear that it was Dtr who used the Jehu story to illustrate the fulfillment of prophecy. He linked it with the Naboth episode as the fulfillment of Elijah's oracle against Ahab's house and incorporated the product within his prophecy - fulfillment scheme. There is nothing to indicate that the two stories were connected before Dtr. He followed the same scheme as with the previous oracles against Jeroboam and Baasha, illustrating how the prophetic curse repeated against each dynasty was effected in that dynasty's annihilation. The only difference in the case of Ahab's house was that Dtr had access to a lengthy narrative about Jehu's *coup* which he incorporated within his scheme as the fulfillment of Elijah's word which he set in the context of the Naboth incident.

CONCLUSIONS

We began this chapter in search of a running prophetic narrative underlying Dtr's version of the book of Kings. Our results in this quest have been decidedly negative. Dtr seems to have used individual prophetic stories as the bases for his accounts in 1 Kings 14 and 21. But others of his sources (e.g., 2 Kings 9-10) were not prophetic. Moreover, there is no evidence that the stories about prophetic activity during the reigns of Jeroboam, Baasha, and Ahab were connected with each other at a level underlying Dtr's composition.

The scheme that currently links the oracles against royal houses in 1 - 2 Kings is Dtr's. He probably borrowed the curse of non-burial from a set of treaty curses. But he applied it to a different context and used it to forecast the fall of the successive Israelite dynasties. He had no prophetic *Vorlage* for any of the oracles against the dynasties. The fulfillments for those oracles were also Dtr's doing, although he drew upon official reports for the details about the downfall of each dynasty. Thus, neither the curse employed by Dtr nor the prophecy - fulfillment scheme offers evidence of a pre-Dtr prophetic narrative. Nor is there evidence for a scheme of anointings or royal designations in a pre-Dtr prophetic document as Campbell contended. Some kings and heads of dynasties receive no prophetic designation (Nadab, Baasha, Elah, Zimri, Omri, Ahab), and there is a good deal of variation among the stories of those who do receive some prophetic endorsement (Saul, David, Solomon, Jeroboam, Jehu). All of these materials were first brought together by Dtr within a rubric which he imposed upon them.

Dtr's creative hand has been involved in every aspect of the development of the narratives analyzed. He has restructured the narratives, revised the oracles, and composed new imitative oracles in order to present a theology of history. This illustrates how Dtr was both an author and an editor. In the case of Dtr these two enterprises are not mutually exclusive. This, as we have seen, was Noth's original understanding (1967:11).

Dtr obviously had sources which he edited to form his narratives (e.g., 2 Kings 9-10). On occasion he also composed narratives out of whole cloth (e.g., 1 Kgs 16:1-4). By both processes he created a new work of history. He shaped all of his narratives with his own theological perspective. His purpose in the book of Kings was to offer a comprehensive theological explanation of the history of Israel and Judah in the divided monarchy.

CHAPTER FOUR

PROPHETS COME LATELY:
PROPHETIC ADDITIONS TO THE BOOK OF KINGS

The stories about Northern prophets in the book of Kings which have not yet been treated fall into the following categories: the Elijah cycle in 1 Kings 17-19, the battle accounts in 1 Kings 20 and 22, the story of Elijah in 2 Kings 1, and the Elisha narratives in 2 Kings 2-8 and 13. Most of these narratives reflect a complex history of development that cannot be reconstructed with certainty. This chapter will attempt to survey in broad terms the more obvious and widely accepted developmental features of these prophetic tales. But my main interest here will be the relationship between these Northern prophetic legends and Dtr's composition of Kings.[1]

1 KINGS 17-19

The material about Elijah in the MT of Kings falls easily into four units: 1 Kings 17-19; 21; 2 Kings 1; 2. I have already dealt with 1 Kings 21. Elijah's ascension in 2 Kings 2 can be eliminated from immediate consideration, because it is really part of the Elisha collection, providing the basis of authority for Elisha's career (Rofé 1970:436). It also contains some peculiarities associated with the Elisha stories but not the other Elijah material. These include the presence of the "sons of the prophets" (Gunkel 1906:31) and the epithet "my father, my father, the chariots of Israel and its horsemen" (2:12; cf. 13:14).

As it now stands, 1 Kgs 17:1-19:18 is a complex of legends about Elijah which have been bound into a cycle. The cycle begins with the introduction of the prophet in 17:1, and ends in 19:17-18 with Elijah's designation of Elisha as his successor.[2] The final three verses of chapter 19 were added to

---

[1] Stipp's 1987 monograph is probably the best attempt to unravel the development of these prophetic narratives. My conclusions in this chapter concerning the relationship of these narratives to Dtr are very similar to Stipp's, though completely independent. I discovered Stipp's volume only after I had completed a draft of this chapter.

[2] Eissfeldt (1953:32-39) stresses the unity of all of 16:29-19:18. His inclusion of 16:29-34, however, does not take adequate account of the abrupt beginning at 17:1 or the differences in language and ideology between 16:29-34 and 17:1-19:18.

link this Elijah cycle with the Elisha stories, particularly the one in 2 Kings
2, replacing earlier accounts of Elijah's anointings of Hazael and Jehu. As
Alt (1912; cf. Seybold 1973:5) pointed out long ago, 19:19-21 report
nothing about Elijah's fulfillment of his commission in 19:15-16 to anoint
Hazael and Jehu. Even in vv 19-21 Elisha is not anointed to be Elijah's
successor as 19:16b leads the reader to expect. Rather, Elisha becomes
Elijah's servant when the latter casts his mantle upon him. Hence, the story
in 19:19-21 is not an appropriate conclusion for v 16b, much less for all of
vv 15-16. It has been borrowed by an editor from the beginning of the
Elisha collection in 2 Kings 2, which alone shares its motifs, and has been
adapted to link the Elijah and Elisha narratives, displacing the original
conclusion to 19:1-18.

Within the cycle at 17:1-19:18 further delineation of units is possible.
Chapters 17-18, on the one hand, and 19:1-18, on the other, betray
originally variant traditions (Gunkel 1906:21). Both accounts deal with
Elijah's flight from Israel. In both, Elijah is miraculously sustained.

The introduction in 19:1-3 presupposes the account in chapters 17-18 but
also stands in tension with it. Chapter 18 climaxes with the recognition by
the people of Yahweh's victory over Baal and the slaughter of the priests of
Baal. But Elijah's fearfulness in 19:3 is not the attitude of one who has just
stood up to Jezebel and slaughtered her 450 Baal prophets. Nothing in
chapters 17-18 prepares the reader for Elijah's discouragement and resultant
retirement in chapter 19. The new concern in chapter 19 is with Elisha, and
Elijah receives Yahweh's reassurance that his successor will destroy Baalism
from Israel (19:14-18). As Stipp (1987:432-435) has also pointed out, the
references to Jezreel in 18:45-46 connect chapters 17-18 with the Naboth
story in chapter 21, but that connection has been broken by the insertion of
chapter 19 and, in the MT, chapter 20.

Smaller, once independent units comprise the two variants. The accounts
of Elijah's dealings with the widow and her son in 17:8-16, 17-24 derive
from the similar tales of Elisha in 2 Kgs 4:1-7, 8-37, respectively (Gunkel
1906:38-39; Rofé 1974:148-149; Schmitt 1977:454-455; Stipp 1987:451-
458). This is suggested by details that seem out of place in the Elijah
stories but are at home in the Elisha ones. For example, although there is
no previous mention of the Phoenician widow, Eiljah's demeanor toward her
and vice versa (17:10-11, 13) seem to assume prior acquaintance. This is
appropriate in 2 Kings 4 where the woman is identified as a widow of one of
the "sons of the prophets." Again, the reference to the woman's household
in 17:15 is out of place in this story where she and her son face starvation
but seems at home in 2 Kgs 4:1-7 where the problem is an impatient
creditor. This latter point also holds true for the second story in 17:17-24
where the destitute widow is now called the "mistress of the house" (בעלת
הבית, v 17), a house with a furnished upper chamber in which the prophet
stays (vv 19, 23). Once more, these are elements appropriate to the story
about the Shunammite in 2 Kgs 4:18-37 but not to the one with Elijah in 1
Kings 17. Other independent stories may lie behind the narratives of

Elijah's sojourn at the Brook Cherith (17:1-7), Elijah's encounter with Obadiah (18:1-16), and the contest on Mt. Carmel (18:17-40). The theme which unites chapters 17-18 is the drought which Elijah announces in 17:1 and which ends in 18:41-46.[3]

As we have seen, chapter 19 was attached to the drought collection by the addition of 19:1-3.[4] The story of Elijah's miraculous sustenance in the wilderness in 19:4-8 is likely a variant of the one in 17:1-7. Then follows the account of the theophany on Horeb (19:9-18). Within the latter account, vv 11-14 are an insertion by *Wiederaufnahme*, as Würthwein (1970) has shown. Yahweh's question in v 9 ("What are you doing here Elijah?") and Elijah's response in v 10 are repeated *verbatim* in vv 13-14. The intervening insertion may reflect a polemic against the use of storm language and divine warrior imagery for Yahweh (Cross 1973:193-194).

One of the motifs peculiar to chapters 17-18 is their polemic against Baalism, a topic which L. Bronner (1968) has explored in a preliminary way. The drought story enclosing the materials in chapters 17-18 illustrates Yahweh's control of the storm and the fertility it brings. It is Yahweh who has power over life and death (17:17-24). Elijah's decisive victory at Carmel in chapter 18 is, of course, Yahweh's defeat of Baal. Yahweh's refusal to reveal himself in traditional storm theophany (19:11-12) is a subtle repudiation of the use of storm god imagery for Yahweh because of its association with Baal. It is noteworthy, then, that this theme is completely missing from 1 Kings 21. The Naboth story deals with Israelite law and social justice. It has no mention of Baal or anything connected with Canaanite religion.

The description of Elijah as Moses is another theme of the Elijah cycle in 1 Kings 17-19 which is lacking in chapter 21. The allusions to Moses have been pointed out by a number of scholars.[5] The provision for Elijah at the brook Cherith (17:6) and then Elijah's provision for the widow (17:8-16) recall the provision of meat and manna in the wilderness (Exod 16:4-36). The narrative in 1 Kgs 17:17-24 presents Elijah as a "man of God" in the tradition of Moses (cf. Schmitt 1977). Elijah's pleading in 17:20 is similar to Moses' technique in pleading on behalf of Israel (e.g., Exod 32:11-14). Obadiah's fear of Elijah's disappearance (1 Kgs 18:12) and Elijah's ascension (2 Kgs 1:11-12a, 15-18) are reminiscent of Moses' death and secret burial (Deut 34:5-8). Elijah's altar on Mt. Carmel (1 Kgs 18:30-32) resembles Moses' altar in Exod 24:4. Elijah's conflict with the priests of Baal is like

---

[3] Alt (1953:135) described the assembled units of chapters 17-18 in the editor's craftful presentation of them as scenes in a great drama. "Die hier eingegliederten Einzelgeschichten nur noch als Szenen im Ablauf eines größeren Dramas erscheinen oder wenigstens nach der Absicht des Bearbeiters erscheinen sollen."

[4] Alt 1912; Seybold 1973:5. For a summary of opinions on the formation of chapter 19 see von Nordheim 1978:153-156. I am following von Nordheim's division of the units in this chapter (1978:171-172).

[5] Alcaina Canosa (1972:especially 324-326); Carlson 1969; Carroll 1969; Cross 1973:191-194; Cohn 1982; Fohrer 1957:48-49.

Moses' competition with the Egyptian magicians. The people seize the prophets of Baal at Elijah's command in 1 Kgs 18:40 like the Levites who follow Moses in the slaughter of the worshipers of the golden calf in Exod 32:24-29. In chapter 19 Elijah fasts 40 days and nights (v 8), as did Moses in Exod 34:28. Elijah then ascends to Mt. Horeb, where Moses received the law, and while standing in "the cave" (cf. Exod 33:21), witnesses the same kinds of phenomena associated with Yahweh's theophany at the giving of the law to Moses (Exod 19:16-25). Elisha ministers to Elijah (1 Kgs 19:21) as Joshua is Moses' מְשָׁרֵת. Outside of 1 Kings 17-19, Elijah's fire from heaven (2 Kgs 1:5-12) recalls the fire from Yahweh at the defense of Moses' authority (Num 16:35). Joshua divides the Jordan (Josh 3:14-16) as Moses divided the sea (Exod 14:21-22). So Elisha divides the Jordan as Elijah had done (2 Kgs 2:8, 14). The spirit of Elijah rests on Elisha (2 Kgs 2:15) as Joshua possesses the spirit and is invested with Moses' authority (Num 27:18-20).

It is striking how much the depiction of Elijah in 1 Kings 21 differs from these other Elijah legends. Elijah does not appear in the Naboth story as the great wonder worker that he is in the other tales (Van Seters 1983a:306). Rather, he appears in a more traditional prophetic role, like Samuel in 1 Sam 13:11-14; 15:10-31, Nathan in 2 Sam 12:1-15, or Ahijah in 1 Kgs 11:29-39; 14:1-16, confronting the king who has sinned and announcing his coming punishment from Yahweh.

These differences in theme and depiction suggest that the Elijah cycle in 1 Kings 17-19, and perhaps the story in 2 Kings 1 as well, have had a different tradition history from the Naboth tale in 1 Kings 21. The major point of difference concerns the question of Dtr's inclusion of these materials in his composition of Kings. We have seen that the Naboth story in 1 Kings 21 was adapted by Dtr as a theological explanation for the demise of Ahab's house. But there is reason to believe that Dtr's History did not include chapters 17-19. Rather, they have been inserted at a post-Dtr level. This is a matter that requires detailed exploration in view of the virtually unanimous consensus of scholars that 1 Kings 17-19 have been edited by Dtr.[6]

In 1923 G. Hölscher wrote that there was no trace of Deuteronomistic editing within the Elijah stories (p. 393). Noth apparently agreed (cf. Hentschel 1977:45). His 1943 masterpiece argued that Dtr included the Elijah stories "in ihrem überlieferten Wortlaut" within his History (1967:82). In his view, Dtr received the Elijah stories already as a collection, and then he divided them into units (especially chapter 21) for inclusion in his work. Scholars since Noth have tended to assume this understanding of Dtr's inclusion of the Elijah cycle.[7] If anything, they have

---

[6] A notable exception to this consensus is Miller's 1966 essay which contended (p. 450) that the Elijah legends in 1 Kings 17-19 were among a series of prophetic narratives that seemed to be post-Dtr additions to Kings because they contradicted Dtr's theological and historical assumptions.

perceived an even stronger Deuteronomistic influence in the Elijah cycle than Noth was willing to admit. E. Nielsen (1954:77), for example, asserted that Dtr's editing in 1 Kings 17-19 had been so thorough as to leave only traces of the original prophetic legends. More recently Smend (1975b:531) has referred to material in 1 Kings 17 as a "fraglos deuteronomistisch redigiertem Zusammenhang."

The assumption that these chapters passed through Dtr's hands was fueled in 1957 by G. Fohrer's presentation of a set of arguments for the Deuteronomistic redaction of the Elijah material (pp. 46-47). To my knowledge, Fohrer's is the only systematic case ever built for the Dtr editing of the Elijah cycle. Since it is frequently cited unreservedly by scholars as proving the Dtr nature of 1 Kings 17-19, his arguments merit careful inspection.[8]

Fohrer lists seven categories of expressions and other signs of Dtr's hand in the Elijah cycle.

1. He contends that Dtr is responsible for the following editorial rubrics within the Elijah narratives. a. Dtr omitted the reason for Elijah's proclamation of drought against Ahab in 17:1, since he provided the motive for that proclamation in Ahab's introductory formula (16:29-33). b. The introduction in 21:1 (ויהי אחר הדברים האלה) is Dtr's, because it presupposes the material in chapters 17-19, chapter 20 being out of place. c. 1 Kgs 21:20bβ-22, 24, 25-26 are from Dtr. d. The framework around the last Elijah story (2 Kgs 1:1, 17aβ-b) is Dtr's.

2. The expression "before whom I stand" (אשר עמדתי לפניו) in 17:1; 18:15 derives from the Deuteronomistic time period and occurs in Deuteronomy (4:10; 10:8) and Jeremiah (7:10; 15:19; 35:19) as well as Dtr's editing in 2 Kgs 3:14.

3. The formula "the word of Yahweh came" in 17:2, 8; 18:1; 21:17 is not found in the older writing prophets and occurs only in redactional sections of Hosea (1:1) and Zephaniah (1:1).[9] It is especially common in Jeremiah, Ezekiel, Haggai, and Zechariah. Fohrer asserts that it is part of Dtr's editing in the narrative about the early monarchy in Samuel (1 Sam 15:10; 2 Sam 7:4; 24:11) and Kings (1 Kgs 12:22; 13:20; 16:1; 2 Sam 20:4) and concludes that it originates in late pre-exilic times.

4. The expression "to bring to remembrance" (17:18) has its juridical meaning, according to Fohrer, only in P material (Ezek 21:28-29; 29:16; Num 5:15) and therefore is late.

---

[7] A refreshing contrast to this trend was the excellent overview of the Elisha cycle in 1964 by Alcaina Canosa. He argued that the "first redaction" of Kings did not include either the Elijah or Elisha materials. In his view this first redaction included only 1 Kgs 16:29-34; 21?; 22:39ff; 2 Kgs 1:18; 3:1-3; 8:16ff; 13:13, 22-23. I believe that he was basically correct.

[8] E.g., Timm (1982) who cites Fohrer on v. 53 and Smend on p. 56n.

[9] Timm (1982:79) also cites this phrase as an example of Dtr's retouching and adds 18:31 to the list of passages that include it.

5. The formula "to know that you are God" (18:37; cf. 17:24; 18:36) forms the basis for Fohrer's fifth point. "To know that you are Yahweh" is most frequent, of course, in Ezekiel. But Fohrer argues that the expansion of the expression with האלהים is Deuteronomistic (Deut 4:35, 39; 7:9; 1 Kgs 8:60; later - 2 Chr 33:13), and its use in the Elijah narrative is from Deuteronomistic editing.

6. Elijah is the only pre-exilic prophet to call himself "the servant of Yahweh" (18:36). Outside of Kings this title for prophets is most common in Jeremiah. Fohrer believes that it was used as an honorific title for prophets only from Jeremiah's time on, after Jeremiah's predictions about disaster for Judah had come true.

7. The expression "the hand of Yahweh came upon" in 18:46 (cf. 2 Kgs 3:15-16) is dependent on the expression in the book of Ezekiel (1:3; 3:22; 33:22; 37:1; 40:1) and belongs to Dtr who used it in agreement with Ezekiel.

Fohrer's first set of points about the framework passages may be dismissed quickly. The first verse of the cycle (17:1) is jarring and unanticipated. While 17:1 may presuppose Dtr's introduction to the evil Ahab in 16:29-33, the latter verses do not prepare the reader for Elijah's advent in 17:1. It appears very much like a piece of tradition severed from its beginning and inserted into Dtr's account of Ahab. The formula at 21:1a does not presume the stories in chapters 17-19. It was probably added to connect chapters 20 and 21 in the MT (so also Baltzer 1965:75). The LXX witnesses which "reverse" the order of these chapters lack the rubric in 21:1a. Fohrer's perception of Dtr's writing in 1 Kings 21 is correct, as we have determined, but that does not make chapters 17-19 Dtr's as well. I shall treat 2 Kings 1 momentarily.

One is struck by Fohrer's frequent citation of parallels from Ezekiel and Jeremiah in the rest of his arguments. These are a good deal like Lemke's arguments in 1 Kings 13. They indicate the late editing of 1 Kings 17-19 by someone who knew and perhaps helped to shape the prophetic books. But none of the arguments points decisively to Dtr's editing in these three chapters. The lack of any clear sign of Dtr's hand is odd if Dtr included these chapters, especially in the light of his heavy editing of the Jehu story in 2 Kings 9-10.

Besides the lack of Deuteronomistic language in chapters 17-19 and their view of prophetic activity which differs from Dtr's, there are other indications that Dtr did not include these chapters. The introduction of Elijah in 17:1 is abrupt and unanticipated in the context of Dtr's formulaic evaluation of Ahab in 16:29-34. He is presented there as "the Tishbite," an introductory epithet that does not occur again in chapters 17-19. In 21:17, however, Elijah is again called "the Tishbite," as though he had not been previously introduced. In other words, the Naboth story seems not to presuppose the earlier Elijah stories.[10] The post-Dtr insertion of these chapters would also help to explain the references to legitimate Yahwistic altars outside of Jerusalem in 18:30-32 and 19:14. Dtr would hardly have left these references unrevised. The references in 18:29, 36 to the evening oblation also indicate the late Jewish editing of these chapters (Timm 1982:77).

Van Seters includes the Elijah cycle in Dtr's history on the basis of its themes.

> The Elijah stories of 1 Kings 17-19, 21, and 2 Kings 1 are quite different [from the Elisha stories]. These are not only integrated into the general chronological framework but also bear the stamp of the Dtr concern about the incursion of the Canaanite cults and the Dtr aversion for the house of Ahab, elements completely lacking in the Elisha collection (1983a: 305).

We have seen how 1 Kings 17-19 break unexpectedly into Dtr's report on Ahab so that they are better described as intruding into Dtr's framework rather than being integrated into it. Certainly Dtr had an aversion to both the Canaanite cults and the house of Ahab. However, in 1 Kings 11-16 Dtr traces the fall of the houses of Jeroboam and Baasha in fulfillment of prophetic oracles against them for the "sin of Jeroboam," i.e., the shrines he erected at Dan and Bethel. In 1 Kings 17-19 the concerns are different. Not only is Elijah more a miracle worker than a messenger (in contrast to Ahijah and Jehu ben Hanani) but there is no mention of the sin of Jeroboam. Elijah is now the focus, not the Northern royal house. Elijah's nemesis is not really Ahab but his alien wife, Jezebel. Dtr would no doubt agree with the perspective of 1 Kings 17-19, but the issues here are different than those Dtr has dealt with heretofore.

The Elijah cycle in 1 Kings 17-19, then, was a late, post-Dtr insertion into Dtr's account of Ahab.[11] Chapters 17-18 were added first and linked to Dtr's account of Naboth. Then, chapter 19 was added to prepare for the transition from Elijah to Elisha. This does not necessarily mean that the legends in the Elijah cycle are entirely of a late composition. Many of the late expressions noticed by Fohrer occur in redactional seams (cf. Dietrich 1972:122-123). The stories themselves may be much earlier,[12] but they were edited and added to the DH in the exile or afterwards.

---

[10] The MT attests three other instances of the expression "Elijah the Tishbite" in the Elijah stories: 1 Kgs 21:28 and 2 Kgs 1:3, 8. In 21:28, "the Tishbite" is a gloss. All LXX witnesses lack it. On the uses of the expression in 2 Kings 1 see below.

[11] Compare the analysis of Hölscher (1923:184-185) who concluded that all of the Elijah material from 17:1-22:38 was an addition to the work of a Deuteronomistic redactor, Rd in Hölscher's terminology.

[12] Sanda (1911:455-456) contends that the unit in 1 Kings 17-19 dates from before 721 B.C.E. on the following grounds. 1. The statement in 19:3 that Beersheba belongs to Judah would be meaningless after the deportation of Israel in 721. 2. The similar statement in 17:9 that Zarephath belongs to Sidon is appropriate only if Israel

1 KINGS 20 AND 22:1-38

Scholars have long recognized that these two chapters go together. This is indicated by the order of the narratives in the Old Greek and Lucianic witnesses. While the accounts in chapters 20 and 22 of the MT are separated by the Naboth story, they occur together in the Septuagint (21, 20, 22 *vis-à-vis* the MT). Also, the statement in 22:1, "for three years Aram and Israel continued without war," presupposes the direct precedence of the battle stories in chapter 20:1-34. This disarray among textual witnesses over the order of chapters 20 and 22 is one hint that the placement of both chapters is secondary.

The stories in the chapters 20 and 22 are completely independent of the Elijah and Elisha legends. Neither of them plays any part in these two chapters. The prophets in chapter 20 are nameless while in 22:1-38 Micaiah ben Imlah is the lone "true" prophet who opposes both the king and his prophetic lackeys. The hero prophets in chapters 20 and 22 are not miracle workers like Elijah and Elisha but mediators of the word of Yahweh. The issues they encounter are different than those in the Elijah - Elisha collections. The conflict in 1 Kings 22, for example, is not between a prophet of Yahweh and foreign (Baal) prophets as in 1 Kings 18 but between prophets of Yahweh. The issues at stake are obedience to the divine word and distinguishing true and false prophecy.

Beginning with Jepsen (1942) scholars over the past four decades have assembled arguments showing that the contents of 1 Kings 20 and 22:1-38 do not fit in the context of Ahab's reign either historically or literarily (Whitley 1952; Miller 1966; 1967b; 1968; Pitard 1987). First, the animosity between Israel and Aram in 1 Kings 20 and 22:1-38 does not fit with the picture from extra-biblical sources of the conditions between the two nations during Ahab's reign. The royal inscriptions of Shalmaneser III recount campaigns against a coalition of Syro-Palestinian kings in his sixth, tenth, eleventh, and fourteenth years or 853-845 B.C.E. (Oppenheim 1969:276-281). The coalition is headed by Hadadezer of Damascus, and Ahab of Israel is a significant member. It is difficult to believe, therefore, that Israel and Aram were warring with each other during this same period or that Ahab was killed by an Aramaean arrow (1 Kgs 22:34-38).

Secondly, the weakness of Omri and Ahab described in 1 Kings 20 and 22:1-38 is contradicted by the portrait of the two kings in extra-biblical sources. Shalmaneser III's Monolith Inscription (Oppenheim 1969:278-279)

---

exists as a parallel state to Sidon and not as an Assyrian province as after 721. 3. The reference in 18:30-38 to Elijah offering a sacrifice on an altar to Yahweh which he had repaired and Elijah's mention of Yahweh's altars in 19:14 would not have been left alone by a writer following Hezekiah's institution of cultic centralization. Sanda (p. 459) dates these stories to ca. 825 B.C.E. and sees them as an explanation for Hazael's subjugation of Israel in thelast days of Jehu and the time of his successors. Hentschel (1977:44-45) also argues for an early origin of these stories.

describes Ahab as fully the equal of the Aramaean kings. Ahab is the primary supplier of chariotry (2,000) for the coalition and contributes a large contingent of infantry (10,000). This description contrasts sharply with the ones in 1 Kgs 20:15, 27 where the Aramaean army far outnumbers Ahab's. Moreover, the Aramaeans in 1 Kings 20 expect to win easily in the plain (vv 23-25), implying that Israel's chariot force is exceedingly weak (Pitard 1987:115-116). In addition to the Assyrian inscriptions, the strength of Omri and Ahab is indicated by their control over Moab referred to in the Mesha stele (Albright 1969:320-321, ll. 7-8) and the Bible (2 Kgs 1:1; 3:5).[13] Architectural remains from Ahab's reign in several Northern cities including Samaria (Kenyon 1971:71-110), Hazor (Yadin 1972:165-178; 1975:158-170), Megiddo (Yadin 1960:62-68), and Dan (Biran:1980: 175-177) further illustrate the wealth and power of the Omride dynasty. The Bible itself briefly reports certain building projects of Omri and Ahab (1 Kgs 16:24; 22:39). Its curt, negative treatment of Omri obscures neither his extensive international relations represented by his treaty with Tyre, sealed by Ahab's marriage to Jezebel (1 Kgs 16:31), nor his effective leadership which forged the first true dynasty in Israel out of the chaos of civil war (16:15-24). All these considerations are in tension with the debility of Omri and Ahab in 1 Kings 20 and the extent to which Ahab is dominated by Aram in that chapter, especially in v 34.

Thirdly, the premise of the story in 1 Kings 22:1-38 is that Ramoth-Gilead is in Aramaean hands and needs to be restored to Israel (vv 3-4). But other texts indicate that it was in Israel's possession throughout the Omri dynasty. There was apparently an Israelite outpost there from which Jehu initiated his revolt (2 Kgs 8:28-29; 9:1, 4, 14). It was not until Jehu's reign that Yahweh began "to cut off parts of Israel" including Gilead (10:32-33). There is no indication that Ramoth-Gilead belonged to Aram before that point.

There are also literary indications that 1 Kings 20 and 22:1-38 do not belong with the account of Ahab. Most persuasive is the statement in 22:40 that Ahab "slept with his fathers." As Hölscher (1923:185) first observed, this formula is used elsewhere only for kings who die in peace (cf. Alfrink 1943:109-110). This means that Dtr was unaware of the story about Ahab's violent death in 1 Kgs 22:1-38.

Ahab is named only three times in the MT version of chapter 20 (vv 2, 13, 14) and only once in 22:1-38 (v 20). Elsewhere, he is simply called "the king of Israel." The name occurs only slightly more frequently in the Old Greek (LXX[B]) and Lucianic witnesses, but not always in the same places.[14] The paucity and irregularity of occurrences of Ahab's name sug-

---

[13] Israel's subjugation of Moab lasted until after Ahab's death according to 2 Kgs 1:1; 3:5. The Mesha stele says that "Omri possessed all the land of Mehdebah and dwelt in it all his days and half the days of his son, forty years" (Albright, ll. 7-8). For explanations of this statement which accept the duration in the biblical notices see Cross and Freedman (1952:39-40, n. 13) and Miller (1974:15-16).

gests that his identification as the king of Israel in these stories is secondary. As with the Elisha stories in 2 Kings, the king of Israel in 1 Kings 20 and 22:1-38 was originally nameless. The concern of the stories originally was with prophets and prophecy. The names of the kings were relatively unimportant. The consistent identification of the king of Aram as Ben-Hadad is stereotypical (Alcaina Canosa 1964:233; Miller 1966:448, n. 34). Chapter 20 credits prophets with bringing about victory and downplays the role of the king. The oracle of Micaiah is at the center of chapter 22.

While the stories in 1 Kings 20 and 22:1-38 are out of place in the reign of Ahab, they are perfectly suited to the reigns of Jehoahaz son of Jehu and Joash son of Jehoahaz in the later Jehu dynasty. The Omride alliance with Aram is over. The Aramaeans under Hazael have annexed territory east of the Jordan formerly belonging to Israel (2 Kgs 10:32-33) and have subjugated Israel so that its army is exceedingly weak (13:7). To be more specific, the three battles in 1 Kgs 20:1-34; 22:1-38 were originally the three victories of Israel over Aram in fulfillment of the secondary oracle in 2 Kgs 13:18-19. Elisha predicted victory for Israel over Aram in Aphek (2 Kgs 13:17), which is specifically identified in 1 Kgs 20:26 as the site of the second battle (Miller 1968:339-340). The Aramaean king whom Israel defeats in three battles is Ben-hadad (2 Kgs 13:24-25), the same king of Aram consistently identified in 1 Kings 20. Finally, in 1 Kgs 20:34 Ben-hadad agrees to restore the cities which his father had taken from Israel. This fits well with the notice at the end of 2 Kings 13 that Joash recovered the cities which his father had lost to Aram.

There is some doubt about the original identity of the king of Israel in the battle accounts. Most scholars who see in 1 Kings 20 and 22 the fulfillment of 2 Kgs 13:14-19 have assumed that the king of Israel was Joash, since he is named in 13:14, 25. However, Miller (1966:442-443; 1968) argues that this king is better identified with Jehoahaz. He contends that the king of Israel in the story in 2 Kgs 13:14-19 was originally anonymous as in 1 Kings 20 and 22:1-38 and the Elisha cycle. The identification with Joash in 13:14 was secondary and led to the harmonizing passage about him in 13:22-25. Miller's view is based in part on his interpretation of 13:5 as a reference to a "savior" in Jehoahaz' own day (possibly Elisha). He finds contradictory information regarding the ascension of Ben-hadad to power -- in the reign of Joash (13:22-25) or in the reign of Jehoahaz (13:3). There is also a contradiction concerning whether it was Jehu (2 Kgs 10:32-33) or Jehoahaz (13:25) who lost portions of Israel to Hazael. W. T. Pitard (1987:122-125) has recently reviewed Miller's position but prefers to see Joash as the king who three times defeated Aram. Pitard suggests that the "savior" of 2 Kgs 13:5 was Joash. He also understands 1 Kgs 10:32-33 and

---

[14] Ahab's name appears in LXX[B], which contains the Old Greek, in 20:2, 14 (twice), and 15. The Lucianic manuscripts (boc_2e_2) have his name in these four places and also in v 34. In 22:1-38 the Old Greek agrees with the MT in reading the name only in v 20. But the Lucianic witnesses also have it in four other verses: 2, 5, 10, and 37.

2 Kgs 13:3-6 more generally than Miller, not limiting the former to the reign of Jehu nor the latter to the period of Jehoahaz.

It is probably impossible to resolve this historical question on the basis of the biblical accounts. However, Miller makes a good case for Jehoahaz as a viable alternative to the more obvious Joash. Stipp (1987:262) concludes that the king in chapter 20 was once identified as Joash (20:34), while in chapter 22 he was once thought to be Jehoahaz. Stipp's observation that 22:26 refers to "Joash, the king's son" adds support to Miller's proposal that the king here was Jehoahaz.[15]

There are two other points in this debate which have not received sufficient consideration. First, the Old Latin, which is an important witness in this section of Kings to the Old Greek text, contains the story of Elisha's death bed oracle (MT 2 Kings 13:14-19) at the end of 2 Kings 10 and identifies the king of Israel in the story as Jehu! It is hard to see how the Old Latin could be historically reliable on this point. But its reading does add force to Miller's contention that the king of Israel in the story was originally nameless and that the identification with Joash is secondary.

Secondly, as Miller (1966:450) points out, the contradictions he observes are from different editorial hands. The passages in 10:32-35 and 13:1-9 are Deuteronomistic. They appear to agree that Aram oppressed Israel under Jehu (10:32) but that during Jehoahaz' reign Israel was delivered (13:4-5). However, the editor who added 2 Kgs 13:14-25 identified Joash as the king who won three victories over Aram thereby freeing Israel from Aramaean domination. This latter editor obviously worked after the time of Dtr, since the material in 13:14-25 stands outside of the Dtr framework formed by the concluding formula for Joash (13:10-13). Thus, the editorial shape of this material appears to support Miller's explanation.

The narrative in 1 Kings 22:1-38 poses special problems. Since Würthwein's 1967 article on this passage scholars have generally supposed that a fundamental battle account has been supplemented by various layers of additions to produce the present account.[16] There is a distinct lack of agreement among scholars when it comes to identifying the original story behind the present passage or its layers of accretion. Indeed, it is probably impossible to recontruct the development of this chapter completely, and we shall content ourselves here with a few broad observations about the unevenness of the account (cf. Schweizer 1979:2-12).

Chapter 22 attests manifold signs of literary reworking. If the basis for 22:1-38 was originally the third victory over Aram, as I have contended, it must not have included the story of the death of the king and the defeat of

---

[15] Stipp does not connect the battle accounts in chapters 20, 22 with the three victories predicted by Elisha in 2 Kgs 13:19, 25.

[16] Cf. most recently Stipp (1987:esp. 152-229) who finds a total of six levels in the chapter (pp. 228-229). See Long (1984:233) and Weippert (1988:459) for bibliography. De Vries (1978), in contrast, finds two independent narratives about Micaiah which he believes have been combined.

Israel. These elements must have come in later with the shifting of the three battle accounts to Ahab's day. Indeed, the story of Joram's wounding and eventual death in 2 Kgs 8:28-9:28 has largely displaced the story of the restoration of Ramoth as the third victory of Israel over Aram (Miller 1966:445). An additional story about the prophet Micaiah has also apparently played a role in the formation of the story as it now stands. Weippert (1988:466-469; cf. Schweizer 1979:13) has shown that this narrative as it now stands borrows many motifs from other biblical texts, particularly in Samuel and Kings.

The original story about the restoration of Ramoth-Gilead to Israel apparently had no mention of Jehoshaphat. Portions of the story indicate a lack of awareness of the king of Judah at an earlier level: vv 1, 3, 6, 9, 11-13, 15-17 (reading with the LXX), 19-28, and 34-35. These verses by themselves provide a relatively coherent narrative for much of the story.[17] Jehoshaphat was probably added to the story at a later level on the basis of the narrative in 2 Kings 3.

My main concern here is with the final stage of the story and its relationship to Dtr's composition in the book of Kings. We have already seen how 22:40 shows that Dtr was unaware of Ahab's violent death in 22:1-38. The narrative in 22:1-38, therefore, whatever its tradition history, is a post-Dtr addition. This point is also supported by the complete lack of Dtr language and themes in 1 Kings 20 and 22:1-38. In fact, 1 Kings 22 was apparently one of the latest additions to the book, since it contradicts the late addition at 21:27-29 which postponed Ahab's punishment. As it stands, 22:38 tries to provide the fulfillment for 21:19, even though that fulfillment is imprecise. The pool in Samaria where the dogs lick Ahab's blood (22:38) is not the same place where Naboth was stoned. Still, the editor who added 22:1-38 is probably the same one who added 21:19b to the Naboth story.

In broad outline the literary history of 1 Kings 20 and 22:1-38 is as follows (cf. Miller 1966:447-450). The battle accounts in these chapters were independent of the Elisha collection but were attached to it, since 2 Kgs 13:17 anticipates Israelite victory over Aram at Aphek. As with the stories in the Elisha collection, the king of Israel was originally anonymous in 1 Kings 20 and 22; the prophets were the heroes. Both chapters underwent further revision from a "prophetic" editor, leading to the addition of 20:35-43 (Stipp 1987:253-267, 361-362) and at least part of the Micaiah story in chapter 22. It may have been this same editor who removed the battle accounts from the Elisha collection, displacing them with 2 Kgs 13:18-19, and placed them in their current setting in the reign of Ahab. At some later point Jehoshaphat was introduced into 1 Kgs 22:1-38 under the influence of the similar story in 2 Kings 3.

---

[17] Compare the conclusions of Schweizer (1979:12-17) and Stipp (1987:228).

The foregoing sketch does not cover the complete traditional and literary development of 1 Kings 20 and 22, which may be impossible to reconstruct. It does, however, discuss the points of greatest concern for the present study, in particular the post-Dtr attachment of most of the material in those chapters to the book of Kings.

2 KINGS 1

Most scholars see vv 9-16 as an insertion into the older account of Ahaziah's death, although some begin the insertion in v 5.[18]   Parts of vv 3-4 are repeated in vv 6 and 16. This could signal an editor's framing device, but it is difficult to believe that this story could have ended in v 4 with no report of Elijah's actual delivery of Yahweh's message to Ahaziah's envoy. Ahaziah's recognition of Elijah in v 8 could be an appropriate conclusion to the story, but there is no literary disturbance or the like that requires one to find an addition beginning with v 9.

At the same time, it is clear that the direction of the story changes with v 9. In fact, there are form critical grounds for seeing vv 9-16 as a distinct unit. The story in 2 Kings 1:2-8 + 17aα draws on a genre which Trebolle (1980:159-160) identifies in 1 Kings 14 as a "consultation in a case of illness." Another example of the genre occurs in 2 Kgs 8:7-15. In all cases, an injury/illness is reported (1 Kgs 14:1; 2 Kgs 1:2a; 8:7), and an emissary is sent to inquire whether the afflicted person will recover (1 Kgs 14:2; 2 Kgs 1:2b; 8:8). In the cases outside of 2 Kings 1 (1 Kgs 14:3; 2 Kgs 8:8) the emissary bears a gift. In 1 Kings 14 Jeroboam's wife goes to Ahijah and receives the message that her son will die (14:4a, 6bβ, 12-13). Similarly, in 2 Kgs 8:9-10 Hazael goes to Elisha and learns that his master will die. But in 2 Kings 1:3-4 Elijah intercepts the emissary with the message that Ahaziah will die. Two of the examples end with the report that the illness proved fatal as predicted by the prophet (14:17-18; 1:17aα). 2 Kgs 8:15 is different as it reports Hazael's murder of Ben-Hadad.

The form is obviously flexible enough to accomodate certain variations: the disguise of Jeroboam's wife (compare 3 Reigns 12:24g-nα), Elijah's interception of the emissary, and Hazael's murder of his master. But there are also elements of the stories that go beyond the flexibility of the form to indicate redactional activity. There is no place in the form for the extended story in 2 Kgs 1:9-16. This suggests, not that vv 9-16 are an insertion by a later editor but that they contain an originally independent account which a single author has incorporated into the story of Ahaziah's consultation.

Further support for this conclusion has been offered by Rofé's study of the language and ideology of this passage (1988a:35-40). He contends that the

---

[18] For bibliography see Begg (1985:85, n. 2).

entire account in 2 Kgs 1:2-17aα is uniform in its use of linguistic and stylistic irregularities which betray it as a late addition to the book of Kings. These irregularities include:

1. the predominance of יה instead of יהו as the suffix for the Yahwistic theophoric names in the passage;

2. the use of אם instead of ה as an interrogative in v 2;

3. the use of חלי זה in the same verse instead of החלי הזה, which is normal in biblical Hebrew;

4. the use of לדרוש ב instead of לדרוש את or לדרוש אל, which are more frequent in biblical Hebrew;

5. the title "king of Samaria" in v 3;

6. the frequent use in the chapter of דבר in place of אמר.

Rofé further lists the following items in the portrayal of Elijah in this story as illustrations of the story's role as a late synthesis of the Elijah narratives: (a) his description in v 8 as a "hairy man" (בעל שער) alludes to his distinctive mantle of hair cloth; (b) his sudden, frightening appearance as in 1 Kgs 18:7, 12; (c) his effrontery before kings as in 1 Kgs 18:8; 21:17-24; (d) the king's unsuccessful attempt to capture him as in 1 Kgs 17:3; 18:1-16; 19;1-3; (e) his zeal in fighting Baal worship as in 1 Kgs 18; 19:10-18; (f) his cruel treatment of opponents as in 1 Kgs 18:40; (g) his ability to call down fire from heaven as in 1 Kgs 18:24-39. In Rofé's view this story is primarily concerned with revering the person of Elijah. It is this characteristic more than anything else which leads Rofé to classify the story as a late elaboration of prophetic *legenda* (cf. especially 1988a:13-26).

The narrative in 2 Kgs 1:2-17aα, then, is another addition to the Dtr book of Kings. It lacks Deuteronomistic language, and its contents bear no relation to Dtr's schema in 1 Kings 11-16, describing the fall of successive Israelite dynasties foreordained by Yahweh because of their continuation in the sin of Jeroboam. As with the Elisha stories and those in 1 Kings 20 and 22, the focus in 2 Kgs 1:2-17aα is on the prophet not the king. It is more concerned with the description of Elijah than with Ahaziah's death. The king was originally anonymous and has been only secondarily identified with Ahaziah in 1:2. This identification was determined by the association of 2 Kgs 1:2-17aα with Elijah and the fact that 1 Kings 22 narrated Ahab's death. The portrait of Elijah here as a wonder working "man of God" is the same as the depiction of Elijah and Elisha elsewhere in secondary passages in Kings.[19] It is, as we have seen, a very different picture of the prophetic role from that found in portions of the book edited by Dtr.

---

[19] The title "man of God" occurs only in vv 9-16. Elsewhere in this story Elijah is called "the Tishbite" (vv 3, 8). Stipp (1987:463-464) contends that "the Tishbite" was Dtr's title for Elijah (cf. 1 Kgs 21:17, 28) and that vv 2-8, 17* were in Dtr's original work. Verses 9-16 contain one of the "man of God" stories that were later inserted into Dtr's History. However Stipp does not discuss the use of "the Tishbite" in 1 Kgs 17:1. In my view, the occurrences of "the Tishbite" are all in secondary passages with the possible exception of 1 Kgs 21:17. Stipp's reason for seeing 2 Kings 1 as Dtr's work

2 KINGS 2; 3:4-27; 4:1-8:15; 13:14-21

The stories about Elisha in 2 Kings generally share several well known features. They depict the prophet as a wonder worker even in death (13:20-21). They refer to him as the "man of God" (4:7, 9, 16, 21, 22, 25, 27, 40, 42; 5:8, 15, 20; 6:6, 9, 10, 15; 7:2, 17, 18, 19; 8:2, 4, 7, 8, 11; 13:19). They describe Elisha's interaction with the "sons of the prophets" (2:3, 5, 7, 15-18; 4:1, 38-41, 42-44; 6:1-7). Some of them name Gehazi, Elisha's servant (4:8-37; 5:19-27; 8:1-6). They generally do not identify the king of Israel by name (3:4, 5, 9, 10, 12, 13; 5:5, 6, 7, 8; 6:9, 10, 11, 12, 21, 26, 30, 32; 7:2, 9, 11, 12, 14, 15, 17, 18; 8:4, 5, 6; 13:16, 18). They sometimes describe Elisha's relationship with the king as cordial (5:8; 6:8-10, 20-23; 8:1-6; 13:14-19), though not always (3:14; 6:31-33). They generally presuppose a state of war between Israel and Aram (6:8-23; 6:24-7:20; 13:14-19, 24-25), though again, not always (5:1-27). In 8:7-15 Elisha is consulted by the king of Aram, suggesting that he is at peace with Israel, but when Elisha foresees how Hazael will distress Israel he weeps.

There is obviously a good deal of literary unevenness in these stories.[20] Still, most scholars agree that the stories form part of a collection about Elisha that was incorporated into the book of Kings at some point.[21] The developmental history of this collection is complex and has not led to any kind of consensus that can be summarized here even in broad terms (compare Schmitt 1972 and Schweizer 1974). My concern for the present is again the relationship of the Elisha stories to Dtr's composition in the book of Kings.

As with the Elijah materials Noth decided that Dtr had taken up the Elisha stories in 2 Kgs 3:4-8:15 "mit dem überlieferten Wortlaut und wohl auch in der überlieferten Anordnung" (1967:83). Noth's proof that Dtr had not changed the language of the Elisha collection that he inherited lay in his continued use of the title "king of Israel" instead of substituting a name. His proof regarding the traditional order was that 8:1-6 had been left in place even though it presupposed Elisha's death (p. 83n; cf. Rofé 1988a:32-33). Again, in spite of the obvious frailty of these arguments most scholars since Noth have assumed that the Elisha stories were in Dtr's history.

As with the Elijah legends, this assumption was first (to my knowledge) called into question by Miller's 1966 essay on the Elisha cycle (pp. 450-

---

has to do with his reconstruction of the order in which the various prophetic stories were inserted into the DH (1987:463-464, 471-472), which depends heavily on seeing 2 Kings 1 as Dtr's. But there are other reasons to question his reconstruction (see below).

[20] Sekine (1975:46-57) provides a useful overview of some of the major literary critical problems in the Elisha collection.

[21] Stipp (1987:470-477) identifies more than one collection of narratives about Elisha which he sees as having been added independently to Dtr's work. See below.

451). Miller's observation of theological and historical tensions between Dtr's work and the Elisha cycle led him to conclude that the narratives about Elisha in 2 Kings, along with the Elijah stories in 1 Kings 17-19 and the battle accounts in 1 Kgs 20:1-38; 22, had been added to the DH by a second redactor.

Several other scholars in recent years have reached similar conclusions. Schmitt's 1972 (especially pp. 131-138) tradition historical analysis of the Elisha material led him to posit a total of fifteen levels of writing behind its formation: five narratives or narrative collections, nine separate redactors or editors, and later additions. Aside from the Jehu narrative in 2 Kings 9-10, the other narrative collections in Schmitt's list concern the Aramaeans (2 Kgs *5:1-14; *8:7-15; *13:14-17), miracles (2 Kgs *4:1-8:6), wars (1 Kings *20; *22; 2 Kgs *3:4-27; *6:24-7:16), and the succession from Elijah to Elisha (1 Kgs *19:19-21; 2 Kgs *2:1-24). All of these collections were pre-Dtr, ranging from the ninth to the seventh centuries B.C.E. All were edited and expanded before being brought into the book of Kings. But only the Jehu narrative was included in Dtr's original edition of Kings. Most of the Elisha stories were not added to the book of Kings until the fifth century B.C.E.

Van Seters (1983:305) holds that "the Elisha stories in 2 Kings 2; 4-7; 8:1-15; 9:21 are a loose collection tied together by statements of the prophet's itinerary from one point to another" (cf. Coats 1972). 2 Kings 3 and 9 are not in this collection. "Here the prophet plays a minor role, primarily as the messenger of Yahweh, quite different from the stories within the Elisha collection." Van Seters does not discuss the Elisha tales in 2 Kings 13.

Even more recently Stipp (1987:especially 470-477) has posited several collections behind the Elisha narratives. The account of the succession from Elijah to Elisha in 2 Kings 2 had already been bound together with the stories about women in 2 Kings 4 before they were added as a whole to the Dtr book of Kings. Similarly, a collection of stories about Elisha "the prophet" (5:1-6:23) came into Dtr's work as a unit. Other narratives, such as the ones behind 3:4-27 and 6:24-7:20 were added independently. In all cases, however, the Elisha stories were understood by Stipp as post-Dtr additions to Kings.

The reasons advanced by these scholars for taking the Elisha stories as post-Dtr insertions into Kings are quite similar. Van Seters puts it succinctly, "The collection of Elisha stories ... has not been integrated in any way into the Deuteronomist's history, nor does it show any signs of his editing" (1983:305; cf. Schmitt 1972:131-136). Rofé (1970; 1974; 1988a) has added further support for this conclusion with his linguistic arguments contending that the Elisha legends represent late genres of prophetic stories. In addition, Schmitt argues from certain theological formulas and ideas for late editorial activity in the collection of war narratives (1972:69-71) and in his "man of God" edition (pp. 127-129).

One need not accept some of the complex reconstructions of the Elisha collection in order to affirm that it has been inserted into Dtr's history. Nor does this necessarily mean that the stories themselves are purely late compositions. Dtr may have known them. But the evidence that he did not include them is compelling. It is not simply that there are no signs of Dtr's retouching in the stories, although this is striking in comparison with the Jehu narrative in 2 Kings 9-10. But several of the Elisha stories also stand outside of Dtr's chronological framework indicating that he did not edit them. The tales in 2 Kings 2 (MT) are between the closing formula for Ahaziah (1:17aβ-18) and the accession formula for Joram (3:1-3). The account in 3:4-27 includes Jehoshaphat, whose reign has already been closed by Dtr (1 Kgs 22:45-50). In 8:16 Dtr reports the accession of Jehoram of Judah in the fifth year of Joram of Israel. But the Elisha stories in 2 Kings 3-8 clearly presuppose more than a five year period (cf. 8:2). Elisha's last oracle to Joash (13:14-19) and posthumous miracle (vv 20-21) are recounted after Dtr's formulaic report of Joash's death and burial (13:13).

Van Seters may be correct that 2 Kgs 3:4-27 was not part of the Elisha collection. But I cannot agree with him that Dtr's history included this episode or the ones in 13:14-21. As indicated above, neither of these passages contains any Dtr language, and both are outside of Dtr's chronological rubric. But both passages are also important because they show how the insertion of the Elisha stories has led to confusion in the MT's chronology. Miller (1966) and Shenkel (1968:esp. 93-108) have shown that the OG contains an older, more original chronology that has been altered in the MT. The information about Joram's accession year in 3:1-3 agrees with 1 Kgs 22:51 but blatantly contradicts 2 Kgs 1:17aβ-18. The latter passage preserves the older chronology, while 1 Kgs 22:51 and 2 Kgs 3:1-3 reflect the revised chronology.

The reason for the shift in the MT was the mention of Jehoshaphat in 2 Kgs 3:4-27. The account in 3:4-27 was placed in its present position out of necessity. Since it presumes Mesha's revolt (3:5) it had to come after the Dtr reference to that revolt after Ahab's death (2 Kgs 1:1). But it also presumes the transition from Elijah to Elisha (cf. 3:11). This dictated the order of material for the editor who inserted the Elisha stories into Dtr's work. He placed the story about Ahaziah in 2 Kgs 1:2-17aα between Ahaziah's regnal formulas (including 2 Kgs 1:1), which were in Dtr's work. He then placed the story of Elisha's succession in 2 Kings 2 and the battle account in 3:4-27 after Dtr's formula for Joram in 3:1-3, identifying the king of Israel in 3:4-27 as Joram.

In the story in 3:4-27 the king of Judah was originally nameless. He was identified secondarily in the MT tradition as Jehoshaphat, while the OG, represented in LXX^L, identified him as Ahaziah.[22] Shenkel believes that this

---

[22] Shenkel (1968:93-101). Stipp's objections (1987:69-77) to Shenkel analysis are not convincing.

identification occurred for two reasons. First, the wicked reputations of Jehoram and Ahaziah precluded the identification of the righteous king of Judah, for whom Elisha intervened with God, with either of them. Secondly, the editor responsible for this identification was influenced by the similar account in 1 Kings 22. Miller sees the identification with Jehoshaphat as the result of "the tendency to ascribe anonymous works and deeds to well-known personalities of the past" (1966:447). He points out that Jehoshaphat's alliance with the Omrides is emphasized by the biblical writers and must have been remembered for generations afterward.[23] Shenkel's second reason cannot be accepted. The role of the king of Judah in 1 Kings 22 is completely secondary and has more likely been influenced by Jehoshaphat's role in 2 Kings 3 than the reverse. The other reasons cited by Miller and Shenkel provide sufficient explanation for Jehoshaphat's presence as the king of Judah in 2 Kings 3. Once this identification had taken place it indicated that Jehoshaphat was still alive in the days of Joram of Israel, an obvious contradiction in the MT of Dtr's chronological rubric in 2 Kgs 1:17aβ-18. This led to the adjustment in the MT's chronological framework as in 1 Kgs 22:51 and 2 Kgs 3:1-3. The development of 2 Kgs 3:4-27, therefore, has had a significant impact on the content and chronology of Dtr's history as it appears in the MT.

Finally, there is no evidence of Dtr's hand in the last stories about Elisha in 2 Kgs 13:14-21. I have already shown how these verses stand outside of Dtr's chronological structure. That is true, in fact, of all of 13:14-25. The battle accounts in 1 Kings 20 and 22 were once associated with the story in 2 Kgs 13:14-17. But the present oracle in 13:18-19 and its fulfillment notice in 13:25b are secondary additions, apparently by the editor who moved those battle accounts to 1 Kings 20 and 22. As observed, the Old Latin version of the story in 13:14-19 names Jehu as the king who is promised a three-fold victory over Aram. The disagreement in the witnesses over the placement of this story is yet another indication of its late insertion into Dtr's book of Kings.

CONCLUSIONS

I have identified most of the long prophetic narratives in the section from 1 Kings 13 - 2 Kings 13 as post-Dtr additions. These include the story of the young man of God from Judah and the old prophet from Israel in 1 Kgs 13:1-32a (Chapter Two), the Elijah cycle in 1 Kings 17-19 and the story about Elijah in 2 Kgs 1:2-17aα, the battle accounts in 1 Kgs 20 and 22:1-38, and the Elisha stories in 2 Kgs 2; 3:4-8:15; 13:14-21 (+ 22-25). I have not attempted here to reconstruct the tradition history of these materials,

---

[23] Miller posits that the identification of the king of Judah with Jehoshaphat in 2 Kgs 3:4-27 occurred in the development of that tradition before it was added to the book of Kings. But this does not account for the variant identification of the king with Ahaziah in LXX[L].

which is very complex, nor to describe the order in which they entered the DH (cf. Stipp 1987:463-480).[24]

This makes an enormous difference in the way that Dtr's history should be regarded (so also Stipp 1987:463). It means that his work on the monarchy was considerably shorter and more focused than is usually understood. After his account of Jeroboam's rise and the division of the kingdom (see Chapter Two), Dtr detailed Jeroboam's apostacy at Dan and Bethel (1 Kgs 12:25-32 + 13:34). He then included Ahijah's oracle against Jeroboam's house in the context of the story of Jeroboam's sick son (1 Kings 14). This set the pattern for Dtr's treatment of the next two Israelite dynasties under the scheme of prophecy and fulfillment.

The oracle against Jeroboam was fulfilled in Baasha's revolt (1 Kgs 15:27-29). Dtr placed a similar oracle against Baasha's house in the mouth of Jehu ben Hanani (1 Kgs 16:1-4). It was fulfilled in Zimri's revolt (1 Kgs 16:11-12). With the Omri dynasty Dtr leveled the deprecating oracle against Ahab (1 Kgs 21:20bβ-22, 24) in the context of the Naboth story. Ahab received this dubious distinction because Dtr saw him as the worst king of Israel, perhaps as a result of the reputation of his Tyrian queen, Jezebel. Like the other oracles against the dynasties, this one was fulfilled in short order. It was only later that the prophetic tales in 1 Kings 20; 22; 2 Kings 2-8, which now delay the fulfillment, were added to Dtr's account. Dtr adapted an older account of Jehu's revolt as the fulfillment against Ahab, showing continously throughout that story how Yahweh vindicated his prophet and vented his fury against the evil house of Ahab. Jehu's dynasty lasted until the fourth generation because of his faithful destruction of the Omrides (2 Kgs 10:30). The only reason it ended at all was because he also "walked in the sin of Jeroboam." The end of his dynasty gave way to the swift decline of Israel (2 Kings 15; 17).

The contrast which scholars have perceived in Dtr's history between the series of evil, Northern dynasties and the continuation of the Davidids surfaces more readily with the removal of the prophetic stories treated in this chapter (cf. Stipp 1987:479). It also becomes clear that the reason for Israel's demise, in Dtr's view, was the sin of Jeroboam, the idolatrous shrines at Dan and Bethel.

There remain in the book of Kings yet two more sets of prophetic stories which have not been treated -- those involving Isaiah in 2 Kings 18-20 and

---

[24] I think it likely, in contrast to Stipp, that the narratives listed above were inserted into the DH essentially as a group. This is suggested by their interdependance. For example, portions of the Elijah cycle in 1 Kings 17 draw on (2 Kings 4) in the Elisha collection and the end of the Elijah cycle (1 Kgs 19:15-21) presupposes the Elisha collection. But the succession account in the Elisha collection (2 Kings 2) also seems to presuppose the Elijah cycle. Again, the Elisha story in 2 Kings 3 (v 13) presupposes 1 Kings 17-19, but 2 Kings 3 has also influenced the account in 1 Kings 22. The interrelationship of the narratives renders any attempt to establish a *catena* of independent insertions too complex to be convincing.

Huldah in 22:15-20. These will be discussed in the context of the reigns of
Hezekiah and Josiah in the next chapter.

CHAPTER FIVE

TRUST AND OBEY:
HEZEKIAH AND JOSIAH IN THE BOOK OF KINGS

The stories about the prophet Isaiah in 2 Kings 18-20 are quite different from those prophetic tales covered in previous chapters. They are set in a different century and a different kingdom. The Isaiah stories obviously do not derive from the North. Prophecy in Judah and the development of the Isaiah stories in particular may have been influenced by Northern prophetic traditions, but that is a topic for another discussion. For our present purposes the point is that the Isaiah stories come from entirely different sources than the prophetic stories earlier in Kings. Unlike most of the stories we have treated heretofore, the prophet is not the real focus in 2 Kings 18-20. Isaiah plays an important role, but Hezekiah clearly stands in the center (Childs 1967:100-101).

ISAIAH AND THE REIGN OF HEZEKIAH

The account of Hezekiah's reign in 2 Kings 18-20 bristles with historical, chronological, and literary difficulties. Fortunately, the account has been well analyzed, and a handful of very helpful studies of the passage have been published in recent years (Childs 1967; Clements 1980; Dion 1988; Gonçalves 1986; Vogt 1986). I cannot begin to address all of the difficulties presented by these chapters. But I can survey some of the conclusions generally held by scholars regarding the literary development of the Hezekiah account, which is my main concern in this study. The account in 2 Kings 18-20, as it has been analyzed by scholars, is an excellent illustration of Dtr's methods of composition.

I shall survey the account in four sections: 1. the introduction (18:1-12), including the review of Israel's fall in vv 9-12, and conclusion (20:20-21) to Hezekiah's reign; 2. the invasion of Sennacherib (18:13-19:37); 3. the extension of Hezekiah's life (20:1-11); and 4. the visit of the Babylonian envoy (20:12-19).

Introduction (18:1-12) and Conclusion (20:20-21)

The account of Hezekiah's reign is incorporated, of course, within Dtr's typical initial and concluding rubrics. Other verses in these sections, such as 18:6-7, 12, are obviously Deuteronomistic. Of course, this does not exclude the possibility of later additions to the account, but it does indicate that Dtr is its primary composer. He also provided a chronological structure where there were dates available to him (18:1, 9, 13).[1] In v 3 Dtr bestows upon Hezekiah the greatest possible accolade: "he did right in Yahweh's eyes according to all that David his father had done."˙ Only one other king, Josiah (22:2), is blameless and likened without qualification to David. The description of Hezekiah's cultic reforms in v 4 is the basis for Dtr's sterling evaluation.[2] The fact that Hezekiah removed the במות allows Dtr to declare him righteous without reservation. Scholars have tended to see the references to cultic centralization in 18:4, 22 as a construct by Dtr writing from a later perspective (cf. Gonçalves 1986:73-74). Dtr's portrait of Hezekiah, particularly his centralization of the cult and his trust in Yahweh, serve as his theological explanation for the fact that Jerusalem under Hezekiah escaped destruction at the hands of Assyria (see below).

Dtr's later theological perspective on Hezekiah is also apparent from the incomparability statement for him in 18:5: "there was none like him among all the kings of Judah after him." At first glance this statement seems to contradict the similar one for Josiah in 23:25: "before him there was no king like him." But the two kings are being judged incomparable in different areas -- Hezekiah in his trust in Yahweh and Josiah in his obedience.[3] Hezekiah's trust is what is meant by the following statement in v 6 that he clung to Yahweh and did not turn from him (וידבק ביהוה ולא סר מאחריו). Josiah's incomparable obedience is specified by the subsequent statement that he returned to Yahweh wholeheartedly according to the law of Moses (שב אל יהוה בכל לבבו ובכל נפשו ובכל מאדו ככל תורת משה). Hezekiah's reforms (18:6) are also exemplary, of course, but the brevity of Dtr's report (18:4) suggests that he saw trust as the primary trait to be admired in Hezekiah. Dtr's focus on Hezekiah's trust in v 5 is a mark of his editorial skill as it anticipates the theme of trust in the narrative of Sennacherib's invasion beginning in 18:17.

---

[1] The notorious chronological problems for Hezekiah's reign cannot be dealt with here. See Gonçalves (1986:51-60) for a review of the issues and proposed solutions. The chronological notices at 20:1, 12 will be treated below.

[2] Provan (1988:84-86) contends that 2 Kgs 18:4aα, הוא הסיר את הבמות, is the climax of an initial, pre-exilic edition of Kings that traced the history of the במות (understood as non-idolatrous shrines to Yahweh) in Judah from Solomon to Hezekiah. He assigns 18:3-4aα, 5, 7-8 to this initial edition and the rest of 18:1-12 to the exilic redactor (1988:121). His theory will be assessed in Chapter Six. But in my view 18:1-12 is best assigned to Dtr. He may have used earlier source material, but it has been thoroughly incorporated within Dtr's presentation.

[3] Cf. Pratt 1982:23-24. Both verses, by the way, contain later additions which round out the comparison. In 18:5 ואשר היו לפניו is an addition, and the same is probably true of ואחריו לא קם כמהו in 23:25.

Sennacherib's Invasion (18:13-19:37) [4]

The A Account
Since Stade's 1886 treatment of this passage scholars have recognized two distinct accounts of Sennacherib's invasion in 2 Kgs 18:13-19:37. The first, known as account A, is in 18:13-16. It is a straightforward historical account without theological commentary and is likely derived from official sources. It is relatively close to the account in Sennacherib's annals and is probably the most reliable of the biblical accounts for the historical reconstruction of Sennacherib's invasion (cf. Dion 1988:5; Gonçalves 1986:367-372).

The B[1] Narrative
Account B in 18:17-19:37 is itself composite. Most scholars isolate one narrative, B[1], in 18:17-19:9a (+ ‏וישב‎) + 19:36-37[5] and a second, B[2], in 19:9b (beginning with ‏וישלח‎) - 19:35. The B[1] narrative consists primarily of the Rabshakeh's speech to the people of Jerusalem. B. Childs (1967:80-82) has pointed out the similarity of this speech to an Assyrian report of negotiations with Babylonian rebels (but cf. also Dion 1988:7). He concludes that both texts are examples of the same genre which he calls "diplomatic disputation." Its function is to wage psychological warfare, i.e., through reason, threat, and ridicule to persuade the residents of the beleaguered city to surrender. Thus Childs believes that the speech contains genuine historical tradition.

As mentioned, the theme of the Rabshakeh's speech is trust or reliance (‏בטח‎). He tries to convince the Jerusalemites that their reliance on Egypt or Yahweh for deliverance (‏נצל‎ is another key word) is misplaced. Gonçalves (1986:409-412) has shown that this theme of trust is not common in the DH outside of 2 Kings 18-19. This suggests that it is not Dtr's contribution but was inherent in his source for the speech.

The allusion to Hezekiah's cultic centralization in 18:22 has been a source of debate with some scholars accepting its historicity and others taking it as Dtr's construct (Gonçalves 1986:72-73). Childs sees it as a combination of the two. "The perplexing feature of this argument [in v 22] is the strange mixture between an intimate knowledge of the cultic reforms of Hezekiah and its blatant pagan point of view" (1967:82). Hence, the verse contains elements from Dtr's source for the Rabshakeh's speech as well as from Dtr himself. ". . . the Assyrian diplomat argues from a genuine pagan perspec-

---

[4] I am excluding the Isaiah 36-39 parallel from my present discussion since there is a general consensus that the Kings version is prior.

[5] There is disagreement about the exact location of the seam of the two narratives in 19:7-9. See Gonçalves (1986:351-354).

tive which has misunderstood completely the character of Hezekiah's religious policy" while Dtr "interprets the removal of Assyrian cult objects and the destruction of foreign elements as part of a programme of cultic centralization in Jerusalem" (1967:83).

I cannot make sense of Childs's argument here. The Rabshakeh's point is that the Jerusalemites cannot rely on Yahweh for deliverance because Hezekiah has removed his shrines. But this point presupposes his familiarity with Hezekiah's removal of Yahwistic shrines. If he knows that Hezekiah actually removed Assyrian cult objects, as Childs contends, the argument is undermined.[6] The Rabshakeh may not have understood Hezekiah's actions, but surely he could tell the difference between the cult of Yahweh and that of Assyrian gods.

Dtr is, of course, very interested in cultic centralization, and we have already seen that he reads it back into Hezekiah's reign in 18:4. The structure of the Rabshakeh's speech in 18:19-25 further suggests that v 22 has been added by Dtr. The speech contains four points: 1. v 21 - the Jerusalemites cannot rely on Egypt; 2. v 22 - they cannot rely on Yahweh; 3. vv 23-24 - they are far outnumbered and must rely on Egypt for reinforcements; 4. v 25 - Yahweh himself has sent the Assyrians to destroy Judah and Jerusalem. Each of these points is introduced with the particle עתה(ו) except for the second one. Verse 22, then, stands out from its context. Also, the point in vv 23-24 depends on v 21. The Jerusalemites are forced to rely for chariots and horsemen on Egypt (v 24), which is weak according to v 21. Verse 22, therefore, appears somewhat intrusive and should be assigned to Dtr.

The end of the Rabshakeh's speech in vv 32b-35 introduces rather suddenly the argument that Yahweh is powerless to deliver Jerusalem. This argument stands in a certain tension with earlier verses (22, 25, 30) which presume Yahweh's power. This has led some scholars (Gonçalves 1986:386-388) to see 18:32b-35 as a secondary development dependent on 18:29-31a and 19:10-13. The added verses introduce prematurely the theme of blasphemy which is central to the B[2] narrative. The difficulty with this understanding is that 19:4, 6 seem to presuppose 18:32b-35. The statement in 19:4 that the Rabshakeh has mocked (חרף) the living God is especially reminiscent of David's words in 1 Sam 17:36, 45 (cf. 17:25, 26). Childs's conclusion (1967:86-89) that 18:32b-35 reflect Dtr's theological concerns is attractive, and vv 32b-35 should be seen as Dtr's handiwork.[7]

Hezekiah's appeal to Isaiah for intercession in 19:1-5 shows his trust in Yahweh and thus fits with the main theme of the B[1] narrative. His appeal is answered by Isaiah's brief oracle in 19:6-7 promising that Sennacherib will

---

[6] Whether the Assyrians compelled their subjects to worship Assyrian deities is a matter of considerable recent debate. Contrast Cogan (1974) and McKay (1973) with Spieckermann (1982).

[7] Van Leeuwen (1965:251) has argued that the expressions "land of grain and wine," "land of olive trees and honey," and "that you may live and not die" in v 18:32a are also Deuteronomistic (cf. Deut 8:8; 32:28).

return to Assyria and be assassinated there. Sennacherib's withdrawal from Judah is reported in 19:8-9a, but his assassination is described only in 19:36-37. This indicates that the intervening narrative in 19:9b-35 is an editorial addition.

The B² Narrative

Within the B² narrative in 19:9b-35, vv 21-31 are widely recognized as a later interpolation. The narrative is resumed with the repetition of the messenger formula in v 32aα. Once this interpolation is removed from consideration the true nature of the B² narrative becomes apparent. As Childs (1967:97-98; cf. Dion 1988:10-11; Gonçalves 1986:478-479) has shown, the B² narrative is literarily dependent on the B¹ narrative. Both have the same basic structure and subject matter. What differences do exist in the B² narrative are minor and usually theologically motivated. The B² narrative, in short, was composed on the basis of the B¹ narrative specifically for the purpose of inclusion at this point.

The nature of the B² narrative can be perceived from its ending in 19:32-35. Some scholars have seen a contradiction between vv 33 and 35 which has caused them to see one (Childs 1967:75-76) or the other (Clements 1980:58-59) as a later insertion. But if the B² narrative is simply an editor's composition it is unnecessary to take either verse as secondary. The author of B² separated 19:36-37 from the B¹ narrative, which they had concluded, in order to insert his own composition. He had used Sennacherib's hearing of a rumor and departure in B¹ as the motive for the letter to Hezekiah in his composition (19:9b-13). Hence, he needed another motive at the end of his composition to impel Sennacherib's return to Assyria in 19:36-37. He added v 33, partly on the basis of v 32a, as a preparation for the conclusion in vv 36-37. Then he added v 35, which he had composed from the traditional *topos* of the advent of the angel of death at night (cf. Gonçalves 1986:471-473), to explain why Sennacherib returned to Assyria.

The B² narrative revolves entirely around the themes of blasphemy and deliverance. The letter to Hezekiah (19:9b-13) treats Yahweh as deceitful and impotent. Hezekiah's prayer (19:14-19) points out that the letter blasphemes (חרף) Yahweh and begs him to save (הושׁיע) Jerusalem from the Assyrians. Isaiah's oracle assures Hezekiah that Yahweh will save the city for his sake (because the Assyrians have blasphemed him) and out of loyalty to his promise to David (19:34).

The reference to the Davidic promise in 19:34 is patently Deuteronomistic and fits with Dtr's emphasis on Yahweh's choice of Jerusalem and David in 2 Samuel 7 and throughout the book of Kings (cf. 1 Kgs 11:12, 13, 36; 15:4; 2 Kgs 8:19). It is the clearest sign that Dtr is the author of the B² narrative. But other Deuteronomistic themes and language pervade B², especially in Hezekiah's prayer. Gonçalves's scrutiny of the prayer (1986:463-470) has made this clear, even though he does not specifically assign it to Dtr. In what follows I depend heavily on his analysis.

Ascribing prayers to national leaders is a common compositional technique of Dtr's (Childs 1967:99; Weinfeld 1972:42).[8] Hezekiah's prayer has many affinities with other prayers in the DH, especially Solomon's in 1 Kings 8. The two prayers have a comparable structure with the pivotal point between explanation and intercession being expressed with ועתה יהוה (1 Kgs 8:25; 2 Kgs 19:19). Hezekiah's request that Yahweh open his ears and eyes (19:16) is found in Solomon's prayer (8:29, 52; cf. Jer 32:19). Hezekiah's plea that Yahweh hear his prayer is a constant refrain in 1 Kgs 8:22-53.

There are other features that Hezekiah's prayer shares with Deuteronomy and the DH at large. The reference to "mocking the living God" which occurs in 1 Sam 17:36, 45 and 2 Kgs 19:4 is also shared by 19:16. The title for Yahweh, "who sits above the cherubim," is relatively rare in the Hebrew Bible. Outside of Hezekiah's prayer it occurs only in stories about the ark in Samuel (1 Sam 4:4; 2 Sam 6:2) and its Chronicles parallel (1 Chr 13:6). The strong monotheism of Hezekiah's prayer (19:15) is particularly striking. It is not, of course, an exclusive doctrine of the DH, but it is a characteristic emphasis in Deuteronomy and the DH (Deut 4:35, 39; 7:9; 2 Sam 7:22). The reference to Yahweh as creator in v 15 has a particularly close parallel in the Deuteronomistic prayer of Jeremiah 32 (v 16). Associated with this monotheistic emphasis in 19:18 is the Deuteronomistic polemic against idols, "the work of human hands, wood and stone" (cf. Deut 27:15; 28:36, 64; 29:16; 31:29; 1 Kgs 16:7; 2 Kgs 22:17; cf. Jer 1:16; 10:3-10; 25:6-7; 32:30; 44:8). In fact, as R. Pratt (1982:9) has shown, the prayer is framed by expressions that are typical of Dtr:

v 15	v 19
אתה הוא האלהים לבדך	וידעו כל ממלכות הארץ
לכל ממלכות הארץ	כי אתה יהוה אלהים לבדך

Thus, the language and ideology both of Hezekiah's prayer and of the B² narrative as a whole point to Dtr as their author.

Hezekiah's Illness and Recovery (20:1-11)

Scholars have long held that the stories of Hezekiah's recovery from illness (20:1-7) and his request for a sign (20:8-11) are originally independent units. However, Gonçalves (1986:332-336) has demonstrated the composite nature of vv 1-7 and suggested a different reconstruction. He posits that vv 1abα, 7 were once a brief legend about Isaiah's healing of Hezekiah. The legend was expanded by the addition of the story of the extension of

---

[8] However, as Pratt (1982:3) points out, David and Solomon are the only other kings whose prayers are recorded in the DH. See below.

Hezekiah's life in vv 1bβ-6aα + 8-11. The entire passage (vv 1-11) was added here and linked with the previous account of Sennacherib's invasion by the rubric בימים ההם in 20:1 and the gift of fifteen years to Hezekiah. The invasion took place in Hezekiah's fourteenth year (18:13), and he reigned twenty-nine years (18:2), so the editor extended his life by fifteen years instead of the ten indicated by the story in 20:8-11. The reference to the Davidic covenant in 20:6aβb is another editorial link with the Sennacherib account.

I find Gonçalves's analysis persuasive and would add only one point to his conclusions. The writer/editor responsible for the present shape of 20:1-11 is Dtr. This is indicated by the Davidic promise in v 6, which is one of several links to Sennacherib's invasion. Also, the language of v 3 is Deuteronomistic, especially the expressions בלבב שלם and הטוב בעיניך עשיתי (Weinfeld 1972:335). Dtr assembled the components described by Gonçalves behind 20:1-11. He edited them into a unified story, provided a chronological rubric for it in the context of his previous account of Jerusalem's deliverance and of his entire history.

The Babylonian Envoy (20:12-19)

Scholars have been almost unanimous in asserting that this pericope is an example of *vaticinium ex eventu*. Two recent dissenters are Nelson (1981) and Begg (1986a). Nelson argues that the story does not presuppose the exile or illustrate Dtr's prophecy - fulfillment scheme. Rather, its purpose is simply to warn about the dangers of an alliance with Babylon. The first part of Begg's article gives reasons for his judgement that the story is pre-Dtr. First, he asserts the historicity of the Babylonians' visit. Secondly, the narrative in 2 Kgs 20:17-18 does not follow Dtr's standard formula for a judgement oracle. Also, since 2 Kings 24-25 lack a specific fulfillment for the oracle in 20:16-17 it does not fit within Dtr's prophecy - fulfillment pattern. Thirdly, the narrative lacks the confession of sin from Hezekiah which one would expect in Dtr's version of such a story. Begg concludes that the story in 20:12-19 is essentially a pre-Dtr unit with no Deuteronomistic reworking. Ironically, the rest of his article is then spent trying to explain why Dtr included this story. Begg finds that the story fits Dtr's interests in the despoliation of royal wealth by foreigners and in the depiction of a prophetic announcement and its reception. The latter item, incidentally, is categorically ruled out by Nelson as a possible purpose of this story.

The arguments of Nelson and Begg carry little conviction. Nelson's mistake lies in his assumption that 20:12-19 show no sign of being secondary. Begg's contention that the story shows no Deuteronomistic influence is well taken, but this certainly does not demand the conclusion that it is pre-Dtr. Indeed, the contortions Begg has to perform in an attempt to explain why

Dtr included the story make one very suspicious that Dtr had nothing to do with it.

While it is true that the story occurs within Dtr's structural rubrics for Hezekiah, this does not automatically mean that Dtr included it. The story is clearly out of place chronologically. If a Babylonian contingent did visit Jerusalem it must have come before Hezekiah revolted against Assyria (cf. Dion 1988:3). In view of the way that Dtr integrated 20:1-11 into his account of Hezekiah and related that passage to Sennacherib's invasion one would expect him to do a better job of integrating 20:12-19. The simple introduction בעת ההיא (v 12) is very weak, and the reference to Hezekiah's illness in the same verse only shows that this account presupposes 20:1-11. More telling is the story's view of Hezekiah. We have seen that Dtr expresses a very high regard for Hezekiah in 18:1-8 and in the accounts of Hezekiah's trust in Yahweh when facing Sennacherib. Dtr never hints at any shortcoming on Hezekiah's part. To find suddenly in 20:12-19 a portrait of Hezekiah as proud, selfish, and apathetic about his nation's future shocks the reader. Yet, Dtr's closing formula for Hezekiah (20:20-21) shows no awareness of these faults. Since the story in 20:12-19 otherwise betrays no sign of Dtr's language or interests it is reasonable to assume that he did not include it in his history. It was inserted later.

Dtr's Portrait of Hezekiah

Dtr's narrative of Hezekiah's reign in 2 Kings 18-20 is an excellent example of his method of composition. He prefaced his account with a lengthy introduction (18:1-8) which contains his typical formulas and evaluations but also glorifies Hezekiah. After a brief comment on the fall of the North dated to Hezekiah's fourth year (18:9-12), Dtr then launched into the story of Sennacherib's invasion. This story exemplifies the paratactic style described by Van Seters. Dtr set one account (A) of Hezekiah's capitulation, probably drawn from official sources alongside another (B[1]) which was more theological in orientation and touted Hezekiah's trust in Yahweh. The latter account explained the fact that Sennacherib did not destroy Jerusalem as the result of Yahweh's intervention on behalf of the faithful Hezekiah. Dtr retouched it adding his theme of cultic centralization (18:22) and introducing the motif of blasphemy (18:32b-35). He then expanded on that motif by composing the B[2] narrative on the basis of and in conjunction with B[1]. His B[2] composition further explained Jerusalem's endurance as the result of Yahweh's faithfulness to David (19:34). The final episode in Hezekiah's reign was that of his illness and recovery. Here Dtr welded a story about the extension of Hezekiah's life into a brief prophetic legend about Isaiah healing the sick king. Dtr linked the product chronologically and theologically with his account of Sennacherib's invasion. Dtr's account ended with his standard concluding formulas (20:20-21). The story of the Babylonian envoy (20:12-19) is a case of *vaticinium ex eventu* which was added during the exile to Dtr's account of Hezekiah's reign.

In a paper that remains, regretably, unpublished R. Pratt (1982) has discovered the key to Hezekiah's place in the DH in his two prayers in 2 Kings 19 and 20. Pratt recognizes the Deuteronomistic nature of the prayers. He also observes that the only other royal prayers in the DH are those of David in 2 Samuel 7 and Solomon in 1 Kings 8. Both of those prayers are "related to important moments for the throne and cult in Jerusalem" (1982:10). In 2 Samuel 7 David expresses the desire to build the Temple and is rewarded with the promise of an eternal dynasty. In 1 Kings 8 Solomon dedicates the Temple. Both passages represent the climax of the reign of their respective kings. Both are associated with the themes of Davidic dynasty and Temple, which are, of course, central to Dtr's theology.

The same themes underlie Dtr's account of Hezekiah, along with a third theme of importance for Dtr -- the contrasting theme of the sin of Jeroboam and the fall of Israel. At the beginning of his account of Hezekiah Dtr reminds the reader that the Assyrians had destroyed Samaria (18:9-12; cf. 17:1-6). What was to prevent them from doing the same thing to Jerusalem? In his account of Hezekiah Dtr shows that "the inevitable is averted by the intervention of Yahweh in response to Hezekiah's prayers" (Pratt 1982:13).

But Yahweh's intervention on behalf of Hezekiah and Jerusalem was also due, in Dtr's theology, to his faithfulness to his promise to David (19:34; 20:6). Pratt (1982:13-20) shows that Dtr's prayers in the mouths of David, Solomon, and Hezekiah form a deliberate pattern of expectation and fulfillment. He lists several connections between Solomon's prayer and those of Hezekiah:

1. Solomon hoped that the Temple would be a center of prayer (1 Kgs 8:27-53); Hezekiah's first prayer is made in the temple (2 Kgs 19:14) and his second with a longing to enter it (20:5).

2. Hezekiah faces the threats of siege and sickness which Solomon's prayer anticipated (1 Kgs 8:37).

3. Solomon's prayer for mercy "to your servants who walk before you with all their heart" (1 Kgs 8:23) is echoed by Hezekiah's claim, "I have walked before you ... with a whole heart" (2 Kgs 20:3).

4. Finally, as we have seen, the image of Yahweh opening his eyes toward the temple (1 Kgs 8:29, 52; 2 Kgs 19:16) and the hope that the nations will come to know Yahweh's uniqueness (1 Kgs 8:43, 60; 2 Kgs 19:15, 19) are found in both Solomon's and Hezekiah's prayers.

For Dtr, then, Hezekiah's confrontation with Sennacherib was the proving of the Davidic promise. Jerusalem's survival demonstrated that the promise could not fail. As such, Hezekiah holds a significant place in Dtr's theological schema in the book of Kings. His incomparable trust in Yahweh and Yahweh's proof of his loyalty to his promise to David set Hezekiah apart from all other kings.[9]

---

[9] I agree with Pratt, who follows Rosenbaum (1979), that the brevity of Dtr's description of reforms under Hezekiah is likely due to his downplaying Hezekiah's reform activity in order to present Josiah as the incomparable reformer. However,

THE REIGN OF JOSIAH

Since the publication of Theodor Oestreicher's *Das deuteronomische Grundgesetz* in 1923 scholars have described Dtr's account of Josiah as the combination of two reports.[10] The first, called the *Auffindungsbericht* or the like is generally found in 2 Kgs 22:3-23:3 with some scholars including 23:21-23 and/or vv 24-25. The second, the *Reformbericht* , is located in 23:4-15 with vv 19-20 sometimes included. I shall discuss this material in slightly different units, simply for the sake of convenience and not because I see different source documents behind each unit. Once more, I shall limit my treatment to the literary development of 2 Kings 22-23 drawing on the wealth of scholarly research in these chapters, especially in recent years.

The Finding the Book of the Law (22:3-14)

Dtr's introduction to Josiah (22:1-2) praises him with the same kind of exalted comparison to David as that found for Hezekiah (18:3): "[Josiah] walked in all the way of David his father and did not turn aside to the right or left." Then Dtr launches into the story of the finding of the law book in Josiah's eighteenth year. He begins with Josiah's order for Temple repairs (22:3-7). Hoffmann (1980:192-197) has shown that this passage is an abbreviated rewriting of the account of repairs to the Temple under Jehoiada and Joash (2 Kgs 12:10-16). But the abridgement is not concerned with Temple repairs *per se*. At v 10 the focus moves to the law book, and no further mention of the Temple repairs is made. This indicates that Dtr composed 2 Kgs 22:3-7 from 12:10-16 specifically as an introduction to the discovery of the law book (Dietrich 1977:20-23; Würthwein 1976:401).

In vv 11-13 Josiah sends an envoy to Huldah the prophetess to inquire about the significance of the law book "for me, for the people, and for all Judah." It is possible that Dtr had oral sources for this information or even first hand knowledge of the event. On the other hand, the names in these verses were readily available for Dtr to create his own account (Würthwein 1976:403).[11] In any case, this passage is "rein dtr" (Würthwein), and there is no reason to posit a written *Vorlage* behind it.

Rosenbaum's optimism regarding the historicity of the Chronicler's account of Hezekiah must be tempered by recognizing the extent to which the Chronicler's *Tendenzen* have shaped that account.

[10] For a survey of treatments of the Josiah account see Lohfink (1985:24-35).

[11] The reference in v 14 to Huldah living in the משנה does not necessitate a post-exilic date for the account (contra Hoffmann 1980:199n), as Spieckermann (1982:59n) points out.

The Oracle of Huldah (22:16-20)

This difficult text stands at the heart of the Josiah account. Most scholars agree that it is composite.[12] Usually they find one oracle in vv 16-17 and another in vv 18-20.[13] The first oracle presupposes the exile, especially in the statement that Yahweh's wrath against "this place" will not be quenched (v 17). But this oracle does not answer Josiah's inquiry "for me, the people, and all Judah." It speaks only about "this place."

Some scholars have found in vv 19-20 the remnant of a pre-exilic weal oracle for Josiah (Cross 1973:286n; Nelson 1981:76-79). The statement that Josiah "will be gathered to your grave in peace" (v 20) reflects no awareness of his death in battle (23:29). As such, the verse comes from a time before Josiah died.

Several recent treatments of this passage (Dietrich 1972:57-58; Hoffmann 1980:183-185; Mayes 1983:129-130; Provan 1988:149) contend that the reference to peace concerns only Josiah's burial and not his means of death. Hence, the prophecy means to contrast Josiah's burial to the Northern dynasties who are cursed with non-burial (Hoffmann:1980:185). Or, it means "not that Josiah will die a natural death, but that he will be buried 'in time of peace', before the events of which the prophecy speaks come to pass" (Provan 1988:149)

This line of argumentation, however, is unacceptable. "... eine solche Exegese widerspricht völlig dem alttestamentlichen Sprachgebrauch" (Rose 1977:59). Being gathered to one's fathers or to one's grave are idioms for death just like being brought down to Sheol (cf. 1 Kgs 2:6). The fine distinction between Josiah being gathered to his fathers and Josiah being gathered to his grave lacks support. Rose points out that the biblical passages which concern non-burial all have to do with sudden, violent death (cf. Jer 8:2; 25:33; Ezek 29:5). This is also evident in the oracles against the dynasties which we have surveyed. Dtr uses a curse of non-burial to threaten the massacre of the ruling house. Again, Rose observes that the Chronicler understood Huldah's oracle to refer to Josiah's death since he took pains to have it occur only <u>after</u> Josiah had been carried out of battle and arrived in Jerusalem (2 Chr 35:24). Granted, the prophecy promises that Josiah will not see "the evil" which Yahweh will bring upon Jerusalem. But Josiah's burial (2 Kgs 23:30) hardly occurs "in time of peace." It takes place in the wake of war with Egypt! The scholarly explanations attempting to avoid the implications of Huldah's errant prophecy depict Yahweh as deliberately out to deceive the righteous Josiah through a kind subtle literalism so that he is slain. Surely this is foreign to the writer's intent.

---

[12] To my knowledge Hoffmann (1980:170-181) is alone in asserting the unity of these verses.

[13] Rose (1977:60n) is probably correct in asserting that the last line of v 18, הדברים אשר שמעת, is a corruption of the phrase בשמעך אשר דברתי in v 19.

The prophecy in v 20, then, should be dated before the exile. Other portions of vv 19-20 are probably retouchings by the same writer who added vv 16-17. The demeaning reference to Jerusalem as "this place" is common to vv 16, 17, 19, 20 and seems to reflect exilic retouching (Nelson 1981:79).[14] It is probably impossible to reconstruct Huldah's original oracle. But whatever it was, it served to impel Josiah to lead the people in renewing their covenant with Yahweh (23:1-3) and in carrying out the cultic reforms in 23:4ff (cf. Nelson 1981:77).

The Renewal of the Covenant (23:1-3)

This passage stands at the center of the Josiah account. It is motivated by the finding of the law and by Huldah's oracle. It, in turn, motivates the cultic reforms that follow. There is also a covenant ceremony associated with Joash (11:17) which leads to his cultic reforms (11:18). But there are important differences between the two covenants. The mediator of the covenant in 2 Kings 11 is the priest, Jehoiada, and not the king, Joash, who is simply a party to the first covenant in 11:17. Also, while religious reform certainly is involved in Jehoiada's covenant, the two-fold reference in 11:17 to the king and the people seems to stress affirmation of political loyalty on the part of the people to the new king which is not apparent in 2 Kgs 23:1-3. This may be the reason for the vague expression of purpose in the covenant in 11:17: "to be the people of Yahweh." Whatever this means, it does not seem to express the same focus on the stipulations of the law as in Josiah's covenant.

Hoffmann (1980:201-203) describes how Dtr presents an ideal scene in the Josiah covenant by full participation by all segments of the community. All the elders of Judah, all the men of Judah, all the inhabitants of Judah, all the priests and prophets, and all the people assemble to hear Josiah read all the words of the book of the covenant. It is, of course, not a new covenant but a renewal of the Mosaic covenant of Deuteronomy (Lohfink 1963:272-273). The description in v 3 of the affirmation made by Josiah and the people is in classic Deuteronomistic language (Hoffmann 1980:203): ללכת אחר יהוה ולשמר מצותיו ואת עדותיו ואת חקתיו בכל לב ובכל נפש להקים את דברי הברית הזאת.

---

[14] Other scholars who argue for secondary revision in vv 19-20 include Dietrich (1977:27), Levin (1984:355), Rose (1977:55), and Spieckermann (1982:58-71). The late motif of humbling oneself expressed by the verb נכנע also indicates exilic rewriting (cf. Jepsen 1970). We have already seen that in 1 Kgs 21:29 it is post-Dtr. 2 Kgs 22:11 says nothing about Josiah humbling himself, and the original grounds for Huldah's weal oracle may simply have been "because you tore your clothes and wept before me." Weeping in such contexts is attested elsewhere in the DH (Hoffmann 1980:179). It may serve to link this account about Josiah's inquiry with the one about Hezekiah's petition in 20:3.

Josiah's Reform (23:4-20)

"Der Reformbericht in 2 Kön 23, 4ff. hat einen gegen das Vorhergehende völlig veränderten Stil." This often quoted observation by Oestreicher (1923:30) expresses the reason that many scholars find an independent document behind the reform account. In addition, the material in this section, especially vv 4-14, does not follow any clear structure or organizational thread.

These factors have led many scholars to posit different sources or levels of redaction, especially in vv 4-15. Most scholars take v 8b as an addition that interrupts the account about the priests of the במות, and many also see vv 16-18 or 16-20 as a later addition. However, aside from these verses there has been very little agreement about the literary critical evaluation of this pericope. Much of the literary discussion has dealt with the presence in vv 4-15 of seven cases of the perfect with the <u>waw</u> copulative, which some scholars have used as a criterion for separating the work of a late editor.[15] But the detailed studies of that form have concluded that it is an integral part of Hebrew narrative and cannot be used to isolate levels of composition (Meyer 1959; Spieckermann 1982:120-130).

One cannot rule out the possibility that Dtr had sources which he simply compiled into this report. At the same time, Hoffmann (1980:209) points out that the content of the report accounts for much of its style and unevenness. It is little more than a list which Dtr could have culled from his earlier accounts of cultic offenses. Whatever the origin of the items in the list, the point for our purposes is that Dtr is the one responsible for it. Rose's survey of the cultic terms in the passage has demonstrated its Deuteronomistic character.[16]

That brings up the most important point about the *Reformbericht* -- its thoroughness. Josiah corrects all the cultic aberrations detailed in Dtr's preceding account -- those of Solomon (vv 13-14), Manasseh (v 12), the kings of Judah (v 5), and even Jeroboam (vv 15-20). The last passage appears distinct from the previous list. Verse 15 is attached with the particle וגם but attests the theme of Jeroboam's sin which plays such a major role in Dtr's history. The same is true of vv 19-20 which refer back to Dtr's diatribe against Jeroboam in 1 Kgs 12:26-32 + 13:34. Verses 16-18, however, presuppose the story of the young man of God in 1 Kgs 13:1-32a. Since that

---

[15] For a list of such scholars see Hoffmann (1980:215, n. 37). Add to his list Hollenstein (1977).

[16] Rose (1977:53n). His survey includes the following words and expressions: גללים, שקצים, זבח, קטר, כל צבא השמים, אשרה, בעל, and he reports the following result. "Die genannten Formeln oder Wörter finden sich nur oder weitgehend jeweils im gleichen Bereich: Königsbücher, deuteronomistischer Rahmen im Deuteronomium, Bearbeitungsschichten im Jeremia-Buch."

story was inserted into Dtr's history the same must be true for 2 Kgs 23:16-18 (see below).

The Celebration of the Passover (23:21-23)

Many scholars have been content to see Josiah's Passover as a part, even an essential part, of the *Auffindungsbericht* (Lohfink 1963:269-275). Würthwein (1976:408), however, argues that these verses are a later addition. His argument is based on the fact that both the finding of the law book and the celebration of the Passover are dated to Josiah's eighteenth year. But since the new year probably began in the Spring there would not have been sufficient time to prepare for the Passover by proclaiming it throughout the land.

It is odd to find Würthwein arguing from historical considerations, since he is out disprove the historicity of the Josiah account elsewhere his article. It is not at all clear just how much time would have been available for preparation or how long preparations for the Passover would have taken. But aside from these points, Würthwein's argument does not allow for Dtr's schematizing of the account. Schematizing is suggested by a comparison of 2 Chr 34:3 where Josiah begins to purge the Temple in his eighth year. The Chronicler undoubtedly has his own *Tendenzen*, chronological and otherwise, but this variation may be due to Dtr's wish to depict the law book as the catalyst for Josiah's reform measures, including the Passover. Dtr's point is that Josiah celebrated the Passover as soon as he discovered the commands about it in the law book. Verses 21-22 also share many of Dtr's expressions and themes from the previous two chapters, including the direction of the king, the participation of all the people, and the precise following of the law book's stipulations (cf. Hoffmann 1980:259-260).

The Summary of Josiah's Reform (23:24)

This verse accords with Dtr's emphasis on Josiah's leadership in following the law. Dtr takes pains in v 24a to show that Josiah also did away with the heterodox practices introduced by Manasseh (21:6). The verse goes on to say that in this, as in all of his reforms, Josiah established the words of the law (הקים את דברי התורה). This expression is patently Deuteronomistic (Weinfeld 1972:350) and serves almost as a fulfillment remark showing that Josiah carried out all the prescriptions of the law book to their fullest extent (Hoffmann 1980:260). The verse then refers to Hilkiah's finding of the book, which is not only a *Leitmotiv* in the entire Josiah story (Hoffmann 1980:260) but also serves here as part of an *inclusio* framing that story.

The Summary of Josiah's Reign (23:25)

As we have seen, this verse praises Josiah as incomparable in his obedience to the law. There could be no more appropriate summary for Dtr's presentation of Josiah. It is evident that the entire account glorifies Josiah (Lohfink 1963:276; Würthwein 1976:42). Every episode has Josiah and his concern for the law at its heart. Lohfink (1963:269-270) and Hoffmann (1980:191, 259) observe that the account is structured around Josiah's commissions concerning the law. He sends (שלח המלך 22:3) Shaphan to begin the process of repairing the Temple which leads to the finding of the law. He commands (ויצו המלך 22:12) the envoy to inquire of Huldah on his behalf regarding the meaning of the find. He sends (וישלח המלך 23:1) to gather all segments of Judah for the covenant renewal. He commands (ויצו המלך 23:4, 21) the reform measures and the celebration of Passover. It is Josiah and not the high priest, Hilkiah, who directs all of these activities including Temple repairs, covenant renewal, cultic reform, and Passover. All other figures in the account play only auxiliary roles. In 23:3-15, 19-20 the verbs are all in the singular, as though Josiah acted single handedly.

Dtr's presentation of Josiah is obviously idealized. But it is not the portrait of a bygone hero to be used as a model for the present. The account as a whole looks to the future with optimistic expectancy. The covenant with Yahweh has been renewed by all the people (23:1-3). The cult has been thoroughly reformed (23:3-15, 19-23). These measures can only lead to good things. The pessimism of Huldah's oracle is out of place, and the fact that it is so obviously composite makes the conclusion that it has been reworked unavoidable. In light of this optimism it is astonishing to read in 23:26 that Yahweh did not turn from the wrath that Manasseh had provoked. How can this be when Josiah has reformed all of Manasseh's apostacies and has led all the people of Judah to rededicate themselves to the covenant with Yahweh? If Yahweh is angry one expects to find that the people of Judah provoked him after Josiah's death. But this verse is still within Josiah's reign, and the blame is placed on Josiah's predecessor.

This complete change in perspective has suggested to some scholars a change of authorship beginning with 23:26. Others have argued that a redactional shift takes place during or after the account of Hezekiah. The next chapter will gather and evaluate the arguments that have been forwarded in support of various dates for the book of Kings and the DH.

CHAPTER SIX

A TIME FOR EVERYTHING:
DATING THE DEUTERONOMISTIC HISTORY

The most difficult and controversial issue in the study of the DH is that of determining its date, or more precisely, the date of its primary edition (DtrH). The date that one accepts for this level fairly well determines one's understanding of the work's purpose and method of composition. Given the history of scholarly debate, it would be foolish and arrogant to presume that this chapter could resolve the issue once and for all. What I hope to do is to focus on the central questions in the debate and to set the issue in its proper perspective in the context of our present concern with the model of the DH's composition.

It is important to recognize, first of all, that the evidential base for addressing this question is very narrow. The debate has focused almost exclusively on the book of Kings. In part, this is because the end of the DH is allegedly the location where literary, structural, thematic, and theological differences indicative of redactional levels would emerge most clearly (cf. Nelson 1981:27-28). It is where pre-Noth scholarship built the strongest case for a double redaction and where the regnal formulas, which have figured so largely in the discussion, are found. But it is also true that outside of Kings there appears to be very little material in the DH that gives any indication of date.

What follows is a summary and critique of the three settings that are most frequently proposed for the composition of DtrH: the reign of Hezekiah, the reign of Josiah, and the exile.

IN THE REIGN OF HEZEKIAH

The arguments for a date during the reign of Hezekiah depend heavily on the regnal formulas for evidence. The development of these arguments is principally the work of two scholars whose approaches are quite distinct.[1] First,

---

[1] Quite a few scholars have hinted at the existence of a Hezekian DtrH (see Introduction), but only Weippert and Provan have put forth detailed arguments for it. Halpern and Vanderhooft are preparing another case for this date, expanding on Weippert's argumentation. Macy's observations of changes in the regnal formulas, mentioned in the Introduction, merit special mention here. These changes constitute important evidence, but they can all be explained by other means than redactional

Helga Weippert (1972) analyzed the regnal formulas for Northern and Southern kings according to various schema which she detected within them. The first such schema, IS1, was used for Southern kings from Jehoshaphat (1 Kgs 22:43-44) to Ahaz (2 Kgs 16:2b, 4), mostly for kings judged to be righteous. This schema contained the elements עשה הישר בעיני יהוה, a comparison with the king's immediate predecessor, and the statement that the במות were not removed, but the people still sacrificed and burned incense (piel of זבח and קטר, respectively) on them. A second schema, IS2, occurred for evil kings of Judah during the same period. It consisted of the expression מלכי ישראל or בית אחאב + הלך בדרך. A third schema, IN, used for Northern kings from Jehoram (2 Kgs 3:2a, 3) to the end of the kingdom (2 Kgs 17:22) used the phrase עשה הרע בעיני יהוה followed by לא סר מן חטאות ירבעם בן נבט אשר החטיא את ישראל. Weippert assigned these three schemas to a single redactor, R^I who came from Israel but worked in Judah during Hezekiah's reign. The destruction of the North forced him to describe all of its kings as evil under the influence of Jeroboam. He was influenced by Hezekiah's policy of cultic centralization to remark on the handling of the במות by Southern monarchs.[2]

Two additional schemas were the work of a second redactor, R^{II}. The schema IIS was employed for Southern kings before Jehoshaphat and from Hezekiah to Josiah. It used the expression עשה הישר בעיני יהוה but was distinguished from IS1 by its further reference to David either as אב or as עבד. It could also be expanded by the use of הלך אחר or הלך בדרך. The examples of schema IIN do not all share one typical element. This schema is very similar to IN, but there are three features that distinguish it: the expression הלך בדרך, the expansion of חטא + חטאת (hiphil) with חטא (Qal) or עשה (Qal), and the use of כעס, noun or verb. This schema further differs from IS1 in its lack of the phrase לא סר מן. In contrast to R^I, R^{II} stresses the culpability of individual kings, the worship of foreign gods as opposed to non-centralization of the cult, and the comparison of

---

shifts. The absence of the expressions "with his fathers" and "in the city of David" from the death and burial formulas for Judahite kings from Hezekiah on could reflect a change in actual burial practice (Bin-Nun 1968) or in the records used by Dtr as sources. The reference to burial "in the garden of Uzza" for Manasseh (2 Kgs 21:18) and Amon (21:26) may be due to more precise knowledge or be theologically motivated. In any case, the base of evidence is very small. There are only four sets of regnal formulas from Hezekiah to Josiah, and three of those kings, Hezekiah, Manasseh, and Josiah, are exceptional in some way in Kings. The disappearance of the queen mother's name from Chronicles' accession formulas for Judahite kings following Hezekiah, may indicate the availability of different sources for the royal records. Whatever the reason for the change in Chronicles, Kings betrays no editorial change at this point.

[2] Barrick (1974) suggests an important modification to Weippert's analysis by adding 1 Kgs 15:14 and 2 Kgs 18:4 to the level of R^I, which he then sees as running from Asa to Hezekiah, inclusive.

Southern kings to David. R[II] began his work under Josiah but finished during the four months of Jehoahaz's reign.[3]

The flaws in Weippert's analysis have been observed by several scholars (cf. especially Cortese 1975; Provan 1988:39-41, 50-53). The major problems are precisely with her distinction between R[I] and R[II]. First of all, the extent of the document proposed by Weippert is bizarre. Why would one begin a historical account with Jehoshaphat or end it with Ahaz? Ending R[I] with Hezekiah, as Barrick proposed, is an improvement, but it is still hard to believe that Dtr would have begun his history with Asa. More fundamentally, the difference between IS1 and IIS is due more to content than to redactional structure. Asa, Hezekiah, and Josiah are the only kings favorably compared to David because they are the only reforming kings. Weippert herself recognized the difficulty of separating IN from IIN, and Cortese has in fact shown that there is no reason for such a separation. In short, the proposal of a Hezekian DtrH cannot be accepted on the grounds proposed for it by Weippert.[4]

Iain Provan's analysis of the במות theme in Kings (1988) begins with the evaluations of the five Southern kings, Jehoshaphat (1 Kgs 22:44), Joash (2 Kgs 12:4), Amaziah (2 Kgs 14:4), Azariah (2 Kgs 15:4), and Jotham (2 Kgs 15:35). Although they are all pronounced righteous (ישר) the same reservation regarding the במות is expressed for each of them: רק/אך הבמות לא סרו עוד העם מזבחים ומקטרים בבמות. The Northern kings for the same period are declared evil (רע) for not turning

---

[3] Weippert assigned a third schema, used for the final four kings of Judah, to a third redactor, R[III]. Characteristic of this third schema are the expressions עשה הרע בעיני יהוה and ככל אשר עשה.

[4] Lemaire (1986) improves on Weippert's theory in several respects. With Barrick, he proposes that the edition identified by Weippert as R[I] extended to the reign of Hezekiah. In the material that Weippert ascribed to R[II] Lemaire finds two redactors. One worked under Josiah and added the formulas for Manasseh, Amon, and Josiah, a characteristic of which is the concern for the "host of heaven." The earlier redactor wrote ca. 850 B.C.E. and was responsible for the kings from Rehoboam to Jehoshaphat in the South and Jeroboam to Joram in the North. Distinctive to this editor are the references to the cult prostitutes in the formulas for kings of Judah and the statement that the Northern kings walked in "the way of Jeroboam." Lemaire concludes that the DH, through its various propagandistic stages, functioned as a course book for the instruction of history in the royal Judean court. Thus, he answers the criticism regarding the beginning point for Weippert's R[II], although the lack of clear distinction between this R[II] and the material which Weippert assigned to her R[I] remains a problem for Lemaire. His view of the function of the DH and the settings of its levels also has a certain attraction, but he does not address the lack of ancient analogies for this kind of historiographic process. Another problem with his view involves the occurrence of the expressions which he considers characteristic of different editors. The reference to cult prostitutes in 1 Kgs 14:24 is probably secondary, as we have seen. Also, Lemaire is forced to assign 2 Kgs 17:16 to his Josianic editor because of its mention of the "host of heaven," even though it is far from evident (and Lemaire does not explain) what interest his Josianic editor would have had in the 2 Kings 17 peroration.

from the sin of Jeroboam.[5] This indicates that the במות in these texts were considered non-centralized, Yahwistic shrines in contrast to Jeroboam's idolatrous shrines which were linked to Baal worship. The same view of the במות is found in the context of Solomon's (1 Kgs 3:2-15; 11:1-8) and Asa's (1 Kgs 15:11-14) reigns. However, a few passages which are secondary from a literary critical perspective (1 Kgs 12:31-13:33; 14:22-24; 2 Kgs 17:7aβ-17) attest a different understanding of the במות as idolatrous shrines to other gods because they refer to them in the context of idol worship. Provan contends that these two views of the במות betray two levels of redaction in the book of Kings. The במות theme in the first edition reaches its climax in the account of Hezekiah with the notice in 2 Kgs 18:4aα that he removed the במות. After that the perspective on the במות changes. Provan concludes, therefore, that the pre-exilic edition of Kings ended with Hezekiah.

Provan next reexamines the references to David in Kings in order to show that they lead to the same conclusion as the במות theme. The references to the Davidic promise in 1 Kings 15 - 2 Kings 15 are best understood as pre-exilic. But an exilic editor has reinterpreted the references to David by the addition of 1 Kgs 11:9-13, 32, 34b-35, 39 and conditionalized the Davidic promise in 2:4; 8:25; 9:4-5. The David theme climaxes in the first account of the deliverance of Jerusalem under Hezekiah (2 Kgs 18:17-19:9a + 19:36-37). The rest of Kings is an exilic addition. It portrays Josiah as the ideally obedient king, but its description of the kings of Judah as evil (22:13; 23:5, 11, 12) betrays a different perspective than the earlier positive comparisons with David.

As mentioned in the Introduction, Provan actually dates DtrH early in Josiah's reign because of the reference to Sennacherib's death in 2 Kgs 19:37 and the comparison in 2 Kgs 18:5 of Hezekiah to the kings of Judah after him. He sees DtrH as a history of the monarchy from Saul to Hezekiah, comprised essentially of the books of Samuel and Kings, but without Deuteronomy - Joshua or Judges.

Provan's proposal is well argued and intriguing. He certainly puts forward the most cogent case yet for a Hezekian DtrH. Still, there are portions of this case which remain less than entirely persuasive. First, given Provan's assumption that the first editor would have begun his work during the reign of the king who is the focal point of the work (cf. 1988:133), he does not adequately account for the place of Josiah in it. Josiah's reign is the final climax (*Zielpunkt*) of a number of motifs, including the במות and David themes, that tie the DH together, as Hoffmann and Friedman have shown (see below). Provan does not directly address this point. His scheme leaves the resumptive nature of Josiah's portrait, as well as the radical shift in the nature of the material following Josiah, unexplained.

---

[5] Jehoram (2 Kgs 8:18) and Ahaziah (8:27) are exceptions. Both are called evil, but the reason given is imitating the house of Ahab rather than the sin of Jeroboam.

Secondly, the distinction which Provan finds between the במות as provincial Yahwistic shrines and as non-Yahwistic and idolatrous seems oversimplified and somewhat artificial. Provan is no doubt correct that the במות in the formulaic reservation about otherwise righteous kings of Judah (רק הבמות לא סרו) are seen simply as provincial shrines. But the same writer can also use במות to refer specifically to shrines for foreign gods, as in 1 Kgs 11:7-8. Provan (1988:68) agrees that this passage refers to במות for foreign gods, and he also assigns it to his pre-exilic editor.

Two other texts also indicate the ambiguity of the במות references. The first is 2 Kgs 17:29-34a. Provan (1988:81n) dismisses this passage as an addition by his exilic editor, contending that its references to the כהני הבמות and the בתי הבמות depend on 1 Kgs 12:31-13:34, which he assigns to the exilic redactor (1988:78-81).[6] But his literary critical conclusions in 1 Kings 12-13 are questionable. As argued in Chapter Two, Dtr's diatribe against Jeroboam included 12:31-32 + 13:34 where the expressions כהני הבמות and בתי הבמות occur. The story in 13:1-32a was inserted into Dtr's diatribe by *Wiederaufnahme*, which involved the resumption of Dtr's language from 12:31-32. In 2 Kgs 17:29 the fact that the foreign settlers from "every nation" install their own gods in the Northern במות suggests that those במות were understood as (illegitimate) Yahwistic shrines rather than shrines to other deities until they are taken over by foreigners. In fact, vv 32-33 suggest that the במות continued to be used for the worship of Yahweh even after other gods were installed.

Again, 2 Kgs 23:4-14 uses במות in different ways. In Provan's reconstruction this chapter belongs to the second, exilic redactor and the במות here must all be non-Yahwistic shrines. That explanation works in vv 5 and 13 where specific gods are mentioned. But vv 8-9 speak of priests who have the option of continuing to serve at the Temple in Josiah's Jerusalem. Dtr could hardly have seen their במות as non-Yahwistic.

These two passages illustrate the ambiguity inherent in the DH's references to the במות. Both passages, especially 17:29, 33, describe the במות as *loci* for both Yahwistic and non-Yahwistic cultic activity. They make no clear distinction between Yahwistic and non-Yahwistic במות. These passages suggest, therefore, that Provan's distinction between two understandings of the במות is artificial. In fact, outside of the few references to במות specifically for foreign gods they can be understood as non-centralized, Yahwistic shrines. Certainly Dtr views these as offensive and often lists them in the context of other cultic offenses including the worship of other gods. But the fact that they are listed in the context of apostate practices does not constitute a different understanding of their nature.

---

[6] Similarly, Stipp (1987:399-407) assigns 17:24-33(34a) to the same later editor who inserted 1 Kings 13.

Another case where Provan's hypothesis compels him to adopt a questionable literary critical stance is 2 Kgs 18:4. Provan's view that v 4aα, הוא הסיר את הבמות, was the conclusion to the במות theme in DtrH forces him to argue that the rest of the verse is an exilic addition since it refers to idolatry (1988:85-86). The literary evidence for this conclusion, the presence of the <u>waw</u> copulative before שבר, is weak. There is no real reason to assign any of 2 Kgs 18:1-12 to anyone other than Dtr. The verse as it stands fits well with the ambiguous way that the במות are characterized elsewhere in Kings. While the idea of an earlier source behind Samuel and Kings discernible in the במות theme in Kings merits further study a more fruitful direction may be to explore how a single writer, Dtr, may have developed the theme to convey his own ideology.

IN THE REIGN OF JOSIAH

The primary case for a Josianic date for DtrH was built by Cross (1973:274-289) on the basis of the major themes that he found in the book of Kings (see Introduction). An assortment of other kinds of arguments for this date have now been added by scholars who accept Cross's basic thesis.

Thematic Arguments

David

It was von Rad, as we have seen, who first pointed out that the Davidic promise is a major theme in the book of Kings; Noth failed to notice it. Wolff also touched on the theme in his later article (1961). But neither von Rad nor Wolff fully appreciated the theme's gravity for the date and purpose of the DH.[7]

The promise to David is articulated in 2 Samuel 7 and then reiterated throughout 1 - 2 Kings. Certain of the righteous kings of Judah are compared with David (Asa - 1 Kgs 15:11; Amaziah - 1 Kgs 14:3; Hezekiah - 2 Kgs 18:3; Josiah - 2 Kgs 22:2). And in spite of the sins of the wicked kings of Judah, Yahweh continues to leave Judah in the control of the Davidic dynasty on account of David's faithfulness (1 Kgs 11:12, 13, 32, 34, 36; 15:4; 2 Kgs 8:19; 19:34; 20:6).

The reference to this promise in 11:36 is particularly significant. It says that Judah will retain one tribe so that David may always have a fiefdom in Jerusalem (למען היות ניר לדויד עבדי כל הימים לפני בירושלם).

---

[7] Wolff, in fact, hastily dismissed it from his consideration of Dtr's theology, arguing that Dtr always made the promise to David contingent on obedience to the Deuteronomic law so that the Davidic covenant was subordinated to the Mosaic covenant.

Noth himself had trouble with this verse, arguing in *Überlieferungs-geschichtliche Studien* (1943:72n) that the sentence was pre-Dtr because of its use of "always," but in his Kings commentary (1968:261-262) that כל הימים means "a very long time." Many scholars since Noth have found it hard to believe that these words could have originated from a writer who had seen the destruction of Jerusalem and the end of the Davidic monarchy. They see Dtr's stress on the promise to David of an eternal dynasty as a good indication that he wrote before the exile (e.g., Provan 1988:94-95).

The David theme reaches its climax in Josiah's reform (2 Kgs 22:1-23:25a). He is the last king compared to David (22:2). He and Hezekiah are the only kings who are perfectly like David (18:3; 22:2) and who (taking 2 Kgs 20:12-19 as an addition) are entirely without fault. But Josiah's cultic reforms outstrip Hezekiah's. He purges not only Judah, but Israel as well, and finally gets rid of the "sin of Jeroboam" (23:15abα, 19-20; see below).

He cleanses the Temple and reinstates the centralized cult according to the book of the Law. This includes a celebration of the Passover which has been neglected since before the beginning of the monarchy (2 Kgs 23:21-23). The promise to David plus the righteousness of Josiah leave one at 2 Kgs 23:25 expecting only good things for Judah in the future.[8]

The Sin of Jeroboam

A second theme isolated by Cross in Kings is the sin of Jeroboam.[9] Because of Solomon's idolatry, the Northern tribes were torn from the house of David and given to Jeroboam (1 Kgs 11:*29-37). Yahweh offered to build for Jeroboam the same kind of "sure house" that he had built for David if Jeroboam would faithfully obey Yahweh as David had done (11:38). But instead of imitating David, Jeroboam provided a contrast to him. Motivated by the fear of losing his subjects Jeroboam erected idolatrous shrines at Dan and Bethel to rival the Temple in Jerusalem (12:26-30). He also did away

---

[8] Provan (1988:114-131) extends the David theme only so far as Hezekiah, finding its climax in the deliverance of Jerusalem from Sennacherib. He takes all of 2 Kings 21-25 as exilic. But this ignores the literary unevenness of 21:1-15 and 22:15-20 (see below) as well as the overall expectancy of the Josiah account. Provan (1988:28-29) also finds discontinuity between the David theme and its climax in Josiah. In 2 Kings 22-23, he states that the stress is on Josiah's obedience to the law as a means of avoiding wrath, not on the promise to David. There is merit to this observation, but this tension is not limited to the Josiah account. It holds true for the Hezekiah account -- Jerusalem survives Sennacherib's invasion not only because of the promise to David but also because of Hezekiah's trust. It may also be true of the גיר theme throughout Kings -- Judah endures not only because of the promise to David but also because some of its kings are ישר. Furthermore, the Davidic promise and the stress on Josiah's obedience to the law can be seen as complementary rather than contrastive. As a Davidid Josiah brings the blessings of the Davidic promise. Like David he adheres to the law, meriting the rewards it promises for obedience.

[9] Evans (1983) has identified this Deuteronomistic theme as an aspect of the *Unheilsherrscher* motif represented in the depiction of Naram-Sin in Mesopotamian literature.

with the exclusively Levitical priesthood, allowing anyone who wished to become a priest, and he changed the cultic calendar (12:31-32).

Just as later kings of Judah are compared with David, so the influence of Jeroboam continued throughout the history of the Northern kingdom. Each king of Israel in turn was condemned for "walking in the way of Jeroboam, son of Nebat, who caused Israel to sin" (1 Kgs 22:52; cf. 15:30, 34; 16:2, 7, 19, 26; 2 Kgs 3:3; 10:29, 31; 13:2, 6, 11; 14:24; 15:9, 18, 24, 28; 17:22).[10] In other words, the shrines built by Jeroboam continued in use under his successors (2 Kgs 10:29). Because of the infidelity of Jeroboam and his successors, the Northern kingdom was not ruled by a single dynasty as in Judah. Rather, there was a series of dynasties, some so short that they hardly deserve the designation "dynasty." The same gruesome oracle was used to condemn each dynasty in turn: "Whoever of PN's house dies in the city the dogs will eat, and whoever of his dies in the country the birds will eat." The climax to this string of evil dynasties came with the destruction of Samaria in 2 Kgs 17:1-6, 21-23.

But the theme of Jeroboam's sin does not conclude with 2 Kings 17 (against Provan 1988:70-73). It is dealt with once more, in 2 Kgs 23:15-20. Most scholars have found two hands in these verses. Some (Gray 1963:671-673; Kittel 1900:303; Skinner n.d.:422) have seen vv 16-20 as secondary, while others have limited the insertion to vv 16-18 (Benzinger 1899:194). Noth argued that vv 16-18 were the conclusion to the story in 1 Kings 13 which Dtr incorporated into his account of Josiah's reforms at Bethel (Noth 1967:81, 97; cf. Jones 1984:624). There is a clear contradiction between v 15 where the altar at Bethel is destroyed and v 16 where it still exists and Josiah burns bones upon it. This contradiction seems too obvious to allow Noth's view that Dtr incorporated an older tradition into his account. Why would Dtr not have adapted the tradition or his narrative for a better fit?

The purpose of v 16 is to fulfill the prediction of the man of God in 1 Kgs 13:2. It is best regarded as an insertion from the same redactor who added 1 Kings 13:1-32a. Verses 17-18 are part of that insertion since they relate directly to the story in 1 Kings 13. The reference to the Asherah in v 15bβ is also part of the insertion since the Dtr diatribe in 1 Kgs 12:26-32 + 13:34 never mentions an Asherah in connection with Bethel and those texts that do (1 Kgs 14:15; 2 Kgs 17:16) are secondary. Verses 19-20, on the other hand, do not contain a precise fulfillment of 1 Kgs 13:2 as do vv 16-18. They refer to the במות and altars of the cities of Samaria in general and not specifically to Bethel. Their language is the same as that found in Dtr's diatribe (1 Kgs 12:26-32 + 13:34) and the imitation of Dtr's language in the*Wiederaufnahme* of 13:32b-33. Thus, Dtr's account of Josiah's reforms

---

[10] There is no reference to the sin of Jeroboam in the evaluations of Shallum (2 Kgs 15:13-16), perhaps because his reign was so brief (one month) or Hoshea (2 Kgs 17:1-6), perhaps because of its proximity to the explanation in 17:21-23 that Israel's demise was the result of the sin of Jeroboam.

in Bethel and Samaria (2 Kgs 23:15abα, 19-20) has been interrupted by the insertion of 23:15bβ-18 which relate back to the inserted story in 1 Kings 13. Dtr's theme of the sin of Jeroboam, then, reaches its final climax not with the demise of Israel in 2 Kgs 17:21-23 but with the reform of Josiah in 2 Kgs 23:15abα, 19-20. It is Josiah, and only Josiah, who wipes out Jeroboam's במה at Bethel, and it is Josiah who finally removes the במות in the cities of Samaria.

Josiah's reign is also the real climax of the במות motif in the book of Kings. Hezekiah removed the במות, or at least some of them (2 Kgs 18:4) according to Dtr's theme of cultic centralization. But the account of Josiah's reform in 2 Kings 23 details the destruction of different kinds of במות. It mentions the במות ten times -- much more than the account of any other king. In 23:5 Josiah deposes the idol priests who burned incense on the במות to other gods. Verses 8a, 9 describe his demolition of the rural במות in Judah. Verse 13 tells of Josiah destroying the במות built by Solomon. This indicates that 1 Kgs 11:1-8 should be considered part of the same level of writing as 2 Kgs 23:13. Josiah's correction of Solomon's idolatries clears the way for the reunificiation of Israel and Judah, since it was they that caused the division in the first place. Josiah then destroys those במות erected by Jeroboam (v 15abα) and other Northern kings (vv 19-20).[11] Thus, the במות have different origins and uses. The point of the writer, however, is that Josiah destroyed all the במות, whatever their type, in Judah and Israel. His reform brings the במות theme in Kings to its final resolution. The במות are not mentioned for the final four kings of Judah.

Although Israel is no more, the writer's outlook on the future is bright. The Davidid, Josiah, has not only reformed the Jerusalem cult but has annexed territory in the North and done what no other king could do -- destroyed the idolatrous shrine at Bethel.

The Sin of Manasseh
The final chapters of Kings presently place the blame for the exile on Manasseh (2 Kgs 21:1-15; 23:26-27; 24:3-4). His crimes were so bad that Yahweh would not pardon Judah in spite of the reforms of good king Josiah. This subtheme, noticed by Cross (1973:285-287), appears as a kind of afterthought and indicates that Josiah was the focus of Dtr's edition. Before the account reaches Manasseh's reign there is no real hint in Kings that Judah's history is in decline toward inevitable disaster. Most of the kings of Judah to that point receive qualified approval: Asa (1 Kgs 15:11), Jehoshaphat (22:43), Joash (2 Kgs 12:2), Amaziah (14:3), Azariah (15:3), Jotham (15:34), Hezekiah (18:3). When an evil king reigns Jerusalem is

---

[11] The MT's phrase וישרף את הבמה in v 15 should be emended with the LXX[B] to read וישבר את אבניו.

preserved for David's sake: Solomon (1 Kgs 11:12, *31-39), Abijam (15:4), Jehoram (2 Kgs 8:19). The references to the Davidic promise give ample cause for a hope which peaks in Josiah's reforming reign. Now, however, the irrevocable condemnation associated with Manasseh's reign makes the enthusiastic account of Josiah anticlimactic. The pessimism of this Manasseh theme, contrasts sharply with the positive tone of the Hezekiah and Josiah accounts which surround it and suggests that the Manasseh theme is a later addition.

Friedman (1981a:10-11) has revised Cross's observation by contending that 21:1-15 actually contains two parts. The second half (vv 8-15) blames the exile on Manasseh, but the sins detailed in vv 1-7 are all corrected by Josiah.[12] The division between vv 7 and 8 seems clear, the former referring to the Davidic promise of an eternal ניר in Jerusalem, the latter making that promise conditional upon obedience to the law of Moses and implicitly threatening exile for disobedience. According to 21:1-7 Manasseh was guilty of the following offenses: rebuilding the במות (v 3), erecting altars to Baal and making an Asherah (v 3), worshiping the "host of heaven" (v 3), building altars to the "host of heaven" in the Temple (vv 4-5), burning his son as an offering (v 6), practicing soothsaying and divination (עונן ונחש v 6) and consorting with mediums and sorcerers (עשה אוב וידענים v 6).

The account of Josiah's reforms in 2 Kings 23 takes pains to show that Josiah corrected Manasseh's offenses. He demolishes the במות, as discussed above. He burns the cultic vessels for Baal, Asherah, and the host of heaven (23:4) and deposes the priests who burned incense to Baal and the host of heaven (v 5). He burns and pulverizes the Asherah that is in the Temple (v 6) and tears down the sites where accoutrements for the cult of Asherah are manufactured (v 7). He defiles the תפת to prevent child sacrifice (v 10). He breaks down Manasseh's altars in the Temple courtyard (v 12). And he puts away the אבות and ידענים. In short, Josiah undoes all of Manasseh's evil innovations. But the stress on Josiah's correction of Manasseh's misdeeds accords ill with the exilic subtheme which blames Manasseh for the exile. It is easy to see how an exilic writer may have added the Manasseh theme to the Josiah account to explain the sudden, unexpected death of Josiah and the subsequent exile. It is not easy to understand how a single writer could be responsible for both the account of Josiah and the Manasseh theme. Why would a writer go to such lengths to show that Josiah corrected Manasseh's sins and then explain the exile as the result of those sins?

---

[12] 21:2b is widely regarded as a later addition. The expression "host of heaven" is also sometimes taken as an addition, but see O'Brien 1989:230-231.

The Distinctiveness of the Account following Josiah

Changes in tone
Inherent in Cross's thematic arguments is the observation that the account of
events following Josiah differs in several important ways from the previous
narrative in Kings. The pessimism of the last two and one-half chapters of
2 Kings is sudden and striking. In view of the generally optimistic perspective of the previous narrative one would expect the final chapters to contain
a sermon or the like instructing the exiles about repentance in hopes of future restoration. There is none. At least, the reader expects to find a peroration on the fall of Jerusalem along the lines of 2 Kgs 17:7-20 and in accord
with the structural framework of the earlier DH. Again, there is none.

Absence of themes
Certain themes which are present throughout Kings or the DH suddenly
cease in the last two and one-half chapters. Von Rad noticed the important
prophecy - fulfillment scheme which runs through and unites most of the
DH (1958:192-195). Yet, that scheme is missing from the material following Josiah (Friedman 1981a:6; 1981b:174) . No prophet is named in the final two and one-half chapters of the book of Kings. The important themes
of cultic centralization and the Davidic promise, which Von Rad's 1958 article also pointed out in Kings, are completely absent in the material following Josiah (Friedman 1981a:6; 1981b:174); neither David nor the במות is
even mentioned in the last two and one-half chapters.

Formulas
In addition, the evaluation formulas for the final four kings (2 Kgs 23:32,
37; 24:9, 19) are rigidly stereotyped: "PN did what was evil in Yahweh's
eyes according to all that his father(s)/PN did" (Nelson 1981:36-41; cf.
McKenzie, 1985a:184; Weippert, 1972). The only real variation between
them is in the final word of each formula. This rigidity contrasts with the
fluidity of the evaluation formula for the previous kings of Judah.[13] But it
is not just the formulas that are rigid. G. Vanoni (1985) has observed that
the rich variety of cultic terminology noticed by Hoffmann in the book of
Kings decreases dramatically after 2 Kgs 25:24 and that the Deuteronomistic
language in the final two and one-half chapters attests slight changes in
meaning and signs of imitation.

---

[13] It is true, as Provan has stressed (1988:48-49), that a similar tendency to rigidity
is visible in the formulas for the final kings of Israel (2 Kgs 15:9, 18, 24, 28). But
the formulas for the final Northern kings are not as rigid as are the ones for kings of
Judah following Josiah. Provan's *caveat* is well taken and shows that this argument
from the evaluation formulas cannot be regarded as decisive. However, it has some
value as one indication, among several, of a change in authorship after Josiah, and
Provan does not deal with most of the others.

The Chronicler's use of the DH

A final argument for the distinctiveness of the narrative following Josiah is based on the Chronicler's account. As is well known, the Chronicler's primary source for most of his history is the DH. But a significant change in his source seems to occur from the point of Josiah's death on. H. G. M. Williamson has proposed that the Chronicler's *Vorlage* of the account of Josiah's death was a variant Deuteronomistic version of the 2 Kings narrative (1982; 1987). His primary argument is based on the observation that in Josiah's reign alone Chronicles does not follow the order of the DH in the placement of the source citation formula. He also contends that the word of Yahweh in the mouth of Neco is unusual for the Chronicler and that the entire account lacks the Chronicler's characteristic vocabulary but does presuppose DH material. Finally, he points out the unlikelihood that laments for Josiah were still being made in the Chronicler's day as stated in 2 Chr 35:25. Williamson concludes that this change in the Chronicler's *Vorlage* supports the proposal that DtrH ended with Josiah's reign, before his death.[14]

The differences just described in several cases represent "a full-fledged change of perspective and manner of presentation of history" (Friedman, 1981a:7). The convergence of these changes in the account of the final four kings raises a serious difficulty in the minds of many scholars for the theory of a single, exilic author of the DH.

Associations Between Josiah and the Earlier DH

Friedman has added a new category of arguments to the discussion favoring the Josianic composition of the DH (1981a:7-10; 1981b:171-173). He has noticed a series of allusions and expressions that connect Moses, the first hero of the DH, directly with Josiah, the final hero of the work. The best known such connection, of course, is the identification of the book of the law found during Josiah's restoration of the Temple with the Deuteronomic law code. This identification has been widely accepted since the pioneering work of de Wette.[15] Friedman elaborates on this link that outside of

---

[14] Begg's (1987) objections to this proposal have been answered by Williamson's second article (1987). I also argued in 1985a (pp. 181-188) that the Chronicler ceased at this point to use the DH as a source. My criticism of Williamson's proposal at that time was hasty. However, I would continue to assert that Williamson does not take the text critical evidence seriously enough, especially where 2 Chr 35:19-20 and its 1 Esdras parallel are concerned (cf. McKenzie, 1985a:18-22). If DtrH does date from the reign of Josiah it may have been supplemented later with different endings explaining the death of Josiah and recounting the subsequent history of Judah. The current book of Kings attests frequent secondary glossing by different writers (see Chapter Seven). Williamson's contention that the Chronicler's source for the account Josiah's death must have been Deuteronomistic in nature remains uncertain.

Deuteronomy and the story of Josiah's zeal for the law, the book of the law
(ספר התורה) is mentioned in the DH only in three passages in Joshua
(1:8; 8:31, 34; 23:6).[16] In Deuteronomy, Moses commands the Levites to
place the book of the law at the side of the ark (31:36). The lawbook then
ceases to have any real place in Israel's history until its discovery by Hilkiah
in 2 Kgs 22:8.

Other associations between Josiah and Moses involve the occurrence of
the same expressions in the contexts dealing with these two leaders. The
Deuteronomic injunction to love Yahweh with all of one's heart, soul, and
strength (לבב, נפש, מאד Deut 6:5) is found in the context of obedience to
the law. Of all the characters in the DH only Josiah is said to have carried
out that injunction, for he kept the law of Yahweh with all of his heart,
soul, and strength (2 Kgs 23:25).[17]

Josiah is also the only king ever to inquire (דרש) through a priest
(Hilkiah) following the guidelines of Deut 17:8-12. In the same context
(Deut 17:11) is the warning not to "turn aside to the right or the left" from
the information gained through inquiry. The same expression about not
turning to the right or left is used elsewhere in Deuteronomy (5:9; 17:20;
28:14) and in Joshua (1:7; 23:6) as an idiom for complete adherence to the
law. It is found only once more in the Hebrew Bible -- in reference to

---

[15] W.M.L. De Wette, *Dissertatio critica*, 1805. The recent attempt of Hayes and Hooker
(1988:87) to associate Josiah's reforms with an early form of P is idiosyncratic. It is based
on a single argument involving their interpretation of the Passover in 2 Kgs 23:21-23 as
an independent celebration and does not consider the reasons which scholarship has
produced over the past century for associating Josiah's reforms with Deuteronomy.

[16] Similar expressions are found in Josh 24:26 (ספר תורת אלהים) and 2 Kgs 14:6
(ספר תורת משה). Cf. Hoffmann, 1980:202, n. 46.

[17] Friedman also argued that the exact statement "there did not arise like him" (לא
קם כמהו) is used only for Moses and Josiah in the DH, and that Dtr used the expression
to link the two great heroes of his work (1981a:7; 1981b: 71). But similar statements
occur for Solomon (1 Kgs 3:12) and Hezekiah (2 Kgs 18:5), and the one for Hezekiah is
closer to the one for Josiah than is the one for Moses (cf. Hoffmann, 1980:205):

Deut 34:10	2 Kgs 18:5	2 Kgs 23:25
	(b) ואשר	וכמהו
	היו	לא היה
	למיו	למיו
		מלך ...
	(a) ואחריו	ואחריו
לא קם	לא היה	לא קם
נביא עוד בישראל		
כמשה	כמהו	כמהו

In each case the statement of incomparability refers to a separate category: Moses as a
prophet, Solomon for his wisdom and wealth, Hezekiah for his trust in Yahweh, and Josiah
for his observance of the law.

Josiah. He is the only king of whom it is reported that he did not turn aside from the way of David to the right or the left (2 Kgs 22:2).

Moses' command to read the law "in the ears" of all Israel (Deut 31:11) is carried out only by Josiah (2 Kgs 23:2). The only other place where the idiom occurs in the DH (Judg 7:3) the verb קרא means "to call" not "to read."

Josiah smashes to dust Jeroboam's במה where his calf stood (2 Kgs 23:15) just as Moses pulverized Aaron's calf (Deut 8:21). Moreover, when Josiah carried out his religious reforms, burning the Asherah in the Temple (2 Kgs 23:6) and smashing the altars of his ancestors (23:12), he followed the Deuteronomic prescriptions for treating such apostacies (Deut 12:3).

Manasseh erected the Asherah image (2 Kgs 21:7; פסל האשרה) which Josiah subsequently burned (2 Kgs 23:6) following the ordinance for the treatment of images of foreign gods in Deut 7:25. The word פסל is relatively common in Deuteronomy and Judges. But outside of these two books it occurs in the DH in only two other places: the description of the foreigners who repopulated the North in 2 Kgs 17:41 and the account of Manasseh's apostacy in 21:7.

To these points of Friedman's associating Moses and Josiah two observations may be added. First, in the Kings account of Josiah's reign the finding of the book of the law provides the impetus for Josiah's reforms. In Chronicles, by contrast, the order of the narrative is different, and some of Josiah's reforms precede the finding of the book. The fact that the lawbook was found in the process of cleansing the Temple may indicate some historical validity to the Chronicler's order. If so, perhaps Dtr has rearranged the material. In any case, the point in the Kings narrative is that the reform was motivated and directed by the law scroll.

Secondly, in 2 Kgs 23:2-3 Josiah makes a covenant, in which all the people join him, to obey the prescriptions of the book of the law with all their "heart and soul." It is not actually a new covenant which Josiah makes here. According to v 3 it is the covenant (הברית) into which Josiah enters. This is a covenant renewal. The covenant being renewed is, of course, Yahweh's initial covenant with Israel through Moses. That covenant is the subject of Deuteronomy, which is itself the account of a covenant renewal on the plains of Moab (Deut 28:69; 29:9-16). Aside from Moses and Josiah the only other person to mediate such a covenant in the DH is Joshua (Josh 23:25). In all three cases the purpose of the covenant renewal is to affirm obedience to the "statutes and ordinances" of the law. This association on such an important matter is yet one more confirmation of the crucial significance of Josiah in the DH and one more indication that his reform was the original focus of the work.

Another set of associations between the narrative about Josiah and earlier material in the DH has been described by Hoffmann (1980). Hoffmann traces the thread of cultic reform in the DH through the monarchy. He defines cultic reform as changes in the cult which affect the exclusive worship of Yahweh whether they are evaluated positively or negatively by Dtr. He finds in the DH a structure which balances positive reform movements with negative ones.

Hoffmann sees the story of Josiah's reform in 2 Kings 22-23 as the real goal of the DH. This is indicated not only by the fact that the account of Josiah's reform is the longest reform narrative in the DH but also by the gathering and climax in 2 Kings 22-23 of the themes and motifs from the earlier DH. The earlier reform of Joash connects with Josiah not only in the covenant ceremony but also in the details for financing repairs to the Temple, as we have seen. What are given in 2 Kgs 12:5-7 as general procedures for collecting money and seeing that it is used for work on the Temple are fulfilled as reality for specific repairs involving specific individuals in 2 Kgs 22:3-7 (Hoffmann, 1980:192-197).

The DH begins its crescendo, in Hoffmann's view, with Hezekiah. Hezekiah's reforms prepare the reader for Josiah's, and the connection between the two is particularly apparent in the similar statements of incomparability for each of them. Manasseh's negative reforms also prepare for Josiah's by way of contrast, as is clear from 2 Kgs 23:26. But the connections between Josiah and previous reformers are not limited to these. The account of Josiah's reform is so full of allusions and direct references to previous narratives that 2 Kgs 23:4-20 comes close in Hoffmann's view to being just a list of ties with earlier kings: Solomon (23:13; 1 Kgs 11:5,7), Ahaz (23:12; 20:11), Manasseh (23:12; 21:5), Jeroboam (23:15; 1 Kgs 12:32), the kings of Judah in general (23:4, 5, 10, 11, 12), and the kings of Israel (23:19). Elements of Josiah's reform also allude to aspects of previous reforms. These include Temple renovation (22:4-7; 12:5-17), an oracle sparing the hearer (22:15-20; 1 Kgs 14:7-16; 21:21-29), a covenant ceremony (23:1-3; 11:7), cultic centralization (23:8; 18:4), and the removal of the "sin of Jeroboam" (23:15-20; 2 Kgs 17:7-23, 24-33).

The connections cited by Hoffmann are of differing values, but together they make clear the climactic importance of the Josiah account for the DH. As Hoffmann puts it, Josiah's reform is the "final conclusion" (*endgültige Abschluß*, p. 207) for the DH. Josiah is the ideal king who executes the model reform (pp. 205-207).

Friedman and Hoffmann, then, have discovered different aspects of the importance of Josiah for the DH and the many correspondences between his reign and the previous narratives. Hoffmann finds the goal (*Zielpunkt*) of the entire DH in Josiah's reform. Friedman sees the Josiah account as part of an *inclusio* for the DH. For Friedman and many other scholars the special place of Josiah in the DH (along with the other arguments gathered above) indicates that the work once climaxed with Josiah and hence was written in his reign. In this view DtrH was extended beyond Josiah in order to bring the narrative up to date and to try to explain the sudden, overwhelming disaster which came upon the nation (Cross 1973:285).

While the arguments just assembled for a primary Josianic level are formidable, it must be remembered that nothing approaching a consensus regarding the date of DtrH has yet been achieved. There are still many scholars who continue to date the DH in the exile. Among them is Hoffmann, who clearly recognizes the importance of Josiah in the DH. Indeed, as we saw in the Introduction, the view that the DH was written in the exile has made something of a resurgence in recent years. The arguments for an exilic date must be examined.

IN THE EXILE

Since the book of Kings brings the reader into the exile it is the most obvious option for a date for DtrH. However, it is clear that a contemporary treatment of the DH cannot simply assume its exilic date. This is one of the major problems with the work of the "Göttingen school" and Hoffmann. An effective case for an exilic DtrH must counter the points made in favor of an earlier redactional break in the DH narrative. Such a case has recently been put forward by Burke Long (1984:15-21), and it is based on models of composition for the DH, which is a major interest in the present work.

Long points out the very narrow evidential base upon which some scholars (especially Weippert and Dietrich) have constructed their redactional theories. He states that the lack of consensus about the dates of proposed redactional levels and the extent of reworking of disputed passages (e.g., 1 Kings 8; 2 Kings 17) does not inspire confidence in redactional explanations.

Long contends that the idea of a pre-exilic DtrH is founded on a misunderstanding of the Davidic promise. 2 Sam 7:19 simply speaks of David's house "for a long time to come" (לְמֵרָחוֹק). The reference to an "eternal" covenant is the hyperbolic language of royal legitimation "rooted in the literary styles of ancient Near Eastern monarchies" (p. 16). It should not be taken literally "for this assumes a denotative meaning for the language that is inappropriate to the social context in which it functioned" (p. 17).

The arguments for a multiplicity of redactions behind the DH make assumptions which Long believes to be incorrect. Several of these assumptions relate to the conclusion of an ancient prose work. Redactional theories assume that such a work should have a climactic conclusion and that the author should invest the conclusion with a density of content and theme in such a way that the materials earlier in the work relate to the conclusion in anticipation. Redactional theories also assume a common model for recensional development. Additions and insertions are made to an essentially fixed document that is not subject to rewriting. The result is a longer document whose internal inconsistencies are the clues of its redactional reworking.

Long asserts that these assumptions are based on modern cultural preferences and literary tastes without any support from ancient historiography. In particular, while there are examples of the complete rewriting of historical documents (inscriptions) there are no instances of minor adjustments to an "unalterable" text. Long cites Chronicles as an example of the complete rewriting of the "history" of Samuel and Kings. Following Van Seters, he points to the paratactic method of composition attested in Herodotus' *Histo-*

ries as the alternative to source critical and redactional explanations of the DH. The work of Herodotus shows that an ancient history need not have a dramatic arrangement of narratives moving toward a sweeping climax. It may consist simply of separate traditions linked in a variety of ways through what the author perceives as analogous connections, and it may end abruptly, as does the *Histories* , at the end of a chain of events.

SYNTHESIS

Long's points significantly undercut the arguments listed above in favor of a pre-exilic DtrH. The observations about the distinctiveness of the 2 Kings account following Josiah's death and the associations between Josiah and the earlier DH can be accomodated within the model of an exilic history work as envisioned by Van Seters and Long.

However, Long's perspective on the Davidic covenant is unsatisfactory. Dtr no doubt made use of the language of royal legitimation in formulating the passages about the promise to David. But it is difficult to see how Dtr's use of that promise could be understood as other than literal. It is questionable whether כל הימים ever means "for a long time" instead of "forever" (cf. Provan 1988:96). Indeed, the fact that the exilic works (e.g., Chronicles; Jer 33:14-26) (re)interpret the Davidic covenant as grounds for hope suggests that they understand the Davidic promise to be in effect "forever." Dtr's use of the Davidic promise differs significantly from that of a passage like Jer 33:14-26. In 1 Kgs 11:36; 15:4; 2 Kgs 8:19 Dtr gives Yahweh's fidelity to his promise that David would "always" (כל הימים; 2 Kgs 8:19) have a ניר in Jerusalem as the reason for the continuation of the Davidic dynasty in spite of the sin of individual members. This is more than hyperbole. These passages are Dtr's own free compositions. How could he write them if he were in the exile, fully aware that there was no Davidid on the throne, and blamed that circumstance on sinful Manasseh? Here it is Long who must assume that Dtr was bound by a fixed tradition and not free to rewrite. In addition, if Dtr saw the Davidic covenant as grounds for hope in the exile, as in Jer 33:14-26, why did he fail to refer to it as a source of hope in 2 Kings 23-25?

Long also downplays the results of literary criticism in the DH. But one cannot escape the fact that there are numerous examples of minor additions and "adjustments" throughout the History, as well as a handful of lengthy insertions into its text (see Chapters Seven and Conclusions). It is true that there is no consensus when it comes to identifying the precise parameters of the secondary additions. But there is general agreement about their location. Thus, while the extent of the additions in 1 Kings 8 and 2 Kings 17 is debated, most scholars see some part of these chapters as secondary. In fact, it is to texts like these where secondary additions had already been isolated that scholars who accept the double redaction theory have generally looked to find the work of later redactors (see Chapter Seven). Any theory of composition for the DH must account for these additions; they cannot be dismissed.

As stated at the beginning of this chapter, dating DtrH is the most difficult issue associated with the study of the DH, and I could not hope to solve it here. Hence, the following conclusions are tentative. In my view, no satisfactory explanation for the place of the Davidic covenant has yet been offered by those who assign an exilic date to the DtrH, and a pre-exilic date remains likely. Then, the observations about the connections of the Josiah account with the rest of the DH and the distinctiveness of the post-Josiah account point to Josiah's reign as the likely setting of DtrH.

The important place of Hezekiah in Kings is best explained as part of Dtr's ideological and historical construct. This is not to deny that Dtr had sources for this material, but he has completely revised and incorporated them. The examples cited by Long of historical documents that are rewritten by later authors may provide a helpful analogy to the relationship of the Hezekiah and Josiah accounts in the DH.

There is nothing in the historiographic model of composition advocated by Van Seters and Long that demands an exilic date and could not hold true for a Josianic DtrH. Cross's initial postulation placed the bulk of the DH at the time of Josiah. The work would still have been composed paratactically. Its purpose could still have been historiographic. Naturally, its treatment of Josiah, as its sponsor, would have been propagandistic.

While, as Long claims, there may be no parallel in comparative historiography for appending material to a document, there is more than ample parallel for this in biblical literature (e.g., Isaiah). Other additions to the work were made in the course of its transmission. Whether or not these additions were the work of one or more later redactors is a question that remains open and will be investigated in the next chapter.

CHAPTER SEVEN

AND DTR^2 TOO?:
THE QUESTION OF A SECOND, SYSTEMATIC REDACTOR BEHIND THE BOOK OF KINGS

Previous chapters have tentatively dated DtrH to the reign of Josiah and found evidence of numerous later additions to the book of Kings. The coalescence of these two conclusions immediately recalls the double redaction theory formulated by Cross. But this theory also assumes that the later additions in Kings (as well as the other books in the DH) all derive from the same hand, an assumption that has heretofore gone largely unquestioned. The purpose of this chapter is precisely to question that assumption. I shall attempt to point out important differences in theme, tone, and even theology between texts that have been identified as secondary by those who subscribe to the double redaction hypothesis.

THE EXILIC EDITOR IN THE DOUBLE REDACTION THEORY

In his proposal of two redactions behind the DH, Cross assigned several passages, besides the account following Josiah, to his exilic editor, Dtr^2 (1973:287). The retouched passages were concentrated in Kings and were isolated by thematic rather than literary criteria. While Cross gave no criteria for isolating Dtr^2 passages, the following categories for the texts he listed seem to follow his reasoning: 1) the account, beginning with 2 Kgs 23:25b, of Judah from Josiah's death on; 2) 2 Kgs 21:2-15 which blame the exile on Manasseh; 3) passages which conditionalize the Davidic promise (1 Kgs 2:4; 6:11-13; 8:25b; 9:4-5); 4) passages that appear addressed to the exiles or call for their repentance (1 Kgs 8:46-53; 9:6-9); 5) passages that seem to presuppose the exile (2 Kgs 17:19; 20:17-18; 22:15-20). Cross found a lesser concentration of Dtr^2 texts in Deuteronomy and the earlier books in the DH.[1] He believed, therefore, that Dtr^2 had carried out systematic, albeit light-handed revision of the entire DH.

Cross's list of Dtr^2 additions was meant to be preliminary and suggestive. Subsequent studies by those who adhere to his theory have used literary arguments to support his suspicions about these passages and to delimit them

---

[1] Including Deut 4:27-31; 28:36-37, 63-68; 29:27; 30:1-10; Josh 23:11-13, 15-16; 1 Sam 12:25. Cross also described Deut 30:11-20 as suspect.

more precisely (Friedman 1981a; 1981b; Levenson 1975; 1981; 1984; Mayes 1983; McKenzie 1985; Nelson 1981; Peckham 1983; 1985). These studies, by and large, increase the number and extent of Dtr^2 additions. Some of them (especially Levenson, Mayes, Peckham) no longer see Dtr^2's editing as light-handed but credit him with a major role in shaping the DH. The focus of these studies has been on distinguishing suspect passages from their immediate contexts not on showing the common authorship of the suspect passages. A given insertion is essentially assumed to be from Dtr^2. On occasion, similarities of vocabulary or expression are pointed out between secondary texts. But this is hardly a foolproof indication of common authorship, since the imitative use of Deuteronomistic terminology is common, as we have seen.

The remainder of this chapter will analyze the passages in Kings which Cross suspected as being the work of his Dtr^2. I will discuss the evidence, literary critical and otherwise, for the secondary nature of each passage. I do not hope to resolve the debates that have raged over the literary condition of these texts. Rather, the purpose is to show that there are good reasons in most cases for seeing secondary reworking in these texts. Then I will concentrate on the question of common authorship, employing some of the arguments surveyed in the last chapter for the Josianic setting of the DH. Especially important are the themes and the distinctive features of the account following Josiah's death. The last two and one-half chapters of Kings will serve as standard against which to compare the other secondary texts. Their differences in theme have been blurred by the focus on secondary additions in specific texts.

2 KINGS 23:26-25:26

Our first task is to delimit and characterize the addition following Josiah's death at the end of 2 Kings. Cross (1973:286) thought that his Dtr^2 supplement began at 23:25b because the expression "none arose like him after him" came from a writer who had experienced other kings. As we have seen, Friedman (1981a:7-8; 1981b:171) argued that this expression connects Josiah with Moses and must be the work of the Josianic writer. But otherwise he agreed with Cross that Dtr^2's work begins with v 26. Nelson (1981:83-84) saw v 24 as a generalizing afterthought, secondarily attached with וגם, whose list of reforms does not fit with the interests of the Josianic historian. He assigned v 24 to Dtr^2 along with 23:4b-5, 19-20, 25b-30.[2]

As detailed in the previous chapter, vv 4b-5, 24 are best assigned to the Josianic DtrH because they describe Josiah's correction of cultic aberrations

---

[2] Nelson uses the terms "historian" and "exilic editor" to refer to Cross's Dtr^1 and Dtr^2, respectively.

introduced by Manasseh in 21:1-7 (Friedman 1981a:10-11; 1981b:176-177). Also, 23:19-20 are his because they match the Dtr diatribe in 1 Kgs 12:26-32 + 13:34. The incomparability statement for Josiah in v 25a is one of a series of such statements throughout the DH (Moses, Solomon, Hezekiah) and is thus part of DtrH. The formulaic nature of the comparison in v 25b with successors as well as predecessors (cf. 1 Kgs 3:12) does not require that the author of that half verse lived after Josiah. But this sentence does appear tangential after the lengthy v 25a (cf. 2 Kgs 18:5). It is probably a gloss whose purpose is to round out the incomparability statement for Josiah. The addition proper begins with v 26.

Concerning the end of the exilic addition, Friedman (1981a:35-36; 1981b:189-191) has suggested that 2 Kgs 25:27-30 are a later addition. He points to the large chronological gap between the events in v 26 and those in vv 27-30 as support for this idea. If he is correct, the account in 2 Kgs 23:26-25:26 was added to the DH shortly after 586, but no later than 562 B.C.E. when Jehoiachin was elevated in the Babylonian court.

The last chapter pointed out some distinctive features of these last two and one-half chapters *vis-à-vis* the earlier material in Kings. But there are others, especially relating to theme and tone. Cross (1973:288) referred to the Dtr^2 addition as a laconic report. It lacks the creative flavor of the previous Dtr narrative. It contains only three brief theological remarks (23:26-27; 24:3-4, 20). The first two of these blame Manasseh for the exile, which appears to be the main point of this addition aside from updating the history. Conspicuously absent from this section is any consideration of the meaning of the exile for the Davidic covenant. Even Jehoiachin's elevation in 25:27-30 is recounted as laconically as the rest of the material in the section. If these three final verses contain any hope that Yahweh will restore Judah for the sake of David it is very faint indeed. Thus, the addition reveals no hope for the future. There is no attempt to explain whether Yahweh's covenant with David is still in effect. Even in 23:27 where the Temple and Jerusalem are specifically rejected there is no mention of Yahweh's chosen king. This writer avoids any discussion of the relationship of the exile to the Davidic dynasty except to say that it is Manasseh's fault.

1 KINGS 2:4; 8:25; 9:4-5

Cross assigned these verses to his Dtr^2 because they add a condition of obedience to Yahweh's promise to David. But Friedman (1981a:12-13; 1981b:175-176) and Nelson (1981:100-105) have each argued that it is occupying the "throne of Israel" and not the existence of Judah or the Davidic dynasty that is made conditional in these verses. Since these warnings are limited to the reign of Solomon, the throne of Israel may be a reference to control of the Northern kingdom. If so, these passages do not presuppose the end of the Davidic dynasty and were in DtrH. This conclusion would also explain the lack of any clear sign of literary retouching in any of these three passages.

Even if 1 Kgs 2:4; 8:25; and 9:4-5 could be shown to be secondary, thematic considerations suggest that they were not the work of the writer who
added 2 Kgs 23:26-25:26. If these three texts are additions, they reflect a
writer's concern to conditionalize the Davidic promise. But that concern is
not reflected in the last two and one half chapters of Kings. There, where
one expects to find a conditionalizing of the promise to David or some other
explanation of it in light of the end of the kingdom, the writer has instead
chosen to ignore it completely.

1 KINGS 6:11-14

These verses interrupt the description of Solomon's work on the Temple.
The repetition of the statement, "Solomon built the house and completed
it," in vv 9 and 14 marks the passage as an insertion (Friedman 1981a:24).
Verses 11-14 are lacking in the Old Greek and Lucianic witnesses, further
suggesting that they are a late, secondary gloss.

Because of the condition attached to the Davidic covenant Cross assigned
vv 11-13 to Dtr^2. Thus, these verses may seem to fit with the passages just
treated which add a condition to the Davidic promise. The difference is that
in 6:11-14 it is Yahweh's dwelling with Israel and not the throne of Israel
which is conditioned upon the king's obedience. The possibility that
"Israel" in v 13 refers only to the Northern kingdom is ruled out by the
casus pendens about the Temple in v 12 (הזה אשר אתה בנה הבית).

The insertion in 1 Kgs 6:11-14 was probably not the work of the author
who added the account after Josiah. Since those last two and one-half chapters nowhere mention the promise to David it is not likely that their author
would have taken the trouble to insert the conditionalizing in 1 Kgs 6:11-
14. Friedman (1981a:24n) notes that v 13 uses P language about Yahweh
dwelling (שכן) among the Israelites. These verses, then, may be a late
Priestly insertion, but they are not from the author of 2 Kgs 23:26-25:26.

1 KINGS 8

Scholars have commonly viewed the final section or two of Solomon's
prayer as a later addition. Along these lines, Cross took vv 46-53 as Dtr^2's
work and Nelson (1981:69-73) vv 44-51. However, other members of the
"Cross school" are at opposite extremes when it comes to identifying the extent of Dtr^2's contribution to this text. J. Levenson (1981) identified all of
8:23-53, 56-61 as Dtr^2 material. He argued that 8:23-53 was a unit and that
vv 56-61 were probably the continuation of Solomon's third petition in vv
44-53. Hence, since one part of the prayer was late (vv 44-53) the entire
prayer had to be late.

What stamps vv 44-53 as Exilic is not that it speaks of exile, but that it strives to awaken in its audience the hope for restoration, secured through repentance. This unambiguous hope of return makes sense only within a community already in exile. (1981:157-158)

R. E. Friedman, on the other hand, did not include any of 1 Kings 8 among his list of Dtr[2] passages. He apparently agreed with the older arguments of J. Gray (1963:197-213) for the pre-exilic setting of this passage. According to Gray, the prayer presumes a settled, agricultural *Sitz im Leben* as shown by its references to disasters such as drought (vv 35-36) and famine (vv 37-40), which would be concerns of people in the land. The hope that Israel will attract foreigners (vv 41-43) also implies that they are still in their homeland. Friedman (1981a:21) adds a theological argument. He states that this chapter constantly refers to the Temple as the channel of blessing for the people. Even in v 48 where the people are imagined in exile, the Temple is envisioned as still standing. Whenever they find themselves in trouble they are to pray toward the Temple so that Yahweh will hear and respond. In Friedman's view, an exilic writer, who knows that the Temple has been destroyed, would hardly make it so important for Israel's access to God.

Whatever the extent of secondary material in Solomon's prayer, there are significant contrasts in theme between it and the addition in 2 Kgs 23:26-25:26. Friedman is certainly correct that the prayer describes the Temple as a channel of blessing, and this doctrine is seriously undermined by the detailed description of the Temple's destruction in 2 Kings 25. It is difficult to see how the same person could have written both. The hope expressed through Solomon that Yahweh will hear the people's prayers directed to him through the Temple contrasts with the lack of hope offered by the end of Kings. This contrast is especially strong if one sees in 8:44-53 an "unambiguous hope of return" (Levenson 1981:158). The final chapters of Kings offer nothing comparable in eloquence or expectation. The difference between the two texts is particularly marked by their respective uses of the verb סלח. Solomon continually asks that Yahweh pardon his people and act on their behalf (8:30, 34, 36, 39, 50). In v 34 this means restoration. Yet the whole point of the addition in 2 Kgs 23:26-25:26 is that Manasseh's sins so angered Yahweh that he refused to pardon (ולא אבה יהוה לסלח 24:4).

There is also a major contrast in the styles of the passages or the involvement of the author in each. The addition at the end of 2 Kings simply reports the events from Josiah's death to the exile with very little editorial comment. But the prayer in 1 Kings 8 is a Dtr composition which sometimes contains passionate pleading to Yahweh on the grounds that the people are his heritage (נחלה) The author of 2 Kgs 23:26-25:26 never mentions the possibility of praying for mercy or relief. Nor does he hint that there is any cause for hope in Israel's status as God's elect. If anything, that status appears to be repudiated in 23:27. It is difficult to reconcile all of these tensions, and the more of 1 Kings 8 that one dates to the exile the harder it is to ascribe it and 2 Kgs 23:26-25:26 to the same writer.

1 KINGS 9:6-9

There are several indications of a different hand beginning in v 6. One is the change of addressee. Verses 1-5 address Solomon (singular verbs), while vv 6-9 suddenly turn to the people (plurals). Another is the shift in topic. The discussion of the Davidic covenant in vv 1-5 does not prepare for the possibility of idolatry in vv 6-9.

The references to the destruction of the Temple indicate an exilic date for the addition, a position long held by most commentators (cf. Nelson 1981:73). Also, the question and answer scheme of the passers-by in vv 7-9 is a common motif in exilic literature.[3]

The focus in 9:6-9 on the destruction of the Temple fits well with the account of that event in 2 Kgs 23:26-25:26, and the finality of the destruction implied in 1 Kgs 9:6-9 accords with the lack of hope in the addition at the end of 2 Kings. But the theological explanations for Judah's demise differ. In 1 Kgs 9:6-9 the people shoulder the blame for the exile because of their idolatry. In the last two and one-half chapters of Kings Manasseh is to blame for the disaster. Since 1 Kgs 9:6-9 are set long before Manasseh's reign one would not expect him to be blamed directly. But the glossator might have indicated primary responsibility on the part of the king, especially after vv 1-5 address Solomon. Instead, he shifts the audience to the people in v 6. If the glosses in 1 Kgs 9:6-9 come from the author of 2 Kgs 23:26-25:26, why did he condemn the people for the exile in Solomon's reign but then hold Manasseh almost exclusively responsible in the few, brief, explanatory remarks that he includes in his final addition?

2 KINGS 17:7-41

Cross (1973:287) assigned only v 19 to Dtr[2]. Friedman (1981a:24-25) suspected vv 19 and 35-40a of being Dtr[2]'s. Nelson (1981:53-69) took most of the chapter (vv 7-20, 23b, 24-40) as the work of Dtr[2].

This chapter has long challenged literary critics, and their conclusions about it have varied widely. Before Noth many scholars saw vv 18, 21-23 as the work of the pre-exilic redactor of Kings and vv 7-17, 19-20 as the exilic editor's contribution (cf. Nelson 1981:55). Noth reversed this position

---

[3] The best extra-biblical parallels actually come from before 587 (cf. Hillers 1964:65, 76-77; Moran 1963:83-84; Weinfeld 1972:114-115), although most biblical examples of are exilic (Lev 26:32; Deut 29:23-26; Jer 18:16; 19:7-9; 25:18; 29:18; 49:17-18; 50:13; Ezek 26:16; 27:35-36; 28:19; Mic 6:16; Zeph 2:13-15; Lam 2:16; 2 Chr 29:8. Nelson (1981:74-76) argues that 1 Kgs 9:6-9 is dependent on Deut 29:23-26, which is itself exilic.

by contending that vv 7-20 were a summary statement by Dtr and one of the texts in his structural framework for the DH. Noth also took vv 21-23 as a secondary addition which viewed Israel's separation from Judah as its major sin (1967:85, n. 4).

Recent scholars have returned, in some respects, to the pre-Noth opinion about this chapter. Nelson (1981:55) and Provan (1988:71) agree that the original apodosis of the circumstantial clause in v 7a comes in v 18a, so that the rest of vv 7-17 are a unit which has been inserted. The unit sketches the history of the whole nation of Israel from the exodus as a long tradition of sin which eventually led to Israel's demise. Provan takes vv 18b-20 as an even later addition, while Nelson sees vv 19-20 as the work of the same hand responsible for vv 7-18. Verses 19-20 make it clear that Judah's guilt is as great as Israel's (cf. v 13) and carry the sketch of Israel's sinful history down into the Babylonian exile when Yahweh rejected "all the seed of Israel."

Verses 7-18 (20) offer a different explanation for Israel's demise than vv 21-23. In the former it is the idolatry of the people that brought about the end of the nation; in the latter, the sin of Jeroboam. The second explanation, the sin of Jeroboam, is the culmination of one of Dtr's main themes in the book of Kings. Every king of Israel except for Shallum and Hoshea is accused of perpetuating the sins of Jeroboam. Israel's fall is his fault. The explanation in vv 7-20 is a later, exilic insertion. The sins in its catalogue occur in the accounts of the kings of Judah (especially from Ahaz on) but are not characteristic for kings of Israel. The author of these verses has culled his list from Dtr's accounts of kings from Ahaz to Josiah and applied these sins to Israel (cf. Viviano 1987:552).

In the second half of the chapter vv 24-28 have generally been regarded as drawn from an older source with vv 29-34a being an expansion on them. Again, there is no consensus as to the party responsible for the expansion (cf. Nelson 1981:63-64). Nelson ascribes the preservation and addition of source material in vv 24-34a to Dtr[2], but his case is not strong. He contends that the uncentralized worship in these verses would not have been left uncriticized by the pre-exilic historian. But Nelson's exilic editor also opposed non-centralization. More to the point, why would either the historian or the exilic editor be offended by the non-centralized worship described in these verses? This account is concerned not with Israelites but with foreigners who were settled in Israel. One might also argue that the condemnation in the account is implicit. The foreigners continue or increase the cultic perversion already in Bethel. In short, there is nothing in vv 24-34a which mandates an exilic date.[4] Verses 24-28 are likely from one of Dtr's sources, and vv 29-34a are his commentary. The references in v 32 to priests of the

---

[4] The reference to the Samarians (הַשֹּׁמְרֹנִים) in v 29 is often taken as an indication of an exilic hand. But as Nelson (1981:63) points out, the term is possible any time after the formation of the Assyrian province in the late eighth century.

במות from among the people and shrines of the במות are reminiscent of Dtr's diatribe against Jeroboam in 1 Kgs 12:26-32 + 13:34.

Verses 34b-40 are usually seen as a late anti-Samaritan polemic, and v 41 has been associated with vv 29-34a or regarded as a late, independent gloss. The tension between vv 33a and 34b concerning whether or not the Samarians fear Yahweh is obvious. The phrase, "they did/do according to their former custom" in vv 34a and 40b marks the extent of the insertion. Verses 34b-40 suddenly change the topic of the narrative from foreigners brought in by the Assyrians back to the Israelites whose apostasy is described in vv 7-20. Their language is similar to vv 7-20, and they may come from the same writer. In sum, the exilic additions in 2 Kings 17 include vv 7-20, 34b-40, and probably v 41.

These verses, and indeed all of 2 Kings 17, stand in strong thematic tension with the addition in 2 Kgs 23:26-25:26. The latter displays no interest at all in the North. More important is Cross's point about the lack of any summation comparable to 2 Kgs 17:7-20 in the final two and one half chapters of Kings. It is difficult to believe that an exilic editor would give a lengthy peroration on the fall of Israel but say virtually nothing by way of summary for Judah. How can Dtr² be "less articulate" (Cross 1973:288) than the historian in 2 Kgs 23:26-25:26 but more expressive in 2 Kgs 17:7-20, 34b-40? It is also noteworthy that the two additions offer different explanations for the ultimate demise of the nation. As noted, 2 Kgs 23:26-25:26 lay the blame for the exile at Manasseh's feet. But 2 Kgs 17:7-20 ascribe the fall of Israel and Judah to a penchant for sin throughout their history. These differences in theme and tone suggest strongly that these two texts are not the work of the same author but should be assigned to different hands.

2 KINGS 20:12-19

My reasons for seeing these verses as an exilic addition to the Hezekiah account were detailed in Chapter Five. They presuppose the sacking of the palace in the context of the exile which is described in 2 Kgs 24:13. However, this latter verse is widely regarded as an insertion into the account of the exile in the final chapters of Kings (Nelson 1981:88). The connection between 20:12-19 and 24:13-14 is not precise. For example, 24:14 does not refer to the Judean princes becoming סריסים in the Babylon palace. Hence, it is not clear that 20:12-19 and 24:13-14 are from the same writer. But even if they are, they cannot be from the author of 23:26-25:26 as a whole, since 24:13-14 have been inserted into that addition.

2 KINGS 21:1-16

Cross gave vv 2-15 to Dtr² and Nelson vv 3c-15, although the latter found remnants from the pre-exilic historian in vv 4a, 6a, and 7a (1981:65-69). Friedman (1981a:10-12; 1981b:176-178) limited Dtr²'s work to vv 8-15.

As Friedman observes, the sins of Manasseh in vv 1-7 -- the במות that he built (v 3), the Asherah that he erected (vv 3, 7), and his altars to the "host of heaven" (vv 3, 5) -- are all corrected by Josiah. Here Hoffmann's observation that Dtr balanced good and evil cultic "reformers" is especially valuable. All the misdeeds of Manasseh are undone by Josiah. But this cannot be the work of the author of 2 Kgs 23:26-25:26. To introduce sins of Manasseh which he knew to be corrected later by Josiah would only undermine his explanation that Manasseh's sins brought about the exile. The name theology in v 4 (cf. 1 Kgs 11:36; 14:21) and the allusion to the Davidic promise in v 7 reflect themes of DtrH (cf. Friedman 1981a: 10-11; 1981b:177-178). The presence of the word "forever" (לעולם) in v 7 also indicates the pre-exilic nature of that verse.

Verse 8 recalls 1 Kgs 9:6 in the way that it shifts the topic from the king to the people and from the Davidic covenant to disobedience. It adds a condition to the Davidic promise, but its real concern seems to be continued occupation of the land. It makes the nation's stay in the land contingent on the people's obedience to the law of Moses. In the light of Manasseh's seduction of the people to do evil (v 9) v 8 implies that exile is immanent. Verses 10-15 make the threat explicit. They contain an oracle announcing the destruction of Jerusalem and the exile of the people (vv 12-15) because of Manasseh's sins (v 11). The oracle is credited to "[Yahweh's] servants the prophets" without mentioning any specific prophet. The weakness of this phrase is also apparent when one realizes that there are no other prophecies about Manasseh's sins. Since 2 Kgs 21:8-15 and 2 Kgs 23:26-25:26 both blame the exile on Manasseh, a subtheme which I have concluded was tacked on to DtrH, both passages likely came from the same writer.[5]

2 KINGS 22:15-20

In Chapter Five I concluded that Huldah's oracle preserves traces of a pre-exilic, individual, weal oracle, but it has been completely revised into an oracle of doom against Judah. The present oracle's view of disaster is incompatable with Josiah's zeal for reform in the surrounding narrative. The function of the original oracle was evidently to provide the incentive for Josiah to carry out the reform in chapter 23. The present oracle gives no clue that the punishment it forecasts can be averted.

The pessimism of Huldah's oracle and its lack of reference to the Davidic promise are similarities to the last two and one-half chapters of Kings. But the two texts differ in their respective reasons for condemnation. Manasseh's

---

[5] 21:16 probably derives from the same writer, since the only other reference to Manasseh's shedding of blood is in 24:4 (cf. McKenzie 1985:192). It is possible, though less likely in my opinion, that v 16 is an even later addition as O'Brien (1989:234) has argued.

wickedness is the cause of the exile in 23:26-25:26. If the same author revised Huldah's oracle, one would expect some mention of Manasseh's sins as the cause for the exile. Yet, as it stands, the oracle cites the disobedience of the people, especially their idolatry, as the reason for the approaching destruction of Judah.

CONCLUSIONS

I have tried to show that there are significant differences in theme and tone between the addition in 2 Kgs 23:26-25:26 and other passages throughout Kings which Cross and others assigned to the same author (Dtr[2]). As a result, 2 Kgs 21:8-15 (16) is the only text in our survey which can be unreservedly assigned to the writer who updated the book of Kings by adding its last two and one-half chapters. At the most, this writer may have retouched one or two other passages toward the end of Kings (e.g., the Huldah oracle). This indicates that the writer of 2 Kgs 23:26-25:26, whom Cross called Dtr[2], had a lighter influence in Kings than even Cross proposed. Basically, he appended to the DH the account of Judah's history from Josiah's death on and revised the account of Manasseh's reign to fit his explanation for the exile. He apparently did not systematically revise the earlier material in Kings.

Two further points in this regard are germane. First, it is questionable whether the passages outside of Kings which Cross assigned to Dtr[2] (Deut 4:27-31; 28:36-37, 63-68; 29:27; 30:1-10; Josh 23:11-13, 15-16; 1 Sam 12:25) could have the same author as 2 Kgs 23:26-25:26. Subsequent studies have reaffirmed and augmented the assignment of these texts to Dtr[2] (Mayes 1983:22-39; Friedman 1981a:13-23; 1981b:178-185; Levenson 1975). A thorough analysis of those texts must await another occasion, but it is worth observing here that the hope held out by some of them clearly contrasts with the pessimism and hopelessness of the last two and one half chapters of Kings. For example, Deut 4:27-31 speak of the people being removed from their land and scattered among the nations (vv 27-28), the text goes on to say that the exiles will find Yahweh if they will seek him with all their "heart and soul" (v 29). They will return to Yahweh and obey him (v 30), and he in turn will not forsake or destroy them (v 31) because of loyalty to his covenant. All of this goes far beyond the laconic ending in the last two and one half chapters of 2 Kings, which foresee no hope beyond exile. The contrast is even sharper in the case of Deut 30:1-10 which has a highly optimistic description of the prosperity and good fortune that Israel will enjoy after Yahweh has restored them from exile. It is hard to imagine that the same writer who paints such a bleak picture of the fate of Judah in 2 Kgs 23:26-25:26 could be responsible for these two passages in Deuteronomy or that he would have painted such a rosy picture of the exiles' fortunes at the beginning of the History only to leave the reader in the depths of despair at the end.

Secondly, previous chapters have isolated other additions in Kings that were not on Cross's list, but there is no reason to believe that these all came from the hand. Some texts, such as 1 Kgs 14:22-24 bear affinities with texts in Cross's list, such as 2 Kgs 17:7-20. But others, including the additions in the Ahijah oracle (1 Kgs 11:29-30), the Shemaiah oracle (12:21-24), and probably 1 Kgs 14:15 and 16:7, appear to be independent glosses. Still others, the tale in 1 Kgs 12:33-13:32a, the prophetic stories in 1 Kings 20 and 22, the Elijah and Elisha legends, and the "anti-Jezebel" retouchings in 1 Kgs 21:1-16, 23; 2 Kgs 9:7b, 10a, 36b reflect an entirely different set of interests from the other additions that have been identified.

It is not my intention to multiply redactors behind the DH. Indeed, I have agreed with Noth's premise that the DH was an original unit. However, Noth recognized that Dtr's original History had frequently been supplemented by later additions. Yet Noth made no attempt to group those additions by author; he did not see them as the work of successive redactional levels. Again, I believe that Noth was on the right track. The quantity and disparate nature of the secondary additions to the book of Kings have not been adequately explained by the redactional theories that have been offered for the composition of the DH; the situation is more complex. In a work the length of the DH, passed on for generations, it is hardly surprising to find many different secondary additions.

NEW AND IMPROVED:
SUGGESTED REVISIONS OF NOTH'S THEORY OF THE DH

MODEL OF COMPOSITION

Noth's model for the composition of the DH -- that it was originally and fundamentally the creation of a single writer who was both author and editor -- was brilliant and remains unsurpassed in its explanation of the DH. Subsequent revisions of Noth's model along the lines of a redactional theories have served only to obscure his real insight. Noth recognized but did not elaborate on the comparative evidence from Greek historiography for his understanding of Dtr's method of composition. Van Seters's study of history writing in the Ancient Near Eastern and Mediterranean worlds has buttressed Noth's model by detailing the parallel method of composition used by Greek historians.

This model has important implications for various issues that have arisen in the study of the DH. This kind of history writing involved the organization of narratives by parataxis and ring composition. Dtr both edited narratives from sources available to him and wrote narratives with little or no source material. Exactly how much of his work was editing and how much invention is a matter for further study. Van Seters's denials of the existence of the source documents outlined by previous scholarship may be extreme, but he is certainly correct that the line drawn by scholars between Dtr's sources and Dtr's own narrative is often artificial and always difficult to defend. In any case, it must be remembered that the DH is Dtr's work, and his influence on it is pervasive, in the selection and use of written sources and in creating narratives without them.

The foregoing study of Kings suggests that Van Seters is correct to claim a larger portion of DtrH for Dtr than is fashionable. Its organization around the series of prophetic oracles comes from Dtr, as do the oracles themselves. The speeches and prayers in Kings, for the most part, are his as well. His account of Hezekiah is an excellent example of these techniques, as we have seen. The net result was a new work of history. There is no evidence for any kind of earlier running history, prophetic or otherwise, beneath Dtr's composition in the book of Kings. The order and content of the book are Dtr's product.

ADDITIONS TO DTR'S WORK

One of the principal causes for the disagreement over the composition of the DH is the presence of so much secondary (post-Dtr) material within it. Noth recognized that there were later additions throughout the DH, some of which were quite long. His list of secondary passages included (but was not limited to) Deut 4:41-43; 32-34 (except for 34:1, 4, 5-6); Joshua 13-22; Judg 1:1-2:5; 13-21. More recent treatments of the books in the DH have argued for even more extensive sections of secondary material, including the entire book of the law in Deuteronomy (Levenson 1975; cf. Clifford 1982:2) and the "Succession Narrative" in 1 Samuel.[1] However one views these latest proposals for secondary material, the postulation of several rather lengthy additions to Dtr's work in the book of Kings is clearly in good company. Perhaps the clearest examples of extensive secondary additions are the Elijah and Elisha collections and 1 Kings 20; 22. The Elisha legends have not been completely incorporated into Dtr's history. While it is not inconceivable that Dtr simply assimilated the Elijah stories, as Noth argued, the absence of Dtr's remarks within them contrasts with his use of sources elsewhere and is a strong indication that he did not edit them.

I have contended that the various additions to Kings do not all come from the same writer and that the book as a whole does not reflect a complete systematic redaction. Again, the same thing appears to be true about the DH at large, i.e., the later additions to various books within the DH are not from the same writer. For instance, the current shape of Deuteronomy 32 and 34 as well as Joshua 13-22 are often assigned to P.[2] But the other long additions in the books of Judges, Samuel, and Kings were not made by P, and there is no reason to suppose that they were all added by the same hand. They appear to reflect different interests and were probably made a different times. Traditions about various periods in Israel's history were simply added to those sections of the DH that dealt with those periods. There are also numerous briefer additions throughout the DH. As argued in the previous chapter, it is difficult to assign all of these additions in Kings, much less in the entire DH, to one or two specific redactors. It is hardly surprising that a work the length of the DH would be supplemented by independent narrative

---

[1] Cf. Van Seters (1983a:249-291). Van Seters delineates the "Succession Narrative" as 2 Sam 2:8-4:12; 9-20; 1Kings 1-2. The recent works by Mayes (1983) and O'Brien (1989) are very helpful for their overviews of the contents of DtrH and how Noth's view of it has been altered by the subsequent work in specific books.

[2] Cf. Boling (1982:58-67) and Van Seters (1983a:331-337). Noth 's attempt to deny P influence in Joshua 13-22 have not convinced many scholars. Van Seters (1983a:337-343) has also argued for assigning Judg 1:1-2:5 to P.

additions and glosses reflecting changes in historical circumstances over the course of its centuries of transmission.

This view of the DH may seem more fragmentary than those that posit multiple redactions. But it retains the essential unity of the DH while providing an explanation for its inner tensions, and it avoids the difficulty of trying to find ties that bind the diversity of secondary texts to one another. It is closer to Noth's initial model of composition. Most of all, in my opinion, this view of the DH best fits the evidence.

DATE

The date of the DH is perhaps the most difficult and controversial aspect of the scholarly discussion on the DH. Noth naturally assumed that the DH was written in the exile because that is where 2 Kings presently ends. But Noth did not take adequate notice of the significance of the Davidic covenant in the book of Kings. Yahweh's promise that David would always have a dominion (נִיר) in Jerusalem and a descendant on its throne fits best before the exile. That theme and others reach their climax in the reign of Josiah. There are further connections between the account of Josiah's reign and earlier material in the DH that point to 2 Kings 22-23 as the culmination of the History.

Even more significant is the sharp contrast between the account from Josiah's death on and the previous material in Kings. The explanation of the exile as Manasseh's fault in 2 Kgs 23:26-25:26 does not fit Dtr's program. Judah survived through previous evil kings because of David's faithfulness. The account of Josiah's reign leaves one with an optimistic outlook for the future. It makes no sense for Dtr to present such a positive picture of Josiah correcting all of Manasseh's wrongs and then to blame Manasseh for the exile. One expects Dtr to explain either that Josiah's efforts were ineffective in curbing the practices begun by Manasseh or that the sins of the people following Josiah brought on the exile. He does neither. The Manasseh theme, therefore, appears tacked on.

Attempts to retain the exilic date for DH and to explain away these two themes (David and Manasseh) have not been very convincing, and it seems better to date the initial composition of the DH to the reign of Josiah, recognizing that the evidence for this decision comes entirely from Kings. The last two and one-half chapters of Kings are a later addition to the DH, similar to additions in earlier parts of it. This same writer retouched the Manasseh account in 2 Kings 21. But the evidence for his having revised earlier portions of Kings is meager.

PURPOSE

The question of the DH's purpose has always been treated in conjunction with its date. Thus, Noth dated the DH in the exile and understood it as a work designed to explain that catastrophe. But the length of the DH and the stress on the Davidic covenant in Kings make this understanding unlikely. Cross also associated the DH's purpose with its date. He saw the original History as a program for the reform of Josiah. But the length of the DH again makes this view doubtful, as Lohfink and Provan have suggested. If the DH was designed as propaganda for Josiah why does it include the books of Deuteronomy through Judges? Why is it not limited to the history of the monarchy?

The question of the DH's purpose is actually one of genre. The books of Deuteronomy through Kings is called the Deuteronomistic History, yet only recently has Van Seters explored the implications of its designation as history writing. His comparisons with Greek historiography suggest that Dtr's purpose in the research (*historie*) and writing of his History was to render an account to Israel of its national traditions. Dtr may have been motivated by a contemporary search for national identity on the heels of the demise of the Northern kingdom. Such a work written during Josiah's reign would inevitably contain propagandistic elements favorable to him.

In short, then, my study has led me to conclude that the book of Kings in the Deuteronomistic History was written by a single author/editor during Josiah's reign in order to recount the history of Israel and Judah. Over the years the work was glossed and supplemented in a number of places, including an updated account of the history of Judah after Josiah's death (2 Kgs 23:26-25:26). But the History as a whole was not systematically edited after its initial composition.

SUMMARY OF DTR'S HISTORY AND POST-DTR ADDITIONS

The following two tables illustrate the passages that were in Dtr's History and were added later according to my analysis. Dtr probably had sources for much of the material in his History (contrast 1 Kgs 16:1-4 where he apparently had no narrative about Jehu's encounter with Baasha). However, he has so thoroughly rewritten them that in most cases it is impossible to isolate the pre-Dtr level with any degree of certainty. An exception is the account of Jehu's revolt in 2 Kings 9-10 where Dtr's frequent additions are fairly evident so that the older story can be isolated. The references given are those in the MT. It should also be recalled that the MT's chronology and placement of certain passages in Kings is secondary *vis-à-vis* the Old Greek.

DtrH

1 Kings
[1-2?]§
3-10 (minus 6:11-14; 8:50b-53(?); 9:6-9)
11:1-8, 14-43 (minus glosses in vv 32, 33 [plural verbs], 34bα, 38bβ-39)
12:1-20 (minus vv 2-3a and Jeroboam's name in v 12), 25-32 + 13:34
14:1-31 (minus vv 22b-24)
15:1-34
16:1-34 (minus v 7)
21:1-16*, 17-24 (minus "who is in Samaria" in v 18a and vv 19b, 23)
22:39-53

2 Kings
1:1, 17aβ-18
3:1-3
8:16-29 (minus glosses in vv 28b-29aβ
9-10* (minus 9:7b, 10a, 14-15a, 27bβ-28, 36b; 10:18-28)
11-12
13:1-13, 22-25
14-16
17:1-7aα, 18a, 21-34a
18-20 (minus 20:12-19)
21:1-7, 17-26
22:1-20 (minus glossing of Huldah's oracle in vv 15-20)
23:1-15, 19-25a

---

§ Contrast McCarter (1981) and Van Seters (1983a:249-291).

Post Dtr Additions

<u>1 Kings</u>
6:11-14
8:50b-53?[§]
9:6-9
glosses in 11:32, 33 [plural verbs], 34bα, 38bβ-39
12:2-3a and Jeroboam's name in 12:12
12:33
13:1-33
14:22b-24
16:7
17-19
20
glossing of 21:1-16*, 18a, 19b, 23
22:1-38

<u>2 Kings</u>
1:2-17aα
2
3:4-27
4-7
8:1-15
glossing in 8:28b-29aβ; 9:7b, 10a, 14-15a, 27bβ-28, 36b
10:18-28
13:14-21
17:7aβ-17, 18b-20
17:34b-41
20:12-19
glossing in 22:15-20
23:16-18
23:25b-25:26
25:27-30

[§] Cf. McKenzie (1985a:204-205)

BIBLIOGRAPHY

The abbreviations used here follow those in the *Journal of Biblical Literature* 95 (1976) 339-346 with the following exceptions.

AJBI   *Annual of the Japanese Biblical Institute*
BIOSCS   *Bulletin of the International Organization of Septuagint and Cognate Studies*
BN   *Biblische Notizen*
EI   *Eretz Israel*
FOTL   Forms of Old Testament Literature
Fs.   Festschrift
HAR   *Hebrew Annual Review*
JSOT   *Journal for the Study of the Old Testament*
JSOTSup Supplements to *JSOT*
KHC   Kurzer Hand-Commentar zum Alten Testament
NCB   New Century Bible
OBO   Orbis Biblicus et Orientalis
OTL   Old Testament Library
Sem   *Semeia*
SVT   Supplements to *Vetus Testamentum*
UCNES   University of California Near Eastern Studies
WBC   Word Biblical Commentary
WuD   *Wort und Dienst*

Aberbach, M. and Smolar, L.
    1969   Jeroboam's Rise to Power. *JBL* 88:69-72.
Ackroyd, P. R.
    1985   The Historical Literature. Pp. 97-323 in *The Hebrew Bible and Its Modern Interpreters*, ed. D. A. Knight and G. M. Tucker. Philadelphia.
Albright, W. F.
    1969   Palestinian Inscriptions. Pp. 320-322 in *ANET*.
Alcaina Canosa, C.
    1964   Panorama crítico del ciclo de Eliseo. *Est Bib* 23:217-234.
    1970   Vocación de Eliseo (1 Re 19, 19-21). *Est Bib* 29:137-151.
    1972   Eliseo sucede a Elias (2 Re 2, 1-18). *Est Bib* 31:321-336.
Alfrink, B.
    1943   L'expression אבותיו עם שכב. *OTS* 2:106-118.
Alt, A..
    1912   Die literarische Herkunft von 1 Reg 19, 19-21. *ZAW* 32:123-125.
    1953   Das Gottesurteil auf dem Karmel. Pp. 135-149 in *Kleine Schriften zur Geschichte des Volkes Israel* I. Munich.
Anderson, F. I.
    1966   The Socio-Juridical Background of the Naboth Incident. *JBL* 85:46-57.
Ap-Thomas, D. R.
    1960   Elijah on Mount Carmel. *PEQ* 92:146-155.
Baena, G.
    1973   Carácter literario de 2 Reyes 17, 7-23. *Est Bib* 32:357-384.
    1974a   Carácter literario de 2 Reyes 17, 7-23. *Est Bib* 33:5-24.
    1974b   Carácter literario de 2 Reyes 17, 13.35-39. *Est Bib* 33:157-179.
Baltzer, K.
    1965   Naboths Weinberg (1. Kön. 21). Der Konflikt zwischen israelitischem und kanaanaischem Bodenrecht. *WuD* 8:73-88.

Barré, L. M.
    1988   *The Rhetoric of Political Persuasion. The Narrative Artistry and Political Intentions of 2 Kings 9-11.* CBQMS 20. Washington, DC.
Barrick, W. B.
    1974   On the "Removal of the 'High Places" in 1 - 2 Kings. *Bib* 55:257-259.
Barth, K.
    1957   *Church Dogmatics.* Vol. II. *The Doctrine of God.* Part 2. Trans. G. W. Bromiley, *et al.* Edinburgh.
Begg, C. T.
    1985   Unifying Factors in 2 Kings 1.2-17a. *JSOT* 32:75-86.
    1986a   2 Kings 20:12-19 as an Element of the Deuteronomistic History. *CBQ* 48: 27-38.
    1986b   The Significance of Jehoiachin's Release: A New Proposal. *JSOT* 36:49-56.
    1987   The Death of Josiah in Chronicles: Another View. *VT* 37:1-8.
Benzinger, I.
    1899   *Die Bücher der Könige.* KHC IX. Leipzig.
Bic, M.
    1954   *maštîn beqir. VT* 4:411-416.
Bin-Nun, S.
    1968   Formulas from Royal Records of Israel and of Judah. *VT* 18:414-432.
Biran, A.
    1980   Tell Dan -- Five Years Later. *BA* 43:168-182.
Birch, B. C.
    1976   *The Rise of the Israelite Monarchy: The Growth and Development of 1 Samuel 7-15.* SBLDS 27. Missoula, MT.
Bohlen, R.
    1978   *Der Fall Nabot. Form, Hintergrund und Werdegang einer alttestamentlichen Erzählung (1 Kön 21).* Trier Theologische Studien 35. Trier.
Boling, R. G.
    1975   *Judges.* AB 6A. New York: Doubleday.
    1982   *Joshua.* AB 6. New York: Doubleday.
Braulik, G.
    1971   Spuren einer Neubearbeitung des deuteronomistischen Geschichtswerkes in 1 Kön 8:52-53. 59-60. *Bib* 52:20-33.
Bronner, L.
    1968   *The Stories of Elijah and Elisha as Polemics against Baal Worship.* Pretoria Oriental Series 6. Leiden.
Brooke, A. E., McLean, N., and Thackeray, H. St. J.
    1930   *The Old Testament in Greek.* Vol. II. *The Later Historical Books.* Part II. *I and II Kings.* Cambridge.
Buccellati, G.
    1967   *Cities and Nations of Ancient Syria.* Rome.
Burney, C. F.
    1903   *Notes on the Hebrew Text of the Books of Kings.* Oxford.
Butler, T. C.
    1983   *Joshua.* WBC 7. Waco, TX.
Campbell, A. F.
    1986   *Of Prophets and Kings: A Ninth-Century Document (1 Samuel 1 - 2 Kings 10).* CBQMS 17. Washington, DC.
Carlson, R. A.
    1969   Élie à l'Horeb. *VT* 19:416-439.
    1970   Élisée - le successeur d'Élie. *VT* 20:385-405.
Carroll, R. P.
    1969   The Elijah - Elisha Sagas: Some Remarks on Prophetic Succession in Ancient Israel. *VT* 19:400-415.

Childs, B. S.
    1963   A Study of the Formula 'Until this Day.' *JBL* 82:279-292.
    1967   *Isaiah and the Assyrian Crisis.* SBT 2/3. Naperville, II.
Clements, R. E.
    1980   *Isaiah and the Deliverance of Jerusalem. A Study of the Interpretation of Prophecy in the Old Testament.* JSOTSup 13. Sheffield.
Cilfford, R.
    1982   *Deuteronomy.* Old Testament Message. Wilmington, DE.
Coats, G. W.
    1972   The Wilderness Itinerary. *CBQ* 34:135-152.
Cogan, M.
    1974   *Imperialism and Religion: Assyria, Judah and Israel in the Eighth and Seventh Centuries B.C.E.* SBLMS 19. Missoula, MT.
Cohen, M. A.
    1975   In all Fairness to Ahab. A Socio-Political Consideration of the Ahab-Elijah Controversy. *EI* 12:87*-94*.
Cohn, R. L.
    1982   The Literary Logic of 1 Kings 17-19. *JBL* 101:333-350.
    1985   Literary Technique in the Jeroboam Narrative. *ZAW* 97:23-35.
Cortese, E.
    1975   Lo schema deuteronomistico per i re di Giuda e d'Israele. *Bib* 56:37-52.
Crenshaw, J. L.
    1971   *Prophetic Conflict.* Berlin.
Cross, F. M.
    1973   *Canaanite Myth and Hebrew Epic.* Cambridge, MA.
Cross, F. M. and Freedman, D. N.
    1952   *Early Hebrew Orthography.* New Haven.
    1953   Josiah's Revolt Against Assyria. *JNES* 12:56-58.
Damrosch, David.
    1987   *The Narrative Covenant. Transformations of Genre in the Growth of Biblical Literature.* New York.
Debus, J.
    1967   *Die Sünde Jeroboams.* FRLANT 93. Göttingen.
De Vries, S. J.
    1978   *Prophet Against Prophet: The Role of the Micaiah Narrative (1 Kings 22) in the Development of Early Prophetic Tradition.* Grand Rapids, MI.
Dietrich, W.
    1972   *Prophetie und Geschichte.* FRLANT 108. Göttingen.
    1977   Josia und das Gesetzbuch (2 Reg. xxii). *VT* 27:13-35.
Dion, P.
    1988   Sennacherib's Expedition to Palestine. *Bulletin of the Canadian Society of Biblical Studies.* 48:3-25
Dozeman, T. B.
    1982   The Way of the Man of God from Judah: True and False Prophecy in the Pre-Deuteronomic Legend of 1 Kings 13. *CBQ* 44:379-393.
    1979   The 'Troubler' of Israel: *'kr* in I Kings 18:17-18. *Studia Biblica et Theologica* 9:81-93.
Eissfeldt, O.
    1953   *Der Gott Karmel .* Berlin.
    1967a   'Bist du Elia, so bin ich Isebel' (1 Kon xix 2). Pp. 65-70 in *Hebräische Wortforschung.* Fs. W. Baumgartner. SVT 16. Leiden.
    1967b   Die Komposition von 1. Reg 16, 29 - 2. Reg 13, 25. Pp. 49-58 in *Das Ferne und nahe Wort.* Fs. L. Rost. BZAW 105. Berlin.
    1968   Amos und Jona in volkstümlicher Überlieferung. Pp. 137-142 in *Kleine Schriften* IV. Tübingen.

Evans, C. D.
1983   Naram-Sin and Jeroboam: The Archetypal *Unheilsherrscher* in Mesopotamian and Biblical Historiography. Pp. 97-125 in *Scripture in Context II. More Essays on the Comparative Method.* Winona Lake, IN.
1988   Did Ahijah Designate Jeroboam Ben Nebat King? Or Why Ten and One Do Not Equal Twelve. Unpublished paper read at 1988 SBL annual meeting, Nov. 20,1988, Chicago.

Fewell, D. N.
1986   Sennacherib's Defeat: Words at War in 2 Kings 18.13-19.37. *JSOT* 34:79-90.

Fohrer, G.
1957   *Elia.* ATANT 31. Zurich.
1968   *Introduction to the Old Testament,* initiated by E. Sellin. Trans. D. E. Green. Nashville.

Freedman, D. N.
1976   The Deuteronomic History. Pp. 226-228 in *IDBSup,* ed. Keith Crim, *et al.* Nashville.

Friedman, R. E.
1981a   *The Exile and Biblical Narrative.* HSM 22. Chico, CA.
1981b   From Egypt to Egypt: Dtr¹ and Dtr². Pp. 167-192 in *Traditions in Transformation.* Fs. F. M. Cross. ed. B. Halpern and J. Levenson. Winona Lake, IN.

Galling, K.
1956   Der Ehrenname Elisas und die Entrückung Elias *ZTK* 53:129-148.
1953   Der Gott Karmel und die Achtung der fremden Götter. Pp. 105-125 in *Geschichte und Altes Testament.* Fs. A. Alt. Tübingen.

Gonçalves, F. J.
1986   *L'expédition de Sennachérib en Palestine dans la littérature hébraïque ancienne.* EBib n. s. 7. Paris.

Gooding, D. W.
1964   Ahab according to the Septuagint. *ZAW* 76:269-280.
1965a   The Septuagint's Version of Solomon's Misconduct. *VT* 15:325-335.
1965b   Pedantic Timetabling in the 3rd Book of Reigns. *VT* 15:153-166.
1967a   The Septuagint's Rival Versions of Jeroboam's Rise to Power. *VT* 17:173-189.
1967b   Temple Specifications: A Dispute in Logical Arrangement between the MT and the LXX. *VT* 17:143-172.
1968   The Shimei Duplicate and its Satellite. Miscellanies in 3 Reigns II. *JSS* 13:76-92.
1969a   Problems of Text and Midrash in the Third Book of Reigns. *Textus* 7:1-29.
1969b   Text-Sequence and Translation-Revision in 3 Reigns IX 10 - X 33. *VT* 19:448-463.
1972   Jeroboam's Rise to Power: A Rejoinder. *JBL* 91:529-533.
1976   *Relics of Ancient Exegesis: A Study of the Miscellanies in 3 Reigns 2 .* SOTSMS 4. Cambridge.

Gordon, C. H.
1963   Review of M. Noth, *History of Israel* , 2nd ed. *JSS* 8:88-95.

Gordon, R. P.
1975   The Second Septuagint Account of Jeroboam: History or Midrash. *VT* 25:368-393.

Gray, J.
1963   *I & II Kings.* OTL. Philadelphia.

Grønbaek, J. H.
1965   Benjamin und Juda. Erwägungen zu 1 Kön xii 21-24. *VT* 15:421-436.

Gross, W.

1979   Lying Prophet and Disobedient Man of God in 1 Kings 13: Role Analysis as an Instrument of Theological Interpretation of an OT Narrative Text. *Sem* 15:97-135.

Gunkel, H.

1906   *Elias, Jahve und Baal.* Religionsgeschichtliche Volksbucher II. 8. Tübingen.

1913   Der Revolution des Jehu. *Deutsche Rundshau.* 40:289-308.

1922   *Geschichten von Elisa erklart.* Meisterwerke hebräischer Erzählungskunst I. Berlin.

Hallevy, R.

1958   Man of God. *JNES* 17:237-244.

Halpern, B.

1976   Levitic Participation in the Reform Cult of Jeroboam I. *JBL* 95:31-42.

1981   Sacred History and Ideology: Chronicles' Thematic Structure - Indications of an Earlier Source. Pp. 35-54 in *The Creation of Sacred Literature: Composition and Redaction of the Biblical Text*, ed. R. E. Friedman. UCNES 22. Berkeley, CA.

1988   *The First Historians. The Hebrew Bible and History.* San Francisco.

Hanson, P.

1968   The Song of Heshbon and David's *Nir. HTR* 61: 297-320.

Haran, M.

1982   Book-Scrolls in Israel in Pre-Exilic Times. *JJS* 33:161-173.

1984   More Concerning Book-Scrolls in Pre-Exilic Times. *JJS* 35:84-85.

1985   Book-Size and the Device of Catch-Lines in the Biblical Canon. *JJS* 36:1-11.

Hayes, J. H. and Hooker, P. K.

1988   *A New Chronology for the Kings of Israel and Judah and Its Implications for Biblical History and Literature.* Atlanta.

Heider, G. C.

1985   *The Cult of Molek: A Reassessment .* JSOTSup 43. Sheffield: JSOT.

Hentschel, E.

1977   *Die Elijaerzählungen.* Erfurter Theologische Studien 33. Leipzig.

Hillers, D. R.

1964   *Treaty Curses and the Old Testament Prophets .* BibOr15. Rome.

Hobbs, T. R.

1985   *2 Kings .* WBC 13. Waco, TX.

Hoffmann, H.-D.

1980   *Reform und Reformen.* ATANT 66. Zurich.

Holder, J.

1988   The Presuppositions, Accusations, and Threats of 1 Kings 14:1-18," *JBL* 107:27-38.

Hollenstein, H.

1977   Literarkritische Erwägungen zum Bericht über die Reformmassnahmen Josias 2 Kön. XXIII 4ff. *VT* 27:321-336.

Hölscher, G.

1923   Das Buch der Könige, seine Quellen und seine Redaktion. Pp. 158-213. *EUCHARISTERION.* Fs. H. Gunkel. FRLANT NF 19. I. Göttingen.

Ishida, T.

1975   The House of Ahab. *IEJ* 25:135-137.

1977   *The Royal Dynasties in Ancient Israel. A Study on the Formation and Development of Royal-Dynastic Ideology.* BZAW 142. Berlin.

Jepsen, A.

1934   *Nabi. Soziologische Studien zur alttestamentlichen Literatur und Religions geschichte.* Munich.

1942   Israel und Damaskus. *AfO* 14:153-172.

1956   *Die Quellen des Königsbuches.* 2nd ed. Halle.

1959   Die Reform des Josia. Pp. 97-108 in *Festschrift Friedrich Baumgärtel zum 70. Geburtstag 14. Januar 1958*. Erlanger Forschungen 10. Erlangen.
1970   Ahabs Buße. Ein kleiner Beitrag zur Methode literarhistorischer Einordnung. Pp. 145-155 in *Archäologie und Altes Testament*. Festschrift K. Galling, eds. A. Kuschke and E. Kutsch. Tübingen.
1971a   Elia und das Gottesurteil. Pp. 291-306 in *Near Eastern Studies in Honor of William Foxwell Albright*, ed. H. Goedicke. Baltimore.
1971b   Gottesmann und Prophet. Pp. 171-182 in *Probleme biblischer Theologie*. Fs. G. von Rad, ed. H. W. Wolff. Munich.

Jones, G. H.
1984   *1 - 2 Kings*. New Century Bible. 2 vols. Grand Rapids.

Keller, C. A.
1960   Wer was Elia? *TZ* 16:298-313.

Kenyon, K.
1971   *Royal Cities of the Old Testament*. London.

Kittel, R.
1900   *Die Bücher der Könige*. HAT. Göttingen.

Klein, R. W.
1970   Jeroboam's Rise to Power. *JBL* 89:217-218.
1973   Once More: Jeroboam's Rise to Power. *JBL* 92:582-584.
1983   *1 Samuel*. WBC 10. Waco, TX.

Klopfenstein, M. A.
1966   1. Könige 13. Pp. 639-672 in *Parresia*. Fs. Karl Barth, eds. E. Busch, J. Fangmeier, and M. Geiger. Zurich.

Knierim, R. P.
1968   The Messianic Concept in the First Book of Samuel. Pp. 20-51 in *Jesus and the Historian*. Fs. E. C. Colwell, ed. F. T. Trotter. Philadelphia.

Kuhl, C.
1952   Die "Wiederaufnahme" - ein literarkritisches Prinzip? *ZAW* 64:1-11.

van Leeuwen, C.
1965   Sanchérib devant Jérusalem. *OTS* 14:245-272.

Lemaire, A.
1986   Vers L'histoire de la Rédaction des Livres des Rois. *ZAW* 98:221-236.

Lemke, W. E.
1976   The Way of Obedience: 1 Kings 13 and the Structure of the Deuteronomistic History. Pp. 301-326 in *Magnalia Dei: The Mighty Acts of God*. Fs. G. E. Wright, ed. F. M. Cross, W. E. Lemke, and P. D. Miller. Garden City, NY.

Levenson, J.
1975   Who Inserted the Book of the Torah? *HTR* 68:203-233.
1981   From Temple to Synagogue: 1 Kings 8. Pp. 143-166 in *Traditions in Transformation*. Fs. F. M. Cross, ed. B. Halpern and J. Levenson. Winona Lake, IN.
1982   The Paronomasia of Solomon's Seventh Petition. *HAR* 6:135-138.
1984   The Last Four Verses in Kings. *JBL* 103:353-361.

Levin, C
1982   *Der Sturtz der Königin Atalja. Ein Kapitel zur Geschichte Judas im 9. Jahrhundert v. Chr.* SBS 105. Stuttgart.
1984   Joschija im deuteronomistischen Geschichtswerk. *ZAW* 96:351.

Liddell, H. G. and Scott, R.
1968   *A Greek - English Lexicon*. Oxford.

Lohfink, N.
1963   Die Bundesurkunde des Königs Josias (Eine Frage an die Deuteronomiums forschung). *Bib* 44:261-288.
1981   Kerygmata des Deuteronomistischen Geschichtswerks. Pp. 87-100 in *Die Botschaft und die Boten*. Fs. H. W. Wolff, eds. J. Jeremias and L. Perlitt. Neukirchen-Vluyn.

1985 Zur neueren Diskussion über 2 Kön 22-23. Pp. 24-48 in *Das Deuteronomium Entstehung, Gestalt, und Botschaft*, ed. N. Lohfink. Leuven.

Long, B. O.
1969 Etymological Etiology and the Dt. Historian. *CBQ* 31:35-41.
1984 *I Kings with an Introduction to Historical Literature*. FOTL 9. Grand Rapids, MI.

Macy, H. R.
1975 The Sources of the Books of Chronicles: A Reassessment. Unpublished Ph.D. thesis. Harvard University.

Mayes, A. D. H.
1983 *The Story of Israel Between Settlement and Exile. A Redactional Study of the Deuteronomistic History*. London.
1985 *Judges*. Old Testament Guides. Sheffield.

McCarter, P. K.
1980a The Apology of David. *JBL* 99:489-504.
1980b *I Samuel*. AB 8. Garden City, NY.
1981 "Plots, True or False" The Succession Narrative as Court Apologetic. *Int* 35: 355-367.
1984 *II Samuel*. AB 9. Garden City, NY.
1986 *Textual Criticism (Recovering the Text of the Hebrew Bible)* Philadelphia.

McCarthy, D. J.
1965 II Samuel 7 and the Structure of the Deuteronomistic History. *JBL* 84:131-134.
1974 The Wrath of Yahweh and the Structural Unity of the Deuteronomistic History. Pp. 97-110 in *Essays in Old Testament Ethics*, eds. J. L. Crenshaw and J. T. Willis. New York.

McKay, J. W.
1973 *Religion in Judah under the Assyrians*. SBT 2/23. London.

McKenzie, S. L.
1985a *The Chronicler's Use of the Deuteronomistic History*. HSM 33. Atlanta.
1985b The Prophetic History in Kings. *HAR* 10:203-220.
1986 1 Kings 8: A Sample Study into the Texts of Kings Used by the Chronicler and Translated by the Old Greek. *BIOSCS* 19:15-34
1987 The Source for Jeroboam's Role at Shechem (1 Kgs 11:43 - 12:3, 12, 20). *JBL* 106:297-300.

Merendino, R. P.
1981 Kleinere Beiträge zu 2 Kön 22:3-23:15. Eine Erwiderung. *BZ* 25:249-255.

Meyer, R.
1959 Auffallender Erzählungsstil in einem angeblischen Auszug aus der " Chronik der Könige von Juda." Pp. 114-123 in *Festschrift Friedrich Baumgärtel zum 70. Geburtstag 14. Januar 1958*. Erlanger Forschungen 10. Erlangen.

Miller, J. M.
1966 The Elisha Cycle and the Accounts of the Omride Wars. *JBL* 85:441-454.
1967a Another Look at the Chronology of the Early Divided Monarchy. *JBL* 86: 276-288.
1967b The Fall of the House of Ahab. *VT* 17:307-324.
1968 The Rest of the Acts of Jehoahaz (I Kings 20. 22, 1-38). *ZAW* 80:337-342.
1974 The Moabite Stone as a Memorial Stela. *PEQ* 106:9-18.

Minokami, Y.
1989 *Die Revolution des Jehu*. Göttinger Theologische Arbeiten 38. Göttingen.

Mittmann, S.
1975 *Deuteronomium 1,1-6,3 literarkritisch und traditionsgeschichtlich untersucht*. BZAW 139. Berlin.

Montgomery, J. A.
1951 *The Books of Kings*, ed. H. S. Gehman. ICC. Edinburgh.

Moore, G. F.
1895 *A Critical and Exegetical Commentary on Judges*. ICC. New York.

Moran, W. L.
  1963   The Ancient Near Eastern Background of the Love of God in Deuteronomy.
              CBQ   25:77-87.
Morgenstern, J.
  1941   *Amos Studies* I. Cincinnati
Napier, B. D.
  1959   The Omrides of Jezreel. *VT*   9:366-378.
Nelson, R. D.
  1981   *The Double Redaction of the Deuteronomistic History.* JSOTSup 18.
              Sheffield.
  1987   *First and Second Kings.* Interpretation.
Nicholson, E. W.
  1967   *Deuteronomy and Tradition.* Philadelphia.
Nielsen, E.
  1954   *Oral Tradition. A Modern Problem in Old Testament Introduction.* SBT 11.
              London.
  1959   *Shechem. A Traditio-Historical Investigation.* Copenhagen:.
von Nordheim, E.
  1978   Ein Prophet kündigt sein Amt auf (Elia am Horeb). *Bib*   59:153-173.
Noth, M.
  1953   *Das Buch Josua.* HAT 7. 2nd ed. Tübingen.
  1967   *Überlieferungsgeschichtliche Studien: die sammelnden und bearbeitenden*
              Geschichtswerke im Alten Testament. 3rd ed. Tübingen.
  1968   *Könige.* I. *I Könige 1-16.* BKAT 9/1. Neukirchen-Vluyn.
  1981   *The Deuteronomistic History.* Translation of part 1 of Noth, 1967.
              JSOTSup 15. Sheffield.
Nübel, H.-U.
  1959   *Davids Aufstieg in der frühe israelitischer Geschichtsschreibung.* Bonn.
O'Brien, M. A.
  1989   *The Deuteronomistic History Hypothesis: A Reassessment.*   OBO 92.
              Göttingen:.
Oestreicher, T.
  1923   *Das Deuteronomische Grundgesetz.* BFCT 27, 4. Gütersloh.
Olmstead, A. T.
  1913   Source Study and the Biblical Text. *AJSL*   30:1-35.
Olyan, S.
  1984   *Haššalom* : Some Literary Considerations of 2 Kgs 9. *CBQ*   46:652-658.
Oppenheim, A. L.
  1969   Babylonian and Assyrian Historical Texts. Pp. 265-317 in *ANET.*
Parzen, H.
  1940   The Prophets and the Omri Dynasty. *HTR*   33:69-96.
Peake, A. S.
  1927   Elijah and Jezebel. The Conflict with the Tyrian Baal. *BJRL*   11:296-321.
Peckham, B.
  1983   The Composition of Deuteronomy 5-11. Pp. 217-240 in *The Word of the*
              Lord Shall Go Forth. Fs. D. N. Freedman, eds. C. L. Meyers and M.
              O'Connor. Winona Lake, IN.
  1985   *The Composition of the Deuteronomistic History.* HSM 35. Atlanta.
Pitard, W. T.
  1987   *Ancient Damascus: A Historical Study of the Syrian City-State from Earliest*
              Times until its Fall to the Assyrians in 732 B.C.E. Winona Lake, IN.
Plein, I.
  1966   Erwägungen zur Überlieferung von I Reg 11:26-14:20. *ZAW*   78:8-24.

Polzin, R.
   1980   *Moses and the Deuteronomist. A Literary Study of the Deuteronomic
             History.* Part 1. New York
   1989   *Samuel and the Deuteronomist. A Literary Study of the Deuteronomic
             History.* Part 2. San Francisco.
Pratt, R.
   1982   The Incomparability of Hezekiah in the Deuteronomistic History.
             Unpublished paper, presented to OT 200 seminar, 2 December 1982.
Priest, J.
   1980   Huldah's Oracle. *VT* 30:366-368.
Provan, I.
   1988   *Hezekiah and the Book of Kings.* BZAW 172. Berlin/New York.
von Rad, G.
   1957   *Theologie des Alten Testaments* 1. *Die Theologie des geschichtlichen
             Überlieferungen Israels.* Munich.
   1958   Die deuteronomistische Geschichtstheologie in den Königsbüchern. Pp.
             189-204 in *Gesammelte Studien zum Alten Testament* I. TBü 8. Munich.
Radjawane, A. N.
   1973   Das deuteronomistische Geschichtswerk. Ein Forschungsbericht. *TRu* NF
             38:177-216.
Rehm, M.
   1970   *Die Bücher der Könige.* Echter Bibel. Altes Testament. II. Wurzberg.
Richter, W.
   1964   *Die Bearbeitungen des "Retterbuches" in der deuteronomischen Epoche.*
             Bonn.
   1966   *Traditionsgeschichtliche Untersuchungen zum Richterbuch.* 2nd ed. Bonn.
Roberts, J. J. M.
   1984   Review of *Juda unter Assur in der Sargonidenzeit* by H. Spieckermann. *CBQ*
             46:328-330.
Rofé, A.
   1970   The Classification of the Prophetical Stories. *JBL* 89:427-440.
   1974   Classes in the Prophetical Stories: Didactic Legenda and Parable. Pp. 143-
             164 in *Studies in Prophecy.* SVT 26. Leiden.
   1988a   *The Prophetical Stories.* Jerusalem.
   1988b   The Vineyard of Naboth: The Origin and Message of the Story. *VT* 38:89-
             104.
Rose, M.
   1977   Bemerkungen zum historischen Fundament des Josia-Bildes in 2 Reg 22f.
             ZAW 89:50-63.
Rosenbaum, J.
   1979   Hezekiah's Reform and the Deuteronomistic Tradition. *HTR* 72:24-43.
Rowley, H. H.
   1963   Elijah on Mount Carmel. Pp. 37-65 in *Men of God. Studies in Old Testament
             History and Prophecy.* London/New York.
Rust, H.
   1938   Elia am Horeb. 1 Kön 19. *EvT* 5:201-215.
Sanda, A.
   1911, 1912 *Die Bücher der Könige.* EHAT 9. Munich
Saydon, P.
   1952   The Meaning of the Expression עצור ועזוב. *VT* 2:371-374.
Schlauri, I.
   1973   Wolfgang Richters Beitrag zur Redaktionsgeschichte des Richterbuches.
             Bib 54:367-403.
Schmitt, A.
   1977   Die Totenerweckung in 1 Kön. XVII 17-24. *VT* 27:454-474.

BIBLIOGRAPHY

Schmitt, H.-C.
  1972   *Elisa. Traditionsgeschichtliche Untersuchungen zur vorklassischen nordis-
           raelitischen Prophetie.* Gütersloh.
Schmoldt, H.
  1985   Elijas Botschaft an Ahab. Überlegungen zum Werdegang von I Kön 21. *BN*
           28:39-52.
Schweizer, H.
  1974   *Elischa in den Kriegen. Literaturwissenschaftliche Untersuchung von 2 Kön
           3; 6,8-23; 6,24-7, 20.* SANT 37. Munich.
  1979   Literarkritischer Versuch zur Erzählung von Micha ben Jimla (1 Kon 22). *BZ*
           23:1-19.
Seebass, H.
  1967/68 Die Verwerfung Jerobeams I. und Salomos durch die Prophetie des Ahia von
           Silo. *WO* 4:163-182.
  1971   Zu 1 Reg XXII 35-38. *VT* 21:380-383.
  1973   Elia und Ahab auf dem Karmel. *ZTK* 70:121-136.
  1974   Der Fall Naboth in 1 Reg XXI. *VT* 24:474-482.
  1975   Tradition und Interpretation bei Jehu ben Chanani und Ahia von Silo. *VT*
           25:175-190.
Sekine, M.
  1972   Beobachtungen zu der Josianischen Reform. *VT* 22:361-368.
  1975   Literatursoziologische Beobachtungen zu den Elisa-erzählungen. *AJBI.*
           1:39-62.
Seybold, K.
  1973   Elia am Gottesberg. Vorstellungen prophetischen Wirkens nach 1. Könige
           19. *EvT* 33:3-18.
Shenkel, J. D.
  1968   *Chronology and Recensional Development in the Greek Text of Kings.*
           HSM 1. Cambridge, MA.
Skinner, J.
  n.d.   *I & II Kings.* The Century Bible. Edinburgh.
Smend, R.
  1971   Das Gesetz und die Völker. Ein Beitrag zur deuteronomischen Redaktions
           geschichte. Pp. 494-509 in *Probleme biblischer Theologie.* Fs. G. von Rad.
           ed. H. W. Wolff. Munich.
  1975a   Der biblische und der historische Elia. *Congress Volume Edinburgh 1974.*
           VTSup 28:167-184. Leiden.
  1975b   Das Wort Jahwes an Elia. Erwägungen zur Komposition von 1 Reg. xvii-
           xix. *VT* 25:525-543.
Spieckermann, H.
  1982   *Juda unter Assur in der Sargonidenzeit.* FRLANT 129. Göttingen.
Stade, B.
  1885   Miscellen 10. Anmerkungen zu 2 Kö. 10-14 *ZAW* 5:275.
  1886   Miscellen 16. Anmerkungen zu 2 Kö. 15-21. *ZAW* 6:156-189.
Stade, B. and F. Schwally.
  1904   *The Book of Kings. Critical Edition of the Hebrew Text.* The Sacred Books
           of the Old Testament 9, ed. Paul Haupt. Leipzig.
Stahl, R.
  1983   Abstract of "Aspekte der Geschichte deuteronomistischer Theologie. Zur
           Traditionsgeschichte der Terminologie und zur Redaktionsgeschichte der
           Redekompositionen." Diss. B, Jena, 1982. *TL* 108 (1983) 74-75.
Stamm, J. J.
  1966   Elia am Horeb. Pp. 327-334 in *Studia biblica et semitica.* Fs. Th. C.
           Vriezen. Wageningen.
Steck, O. H.
  1968   *Überlieferung und Zeitgeschichte in den Elia- Erzählungen.* WMANT 26.
           Neukirchen-Vluyn.

Steinmann, J.
1956   La geste d'Élie dans l'Ancien Testament. Pp. 93-115 in *Élie le Prophete* I. Tournai.

Stipp, H.-J.
1987   *Elischa - Propheten - Gottesmänner*. Arbeiten zu Text und Sprache im Alten Testament 24. St. Ottilien.

Strange, J.
1975   Joram, King of Israel and Judah. *VT* 25:191-201.

Talmon, S. and W. W. Fields
1989   The Collocation משתין בקיר ועצור ועזוב and its Meaning. *ZAW* 101:85-112.

Timm, S.
1982   *Die Dynastie Omri. Quellen und Untersuchungen zur Geschichte Israels im 9. Jahrhundert vor Christus*. Göttingen.

Trebolle Barrera, J. C.
1980   *Salomón y Jeroboán. Historia de la recensión y redacción de 1 Reyes 2-12, 14*. Bibliotheca Salmanticensis. Dissertationes 3. Salamanca.
1984   *Jehú y Joás. Texto y composición literaria de 2 Reyes 9-11*. Institución San Jerónimo 17. Valencia.
1989   *Centena in Libros Samuelis et Regum. Variantes Textuales y Composición Literaria de Samuel y Reyes*. Madrid.

Vanoni, G.
1984   *Literarkritik und Grammatik. Untersuchungen der Wiederholungen und Spannungen in 1 Kön 11-12*. St. Ottilien.
1985   Beobachtungen zur deuteronomistischen Terminologie in 2 Kön 23,25-25, 30. Pp. 357-362 in *Das Deuteronomium Entstehung, Gestalt, und Botschaft*, ed. N. Lohfink.

Van Seters, J.
1981   Histories and Historians of the Ancient Near East: The Israelites. *Or* 50: 137-185.
1983a   *In Search of History*. New Haven.
1983b   Review of *Reform und Reformen* by H.-D. Hoffmann. *JBL* 102:131-132.

Van Winkle, D.
1989   1 Kings XIII: True and False Prophecy. *VT* 29:31-43.

Vater, A.
1979   Narrative Patterns for the Story of Commissioned Communication in the Old Testament. *JBL* 99:365-382.
1980   Story Patterns for a *Sitz*: A Form- or Literary-Critical Concern? *JSOT* 11: 47- 56.

de Vaux, R.
1956   Le cycle d'Élie dans les Livres des Rois. Pp. 53-79 in *Élie le Prophete* I. Tournai.

Veijola, T.
1975   *Die ewige Dynastie. David und die Entstehung seiner Dynastie nach der deuteronomistischen Darstellung*. Annalae Academiae Scientiarum Fennicae B. 193. Helsinki.
1977   *Das Königtum in der Beurteilung der deuteronomistischen Historiographie*. Annalae Academiae Scientiarum Fennica B. 198. Helsinki.

Viviano, P. A.
1987   2 Kings 17: A Rhetorical and Form-Critical Analysis. *CBQ* 49:548-559.

Vogt, E.
1986   *Der Aufstand Hiskias und die Belagerung Jerusalems 701 v. Chr*. AnBib 106. Rome.

Wallace, H. N.
1986   The Oracles Against the Israelite Dynasties in 1 and 2 Kings. *Bib* 67:21-40.

Weinfeld, M.
1972   *Deuteronomy and the Deuteronomic School.* Oxford.
1985   The Emergence of the Deuteronomic Movement: The Historical Antecedents.
        Pp. 76-98 in *Das Deuteronomium Entstehung, Gestalt, und Botschaft*, ed. N.
        Lohfink. Leuven.
Weippert, H.
1972   Die 'deuteronomistischen' Beurteilung der Könige von Israel und Juda und das
        Problem der Redaktion der Königsbücher. *Bib* 53:301-339.
1983   Die Ätiologie des Nordreiches und seines Königshauses (I Reg 11 29-40).
        ZAW 85:344-375.
1985   Das deuteronomistische Geschichtswerk. Sein Ziel und Ende in der neueren
        Forschung. *TRu* 50:213-249.
1988   Ahab el campeador? Redaktionsgeschichtliche Untersuchungen zu 1 Kön 22.
        Bib 69:457-479.
Weiser, A.
1964   *The Old Testament: Its Formation and Development.* New York.
Wellhausen, J.
1963   *Die Composition des Hexateuchs und der historischen Bücher des Alten
        Testaments.* 4th ed. Berlin.
Welten, P.
1973   Naboths Weinberg (1. Könige 21). *EvT* 33:18-32.
Whitley, C. F.
1952   The Deuteronomic Presentation of the House of Omri. *VT* 2:137-152.
Williamson, H. G. M.
1982   The Death of Josiah and the Continuing Development of the Deuterono-
        mistic History. *VT* 32:242-247.
1987   Reliving the Death of Josiah: A Reply to C. T. Begg. *VT* 37:9-15.
Wilson, R. R.
1980   *Prophecy and Society in Ancient Israel.* Philadelphia.
Winckler, H.
1892   *Alttestamentliche Untersuchungen.* Leipzig.
Wolff, H. W.
1961   Das Kerygma des deuteronomischen Geschichtswerk. *ZAW* 73:171-186.
1970   Das Ende des Heiligtums in Bethel. Pp. 287-298 in *Archäologie und Altes
        Testament.* Fs. K. Galling, eds. A. Kuschke and E. Kutsch. Tübingen.
Würthwein, E.
1962   Die Erzählung vom Gottesurteil auf dem Karmel. *ZTK.* 59:131-144.
1967   Zur Komposition von 1 Reg 22, 1-38. Pp. 245-254 in *Das Ferne und Nahe
        Wort.* Fs. Leonhard Rost, ed. R. Maass. BZAW 105. Berlin.
1970   Elijah at Horeb: Reflections on I Kings 19, 9-18. Pp. 152-166 in
        *Proclamation and Presence. Old Testament Essays in Honour of Gwynne
        Henton Davies,* eds. J. I. Durham and J. R. Porter. London.
1973   Die Erzählung vom Gottesmann aus Juda in Bethel. Zur Komposition von 1
        Kön 13. Pp. 181-189 in *Wort und Geschichte.* Fs. K. Elliger. AOAT 18.
        Neukirchen - Vluyn.
1976   Die josianische Reform und das Deuteronomium. *ZTK* 73:395-423.
1978   Naboth-Novelle und Elia-Wort. *ZTK* 75:375
1984   *Die Bücher der Könige. 1. Kön. 17 - 2. Kön. 25.* ATD 11,2. Göttingen.
1985   *Die Bücher der Könige. 1. Könige 1-16.* ATD. 11,1. 2nd ed. Göttingen.
Yadin, Y.
1960   New Light on Solomon's Megiddo. *BA* 23:62-68.
1972   *Hazor: The Head of all These Kingdoms.* Schweich Lectures 1970. London.
1975   *Hazor: The Rediscovery of a Great Citadel of the Bible.* New York.
Zevit, Z.
1985   Deuteronmistic Historiography in 1 Kings 12 - 2 Kings 17 and Reinvestiture
        of the Israelian Cult. *JSOT* 32:57-73.

INDEX OF AUTHORS

INDEX OF BIBLICAL REFERENCES

SUPPLEMENTS TO VETUS TESTAMENTUM

2. POPE, M.H. *El in the Ugaritic texts.* 1955. ISBN 90 04 04000 5
3. *Wisdom in Israel and in the Ancient Near East.* Presented to Harold Henry Rowley by the Editorial Board of Vetus Testamentum in celebration of his 65th birthday, 24 March 1955. Edited by M. NOTH and D. WINTON THOMAS. 2nd reprint of the first (1955) ed. 1969. ISBN 90 04 02326 7
4. *Volume du Congrès* [International pour l'étude de l'Ancien Testament]. Strasbourg 1956. 1957. ISBN 90 04 02327 5
8. BERNHARDT, K.-H. *Das Problem der alt-orientalischen Königsideologie im Alten Testament.* Unter besonderer Berücksichtigung der Geschichte der Psalmenexegese dargestellt und kritisch gewürdigt. 1961. ISBN 90 04 02331 3
9. *Congress Volume,* Bonn 1962. 1963. ISBN 90 04 02332 1
11. DONNER, H. *Israel unter den Völkern.* Die Stellung der klassischen Propheten des 8. Jahrhunderts v. Chr. zur Aussenpolitik der Könige von Israel und Juda. 1964. ISBN 90 04 02334 8
12. REIDER, J. *An Index to Aquilla.* Completed and revised by N. Turner. 1966. ISBN 90 04 02335 6
13. ROTH, W.M.W. *Numerical sayings in the Old Testament.* A form-critical study. 1965. ISBN 90 04 02336 4
14. ORLINSKY, H.M. *Studies on the second part of the Book of Isaiah.*—The so-called 'Servant of the Lord' and 'Suffering Servant' in Second Isaiah.—Snaith, N.H. Isaiah 40-66. A study of the teaching of the Second Isaiah and its consequences. Repr. with additions and corrections. 1977. ISBN 90 04 05437 5
15. *Volume du Congrès* [International pour l'étude de l'Ancien Testament]. Genève 1965. 1966. ISBN 90 04 02337 2
17. *Congress Volume,* Rome 1968. 1969. ISBN 90 04 02339 9
19. THOMPSON, R.J. *Moses and the Law in a century of criticism since Graf.* 1970. ISBN 90 04 02341 0
20. REDFORD, D.B. *A study of the biblical story of Joseph.* 1970. ISBN 90 04 02342 9
21. AHLSTRÖM, G.W. *Joel and the temple cult of Jerusalem.* 1971. ISBN 90 04 02620 7
22. *Congress Volume,* Uppsala 1971. 1972. ISBN 90 04 03521 4
23. *Studies in the religion of ancient Israel.* 1972. ISBN 90 04 03525 7
24. SCHOORS, A. *I am God your Saviour.* A form-critical study of the main genres in Is. xl-lv. 1973. ISBN 90 04 03792 2
25. ALLEN, L.C. *The Greek Chronicles.* The relation of the Septuagint I and II Chronicles to the Massoretic text. Part 1. The translator's craft. 1974. ISBN 90 04 03913 9
26. *Studies on prophecy.* A collection of twelve papers. 1974. ISBN 90 04 03877 9
27. ALLEN, L.C. *The Greek Chronicles.* Part 2. Textual criticism. 1974. ISBN 90 04 03933 3
28. *Congress Volume,* Edinburgh 1974. 1975. ISBN 90 04 04321 7
29. *Congress Volume,* Göttingen 1977. 1978. ISBN 90 04 05835 4

30. EMERTON, J.A. (ed.). Studies in the historical books of the Old Testament. 1979. ISBN 90 04 06017 0
31. MEREDINO, R.P. *Der Erste und der Letzte.* Eine Untersuchung von Jes 40-48. 1981. ISBN 90 04 06199 1
32. EMERTON, J.A. (ed.). *Congress Vienna* 1980. 1981. ISBN 90 04 06514 8
33. KOENIG, J. *L'herméneutique analogique du Judaïsme antique d'après les témoins textuels d'Isaïe.* 1982. ISBN 90 04 06762 0
34. BARSTAD, H.M. *The religious polemics of Amos.* Studies in the preaching of Amos ii 7B-8, iv 1-13, v 1-27, vi 4-7, viii 14. 1984. ISBN 90 04 07017 6
35. KRASOVEC, J. *Antithetic structure in Biblical Hebrew poetry.* 1984. ISBN 90 04 07244 6
36. EMERTON, J.A. (ed.). *Congress Volume,* Salamanca 1983. 1985. ISBN 90 04 07281 0
37. LEMCHE, N.P. *Early Israel.* Anthropological and historical studies on the Israelite society before the monarchy. 1985. ISBN 90 04 07853 3
38. NIELSEN, K. *Incense in Ancient Israel.* 1986. ISBN 90 04 07702 2
39. PARDEE, D. *Ugaritic and Hebrew poetic parallelism.* A trial cut. 1988. ISBN 90 04 08368 5
40. EMERTON, J.A. (ed.). *Congress Volume,* Jerusalem 1986. 1988. ISBN 90 04 08499 1
41. EMERTON, J.A. (ed.). *Studies in the Pentateuch.* 1990. ISBN 90 04 09195 5
42. McKENZIE, S.L. *The Trouble with Kings.* The composition of the Book of Kings in the Deuteronomistic History. 1991. ISBN 90 04 09402 4